To Emma's Aunty
Love Rebekah

dying to live

by rebekah simpson

First published in Great Britain as a softback original in 2018

Typeset in Sabon LT Std

Illustrations and cover design by Richard Brown

Editing, typesetting and publishing by UK Book Publishing
www.ukbookpublishing.com

ISBN: 978-1-9998743-1-5

www.ladiesinpinkscarves.wordpress.com
Charity no. 1141443

This book is available on Amazon as a paperback and ebook

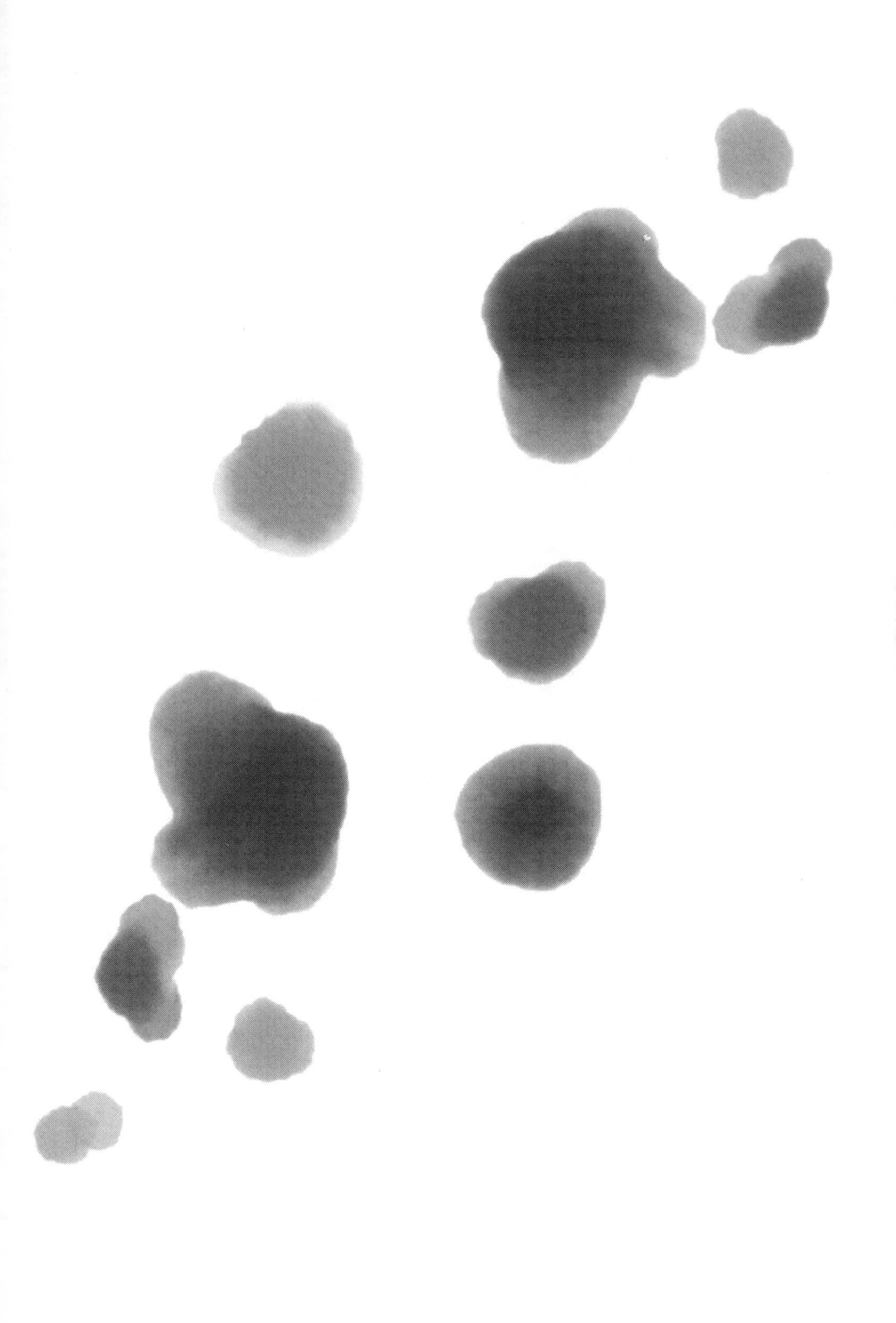

Acknowledgements

Mark:

I want to specifically thank my husband Mark for all he has done to support me. Mark is the unsung, silent and often forgotten about hero behind my story. He, in my mind, is the person who has kept our family ship floating, and when I've felt like I'm drowning, it has been him who has known I need a life float and has known exactly which version to throw me.

He has continued to be a success in his job, receiving promotions at the expected times, thus acknowledging his hard work and success despite the difficult trials he has, and still is, subjected to on a continuous basis. I want to thank him for being so steady and solid. He leaves for work at 6.30am – often missing his lunch in order to keep on top of his job – he then picks the children up from school, helps them with their homework, does the laundry, tea, any miscellaneous chores, then finally bedtime. When all this has finished, he can often be found late at night after we've had some 'alone' time, on his laptop completing some work or church task (he's Chair of Trustees at church) that simply has to be done in order to keep two important areas of our lives functioning.

I want to tell you that he never, ever complains or moans or ducks out of his responsibilities. He really is by my side in sickness and has supported me physically, emotionally, spiritually and mentally. I do sometimes, far more than he deserves, find reason to complain about something he has forgotten, but as I write this I am so sorry that the perfectionist control freak in me far too often focuses on what he hasn't done rather than on all that he has done.

Mark, I want to say sorry for all the times I've failed as a wife by whining when you don't get things 'quite right' and for often 'pointing out' your faults. I love you so much and when I'm alone, like now, I'm overwhelmed by how much you've loved me, and how blessed I am to have had a husband who has such an ability to shoulder so much as you do and always make me feel so loved and that it's not a problem. I wish I'd been able to show that to you more than I feel I have. You really are my best friend and I'm so grateful for the 15 years we've had. Nothing that I've achieved has been on my own – you're behind everything I've managed. I really love you, deeply, very deeply.

Sarah:

I've never known life without you. You know me so well, and have always been there for me. I want to thank you for always stepping up to the mark, for being so adaptable to my needs, for making me laugh, or crying with me, or being so practical, when that's been what's called for.

We have been the greatest friends throughout our lifetime and will continue to be so for the rest of our lives and into eternity, and I know you will continue to look after Mark and the children as their lives unfold.

Philip:

The final specific thank you has to go to my brother Philip, who enabled me to write this book. He rang one day and suggested I write a book about the experience I had had and indeed was still having. I know for certain that there was something in the way he said it, or perhaps it was because it came from my big brother, that filled me with pride and confidence, and gave me the belief in myself that I *could* do it. I had in fact attempted twice before to write my story and had given up. I had not felt it flowed, or had the right 'feel' about it.

Philip's suggestion released something within me and I started almost immediately. Where I had failed on the previous attempts to find the flow and my own voice, this time I didn't. When I emailed back nervously with my effort, it was his response that encouraged me to press on. "It's amazing," he said. You know on X-Factor when people do a really bad audition and you wonder why their family allowed them to embarrass themselves in that way? Well, Phil is that family member who is responsible if I've embarrassed myself publicising this tale. So, if you have not enjoyed my efforts then it is really his fault! Thank you, Phil, for releasing something in me that enabled me to achieve the seemingly impossible.

Everyone else:

I have been blessed throughout this entire experience by many, many people. Impossible to name you all, some have helped me in particular chapters that have now passed, others have come into my life after the book was completed.

I could not have mentioned everyone by name. I'm trusting that no-one feels I've overlooked them. I give thanks to God regularly for all the many people who we know support us or have supported us, and for those who still arrive in our lives just when we need you. You are known, appreciated and loved by us.

Anyway, I had my brain blammed, you know; so I can genuinely use 'brain damage' as a legitimate excuse for any errors, people overlooked, or having written a rubbish book and guilted you into reading it!

Bless you and love you all

Rebekah

Foreword: To the Children

A long, long time ago when I was a little girl, maybe about 8 years old, I used to creep up the two flights of stairs to the attic in the old house I grew up in and go into the room that was my mummy and daddy's. It was right at the top of the house under the roof. Next to my room, in fact, but mine was a lot smaller and only had a little window high up on the sloped ceiling. I could see a small square of sky out of it if I lay on my bed. Their room had a sizeable window that they'd had put into the lower part of the sloping ceiling. I could open it wide and hang out feeling the wind, rain or sun on my face while looking out over the roof tops of the hundreds of Carlisle terraced houses that defined the area we lived in.

Our house wasn't a fancy place, and it contained lots of strange random clutter. To me, most of it looked like junk but to my mummy it was all terribly special. I didn't mind it when I was young, but as a teenager I hated it. I found the clutter so embarrassing. Other people's homes didn't have all this 'stuff' – they had clean carpets, hoovered by house-proud mothers, mantlepieces, polished and shiny with, at most, a clock on one end and a vase of silk flowers on the other. Living rooms that had matching furniture, a basket for papers and magazines and framed photos of family on the unscuffed, spotless walls; calm and peaceful and ordered.

Not so in ours: every dusty space was covered in debris, garden spades sat alongside decrepit pieces of antique furniture probably worth nothing, fit for a charity shop at best. Little pots, boxes, cartons and dishes adorned any available surface. Unused bolts, nails, stones gathered by someone sometime, the odd gem stone sparkled out or a broken bracelet. Bits of Lego, tiny toys, a mini screwdriver, buttons, thread, all thrown together in old ice cream tubs. Every drawer held more – every cupboard rammed untidily with more, every surface contained more and more and more. All of it I suppose had sentimental value to my mother, but it was so messy and it unsettled me inside, and I promised myself that one day I would live in a house that was organised and, in the organisation, I would find a sense of inner quiet, and that is what I have done in my own uncluttered house. I've made a home where furniture matches and there is space to put away toys, sewing stuff, paper and pens and all the other multiple resources needed for a large family. Pegs to hang all the coats on, boxes for shoes in the garage, shelves for suitcases, somewhere for everything to belong. There is one advantage for a child who lives in a very disorganised non-house-proud house: nobody ever tells you to tidy up. I can see in my mind you all chattering about how good that would be, how fantastic and so much more fun to have a mum who never asked you to tidy up your bedroom or put the Lego and Hexbugs back into the cupboard in the living room. I have no recollections of ever being asked to tidy my things away after I had spread them over the entire floor. It wasn't even my own bedroom floor, it could be any floor; I don't think Mummy even noticed – I suppose it would be there for a while before it was just gathered into all the other clutter and lost forever.

This was a time when we didn't have TV, iPhone, iPad, PlayStation or even DVDs, so I just played. I played for hours, often with Sarah, but frequently alone. When young, it was dens and dolls; a den was my little house, a home for my many baby dolls and all their paraphernalia, high chairs, feeding stuff, home knitted or crocheted by Mummy dolly outfits for all occasions, prams, makeshift beds from leftover fabric wrapped around toilet paper to make them more comfortable. Hours just whittled away in this fantasy of a roleplay world. Right up your street, Josie – not a football in sight.

Aside from visiting Granny and Grandad in Nottingham about twice a year, the Keswick convention (a Baptist Christian event) once a year, and one possibly two-week summer holiday and various Saturday trips into the Lake District to climb up mountains – and the weekend trips to the allotment – the rest of the endless hours outside of school time were my own. We didn't have the money to spend on taekwondo, tennis lessons, swimming lessons and all the other stuff that you guys get to do. An old lady in the church had picked up on a talent that myself and Sarah had for poetry reciting, acting and singing, and she had some experience in elocution and took us on as a charity case. We were quite good at it and after a few months of vocal work, we were entered for the Carlisle District Music Festival and won or came in second place in all our categories. We loved going to her house because she put an entire plate of biscuits out and literally told us we could eat them all. I wonder if you would do elocution if you got to eat a whole plate of biscuits! And that, along with church, was really the only activity we did outside of school and the family.

When I grew out of dolls – baby ones that is – Cindy (a bit like Barbie) made an appearance for several years. Through Cindy, I lived out the fantasy of my own longings for a glamorous life. I'd save every penny I could and go off to Woolworths to buy Cindy her latest nightdress or fur coat. Christmas and birthdays were lists of Cindy wardrobe sets, a bedside table with a real push button which switched on a tiny bulb shrouded by a frilly pink gauze lampshade. My Cindy lived the life of Riley, out in her yellow beach buggy, to me she was a real living, talking, walking doll, she even had a real action man as her boyfriend courtesy of having three older brothers. But the most significant progression was into the world of the doll's house. A miniature kingdom that engrossed me all the way into adulthood. Up there in my parents' bright, sunlit room with the dust particles floating in the light from the Velux window, high up in the gods of the house was where it lived. My Lundby doll's house, the first doll's house to have electrical lights inside the house – mine was a Stockholm – I loved it. It's in our own garage now, with all its furniture and its lights that still work. It was my pride and joy, my secret pleasure that still engrossed me well into 1985, when I was 14-15. I expect if I had time now, I would still play with it.

Up in the sanctuary of my parents' bedroom, where nobody ever came during the day; in the distance I could hear the muted sound of Blondie on Stephen's record player, whose bedroom was beneath, but aside from that, nothing. This was my world, where my imagination and dreams were created and dashed and recreated, constantly reincarnating the tiny dolls' destinies.

I guess it was a form of escapism, a therapeutic world in a way. I have a mental picture of myself as a child and as a teenager staring in a window at the tiny dramas that I made happen in the beautiful, perfect rooms that I had created, calm spaces that I could somehow hide away in from the chaos of real life.

The details I could create in these rooms were exquisite. I had the basic, standard, shop bought essentials, e.g. sofas, beds, bathroom and kitchen sets, but the real joy for me lay in making tiny objects and tiny outfits myself, made from stitching by hand leftover scraps of fabric and ribbon. I could make miniature party dresses and small suits, curtains and bedcovers. The actual house mattered less to me than the inhabitants, their lives and the reality I could breathe into them. I could create their destinies; the family could expand or on occasion suffer losses and I could constantly and radically change their historical or social place. I believe my instinct towards dolls and dolls' houses were the early and instinctive expression of a person who longed for a family of her own.

Right from as far back as I can remember, shown in my love of the dolls' house, my one and only ambition was to be married, look after my home and be a mummy. It was all I ever wanted, it was the only specific goal I have ever had. Everything else was just filling in time.

Unfortunately the whole process took a decade longer than I had wanted. This delay was absolutely not me finding a more modern woman's career-oriented set of aspirations; but entirely down to simply not finding a fella who had serious possibilities of being a good husband and father. I often ponder that decade especially in the light of my current 2018 situation. If I'd met 'him' sooner, you'd all be a decade older and life with cancer would have been much easier on us all. The 20s-30s decade contained a lot of life-changing events such as graduating, qualifying to be a teacher, being a financially independent owner of my own cosy, adorable, funky flat. I was creative, friendly, adventurous, well travelled, and reasonably attractive, but still held on to being just a girl who wanted a boy to love her enough to want to marry her and make a love nest for at least two babies to share. I had great friends and lots of boys liked me, some professed to love me, but none of them were close to fitting the concept I had, my only true goal. I wasn't needy, or a freak, or weird, or too intense; I lived the single life because I had to, and I made the best out of that time. I used the time positively, on travelling to various far-flung destinations. I know I had times of desperation and loneliness and I remember some very dark seasons of the soul when the latest (flame) had died and many friends were either engaged, married and even having babies. I felt like the "old maid" and fear of being forever single seeped into the edges of my mind. I don't know if I ever really TRULY believed that I, "Rebekah Mells", would actually be the one "left on the shelf". It couldn't happen to me because I had no other goal, there was no plan B, only plan A. I wanted a family of my own and I had always wanted one, and nothing else had ever entered my mind. How I didn't come across as total desperdado (or maybe I did) I'll never know – maybe the 'actor' in me, darling! It wasn't until I was in my late 20s that the potential reality that some people didn't marry hit me. And this was not always because they chose not to, but quite simply they didn't meet anyone. They didn't meet their Mr Right, their perfect match – this concept really frightened and unsettled me.

It took until I was 33 to meet Daddy, and I guess I can say that my dream began to come true. He came with a bonus of a little girl called Emma who became your eldest sister. We married on 3rd September 2006 and this section of a poem I wrote almost a decade later describes the way I feel about him.

"You're the rudder to my wayward boat
You're the solid vessel that keeps me afloat
You're the cup that matches my saucer
You're the amazing father to our son and daughters
You're the clear full-stop on my rambling sentence
The warming soul that melts my indifference

Our love has not been a walk in the park
More like sliding, slipping and spinning in the dark
Often not sure of the direction we're heading
Or how solid the ground on which we're treading
Our secret – friendship – we hold tight to each other
We know we were made for one another

But our solid foundation is built on nothing less
Than Jesus and his righteousness
In the darkest days or in times full of joy
Jesus is our peace that NOTHING can destroy
His love for us both has been patient and kind
We can stand united – in his word always aligned

So – Mark, my 6ft 3 hazel eyed Ginger Ninja man
My flame coloured head to our amazing clan

My counsellor, strengthener, repairer,
My forerunner, fire, defender,
My fighter, shelter, helper,
My protector, inspirer, provider,

My friend, confidante, believer,
My companion, explorer, inventor
My buddy, soul mate, instructor
My wonderful, wonderful man
My truly awesome, faithful, constant,
Dependable, hilarious, wonderful man."

We do argue sometimes as YOU all know, but it's never over anything important, usually over Dad eating all the chocolates and biscuits! I do think there's no better daddy, no man who could have been such an awesome father to you all. I didn't have to wait long after Dad and I got married for you three babes to come along. Evie, you entered the world less than a year after we were married, Josie followed two years later, and Archie a year later, and we were complete. My longed-for dream had happened.

I gave up teaching, Evie, when I was pregnant with you. I knew I would never-ever want someone else looking after my children; I had waited too long, I wanted to be the person who shared all your experiences that you were going to have, standing at the side of the sports field cheering you all on, being there when you cried and laughed, bathing you all, singing to you all, and feeling such pride at every step you all took.

Like anything one longs for it rarely turns out how you imagined it would be and so it was with being a mummy. I mention in the book some of those difficulties and they were real and true. I don't know many mums and dads who have not found that being a parent is the most stressful thing they ever did, and I was no exception. Having said that, it is also the best thing that ever happened to me, and I want to use this section of writing to tell you how much I enjoy you, not how stressful it has sometimes been. You all make me laugh so much and I quite simply adore you. When you were babies I would sit for a long time with you in my arms and be in awe of what I'd created; my heart melted when I studied your uniqueness. When you could talk I loved the way you'd try and tell me things and now you are older I love listening to your opinions and personal experiences that matter to you.

I never look at you with disappointment, I always see what you are worth to me. I see your potential and I do my best to draw that out of you. I make lots of mistakes, my impatience and stress sometimes get the better of me and I shout – I am always sorry, I have always apologised to you when I reflected afterwards and realised that I had reacted badly. I have always aimed to see each new day as precious and fresh with no mistakes, with the goal of prioritising your needs and what is best for you. I pray that for all the mistakes I have made, that by some miracle the love and the good I try to do for you far out-weighs the bad.

My life's Passions

Emma Kate, your smile lights the room
A gentle spirit that blossoms and blooms
Such a bonny lassy and so amendable
Bringer of reason and always peaceable
Your singing voice will add joy to your life
A positive gift to turn to in times of strife

Evie Rose, my strong but fragile flower
Brave and courageous, an admirable power
Dwells within your sensitive caring heart
I saw a warrior spirit right from your start
Harness your passion, it's a positive force
Embrace your convictions and find your life's cause

My wonderful, cuddly bundle, Josie Grace
Sparkly green eyes gaze from bewitching freckled face
Brimming with life and bouncing love
The kind heart of an angel sent to me from above
Wherever you go friendship will too
Joy, blessings and love will always follow you

Archie Isaac, my bespectacled, smiley faced, golden haired lad
My singing 'sunny Jim' who makes me laugh when times are bad

Your dearest treasure 'Rabbit' – best pal since birth
Priceless to you, of unfathomable worth
It demonstrates how much loyal love lies deep within
You'll defeat life's adversaries with your love and beaming grin.

My amazing children – how can it be
That God saw fit to entrust you to me
But he did – and I handed your lives back to him
Confident that he would one day bring
You all back together united to me
Having won ALL life's battles victoriously

You birds of a feather
Please stick together
Look out for one another
Your strongest allies are your sisters and brother
Direction will be found by seeking God's face
Only in him will you find true freedom and grace.

By the time you are old enough to read this, I may not be here for you and I want you to know how heartbroken I am about that concept. What do I say to you – how do I impart a sense of how much I loved you and longed to be there for the many events of your lives whatever they turn out to be? I've tried to express to you by telling you that right from the beginning of my life I've had a 'mother's heart' that I believe couldn't be satisfied until I became a mother and you guys have been a completion of that dream. You've exceeded my dream.

I lost both my parents before I was 35, far too young. You never met them, so I do have some insight into what you may go through. I have no choice but to put my faith in God and know that you will all be okay because He will look after you. And I know that Daddy and Aunty Sarah will do an amazing job of taking care of you. Life will have its challenges, but it will go on and so will you; I believe that you will all have fruitful and abundant lives, yes there will be pain and tragedy, but overall, I believe you will conquer life's hurdles and be victorious. I hope, like me, that you learn to see the good within the bad.

You will all have your own personal memories of me. The main reason that I wrote this book was to help you surround what you remember of me with a story of what I was going through whilst trying to raise you. Evie said to me recently, "I wish you could spend more time with us, I wish you could be well." I have the same wish. I know that cancer, as much as it cost me, has cost you more.

Despite the battle I have had with my physical health, I never gave up trying to do my best, trying to be the best mummy I could be despite my physical limitations. I hope it conveys my deep love and my authentic apology that I had to leave you far too soon. I have one bit of life advice that I want to share with you, that I hope you will find faith in God in your lives – a relationship of love with the eternal father and his son Jesus Christ – I pray every day for you, that you will find in God the same hope, life and love that I have found, that you discover true security in knowing that He is your closest companion and reliable friend. He chose you and knew you before I have ever thought of you and in my absence, I am trusting Him to be with you and look after you. So, look upwards to Him and allow Him to draw you close, turn your eyes upon Him and look full in His wonderful face and His saving grace. The pain that you may suffer on Earth will grow strangely dim in the light of His glory. You will find the meaning of your life and your purpose for being here when you allow Him to guide you. Always trust and believe that He is a good father and you will find solid ground to stand on, always, I promise, and we will meet again in that glorious heavenly place.

I am not a writer! I want to say sorry if there is anything in any part of this book that you don't like or are not happy with how I have described a memory or an experience. I started the book in 2016 and because I was often too poorly to write, it has taken me almost three years to get to the final stages. I think that has affected my flow and perhaps the style. It's now 2018 and I've been unable to even read it through myself, and have handed it over to Dad to correct and guide it through to be printed. I wish I could have done it myself, and made sure it is good enough for you.

I love you all so much and we will meet again, I am sure of it. Lots of love from your greatest admirer and number one fan.

Coorie doon, my darlings (Snuggle in and settle)

I love you

Mum(my) x.

Dying to Live

I'm Rebekah Simpson, I was born 30th January 1971; at the time of beginning this tale in 2016 I am 45. Numbers, dates, figures of any type are a struggle for me, so you won't find a lot of dated detail in this text; I'm more an estimation type person. I failed 'O' Level Maths quite dramatically with an unclassified result; however, I am the proud owner of a Maths CSE grade one! This is the exam they entered the – I'm not sure what the politically correct term is – I'll go for 'bottom of the class' pupils in case they failed the 'O' Level. It's the equivalent of a C grade at O Level so it didn't hold me back in terms of further education but is definitely evidence that I was educationally challenged mathematically!

Goodness only knows what that all translates to in GCSEs today where an A isn't really an A because there's an A* and recently they've turned it all into numbers with a number 9 as the highest, which I'm told is even better than an A* – makes no sense to me at all.

Given that I'm not so good with figures I have to recall past events based on conversation, feelings and the general essence of the time. Dates – they just don't rank highly when I relate a tale, so go easy on me there, I will definitely have made mistakes – please allow me some creative licence.

Anyway, apparently, I have a story. Wow, I have a story. That makes me want to smile, I don't really know why. It sounds so important and I'm really not. And when you begin to read my story I have a feeling you'll be very relieved that you DON'T have a story, if in order to have a story it has to be similar to mine. Like any story there's some key characters, there's definitely a whole load of things that happen, drama, cliff-hangers, tears, laughter, love and tragedy – so I guess that shapes up for quite a good read. There's a reasonably clear beginning, but we're still living our story and I have no sense of whether we're in the middle or near the end and absolutely no idea what the end may look like. This story is the life I've led for the past nine years with my husband and band of four little merry Simpsons, maybe more of the moody than the merry – but that would have seemed such a downbeat thing to share at this early stage so we'll stick to merry for now.

Many people have encouraged me to tell this story. They say they think I'm amazing and they don't know how I've coped and remained so positive, what's my secret? How do I keep going? Maybe I have no secret, maybe, I AM super woman.

After all, I'm a mother who is raising four spirited, strong minded, hilarious, talented children. I never ever feel frustrated, mad, lose the plot with them or question their or my own sanity. Nope, never, it's happy families all the way in the Simpson home. My amazingly calm husband Mark has NEVER had to play a significant role in the prevention of blood-shed between me and our four emotional, feisty children. Nope – never ever.

I'm still married after 12 years to an incredible man, that's Mark. (Hey, it's an achievement these days, although if I'm honest that's probably down to him too.)

I have some really long-term quality friendships with beautiful people who call me a friend even though they've lived real life with me; they've definitely seen me at my worst, so that's got to say something about my personality, hasn't it?

And I absolutely have to take this moment of glory to tell you that I am the woman who took up running for the first time after she was diagnosed with a life threatening illness and then went on to achieve competitive times in her age category in 5k and 10k races – yup, that's me. PB 22.05 in a 5k aged 42; PB 47.25 in a 10k, not long after. I am sure that will impress somebody.

I am also the awesome chick who harnessed her newfound running skills, dug out a few of her dormant creative abilities and successfully organised four charity fundraisers raising thousands of pounds. Hey, I just squeezed those little events between caring for my family of six and a few hundred trips to the hospital to keep me alive. Of course, such skills don't go unnoticed and these little achievements caused a friend to nominate me for The Chronicle Woman of the Year award. When all the votes were counted – in the entire North East – it was yours truly who drank a little too much Prosecco and had to be picked up off the pavement by her children, waving the trophy and demonstrating exactly how Woman of The Year behaves. It now has pride of place in my kitchen.

Woman of the Year! Just in case you didn't take that in.

I **am** that lady you see dressed in matching clothes AND with make up on, briskly marching two young children to school at 8.40 am, smiling (the smile might be a bit fake), to the school yard, or sitting across the café table from a friend sharing stresses and strains – yup, that's me. My mantra, 'if the day comes when I'm not wearing any make-up or involved in some project or other then you'll know I'm in a baaaaaaaaaad way'.

I eat well and look after myself, I'm in reasonable shape for a 40 something – and I will DEFINITELY take the credit for that. It takes nothing short of steely determination and willpower to lose three stone of child-bearing flab at age 40 and keep it off, WHILST continuing to age, and – here it comes again – 'fighting a life threatening illness'. Do you know how many 'deserves' and 'needs' that gives me?

'Another trip to hospital – I deserve that cream cake.'

'More needles – I need that chocolate bar.'

'I deserve to have a pizza; various surgery and horrendous biopsies deserves pizza. Heck not just pizza…I need sweets, crisps, cake, alcohol, alcohol, alcohol…every day, forever and ever, Amen.'

But no, virtuously I generally resist, I am human, so every so often Mark and I surrender to an all- out chocolate binge when we easily consume an entire family size tub of Celebration. I confess also that I have a private emergency stash hidden in the house which I will never reveal to anyone; and a bottle of Baileys in the fridge door that I swig from during meal times when the children are doing my head in. But most days I am careful with my diet and as this is **my** story I am going to let everyone know who thinks skinny people are 'lucky', IT IS A LIE! We are not lucky, well not many of us, we just put a lot of effort in. Eventually we all have to stay in good shape by making good choices over food and exercise. There is no other way. I try to make those choices, painfully at times, and with great sacrifice- and – wait for it… 'whilst fighting a life threatening illness'. I bet you haven't got an excuse greater than that to eat and drink what you like and do no exercise.

One last thing, slap yourself if you think the following about skinny people:

'She can do it because she's so strong.'

'It's alright for her because she's a different personality to me.'

'Bet she has a fast metabolism.' (Nine years on the cocktail of drugs I've been on makes my metabolism work on 'go slow and stop' – I should be as large as a house.)

Listen, if I can do it 'whilst fighting a life threatening illness' (I couldn't resist it) you can too; set a goal, and do not give up. Boy! Off-loading that one was tough! Surely I deserve that super-sized bag of crisps now?

I'm reading back on the last few paragraphs and I'm feeling I COULD (on the surface) legitimately see myself as Super Woman. There's certainly reason to believe that I am a woman, wife, mother, friend who has attributes that people could look at and possibly admire. What this story will explain is the real secret behind my 'success'.

At the times I have needed it the most, I have received an instant mountain of support from family, friends and community folk from around the country and world who help me to function. My day to day needs are met by such a swarm of wonderful helpers that at times it makes me weep to see love in such literal and practical action. I could not cope if I were not provided for by these angels, I really couldn't. You know who you are: the child carers, the cooks, the cleaners, the laundry ladies, the bed changers, the letter and card writers, the kids' school runners, the coffee and chat buddies and the all-round day or night spontaneous responders.

These people have been a huge unseen part of why I am still standing. I know this. But in actual fact they're still not the total reason for my tenacity and ability to see the positive in the darkest of circumstances. I could not have managed any of the previous stated achievements without the love and power I receive from an additional source, a supernatural source. And there's no way I would still have hope after what I've been through if it was down to me and simply a positive determined outlook, a strong personality, and a dedicated group of people who virtually run my life on a practical basis.

Eventually, friends and family let you down, in big ways and small ways, and boy, do you get hurt by people's insensitive comments and thoughtlessness. Eventually, you can't sustain yourself on your own resources. Not when the fight goes on and on and on, and the things you're fighting get bigger and bigger and bigger. Believe me, I know, you simply run...out...of...energy. And so do people around you.

I don't find it easy to openly confess what I'm about to reveal, but for this to be authentic I will have to go public over one of my well-kept secrets. The reason that my hope has never completely run out despite the most traumatic and extreme life challenges is the following. I have a person in my life that is more important to me than my husband, my children or any friendship. He is everything to me; the most common name for him is God. I'm a bit freaked now by what might be running through your mind, but it's out there now – no turning back.

Look, I am not some raving Bible Basher, in fact before my life was turned upside down by my life threatening illness, acknowledging publicly that I was a Christian was a big 'No No'. I didn't want to scare anyone away from being my friend.

However, I am unable to tell you my story if I am not honest about my beliefs. I'll try not to preach, or come across as a real weirdo, and I am not trying to manipulate you into joining a gang of 'happy clappy' Christians. I promise. So I'm just going to say it real fast and then we can, for many of you reading this, get onto some more comfortable ground. I can't promise you that the God word won't come up again but we all have some type of belief in something, and I challenge anyone to attempt to write about a very personal journey without revealing what or whom they believe in.

Here goes, speed read if you need to; or if you're really brave, soak it in and then file it away under 'this lady is a bit crazy, but I'll roll with it'.

Deep breath, Rebekah. I have a tangible, real relationship with God and the Holy Spirit – she's really lost it now, you're thinking; it gets worse! When I pray, God speaks to me; bet you're on the verge of closing this book. I'd better explain this one. I am not rocking in a corner hearing spooky voices in my head; it's not often an audible voice, it's an inner feeling. A deep sense of 'knowing' that something or someone is speaking to me. Oh boy, this sounds so insane. For example, I might be doing the dishes and I feel something inside prompting me to text my daughter and tell her I love her and I'm sorry that I nearly combusted when she asked me to find her PE bag that she is constantly losing because she won't leave it in the right place! However, screeching the way I did was not really acceptable. Or it's the feeling I have when I'm standing on top of Helvellyn, my favourite mountain in the Lake District, and I just want to shout out 'Thank you for this amazing mountain'. It's not my voice, it's something else. In Portugal last summer we stopped at a café and as I was about to leave the car, I heard this inner voice say 'leave your sunglasses in the glove compartment'. I pushed it aside because I wanted some cool photos of me and the kids on the beach in the evening sun wearing my Versace glasses. After I'd eaten and we arrived home I realised I'd left them there. I was devastated; I made Mark drive back, but they'd gone, stolen. It's a small example of 'the voice' but a real one; on this occasion I wish I'd heeded it then I wouldn't have had to settle for the local supermarket's finest.

This voice prompts me to be nice to my husband when he comes in from a hard day at work; it encourages me to carry on listening for another hour even though I have 100 chores to do; while my teenager moans on about revising. Or it persuades me to meet a friend for coffee when I'd rather stay tucked up at home with my latest novel only then to discover she really needed that coffee because she'd just discovered her daughter had been bunking off school and she needed a friend. Finally, but probably most importantly: how to manage my illness and my attitudes and thoughts, so that despite all that me and my family suffer we can still have a full and joyful life.

I don't always pay attention to the small voice inside, call it your 'conscience' if you like; that inner sense of just knowing that something is right or wrong and knowing that really one should listen to it. I would call it the Holy Spirit; the supernatural aspect of God and Jesus, who when you believe in God resides within you and helps you on an everyday level (blimey, I bet you think I'm a raving lunatic now!). Seriously I am not your archetypal bead-wearing Christian with a sticker of a fish in the car and I'm really not a goody two shoes sort of character; it often takes me a long time to do what I know is the 'right' thing. I like being a little naughty if the truth be told, being a bit feisty or pushing humour to its socially acceptable boundaries, and sometimes simply enjoy defying or at least challenging the protocol around me despite the winding roads that being this way have often led me to. And I am definitely not moralistic or religious; I simply believe that there is enough evidence to prove that God is real, that Jesus was God's son and the truth in those statements mean certain choices for the way I live.

I have spent hours and hours and hours over the last nine years in various types and stages of suffering. Believe me when I say, that when life is like that, you eventually, and often, find yourself alone. Head in hands wondering how you've ended up here. No husband, no child, no friends, no hobbies, no chocolate bars, no drugs can bail you out of the endless abyss you find yourself in. You face the darkest parts of yourself, alone. When this has occurred to ME, this inner voice has stepped in and helped me.

I am so grateful for the solidity that this has given me, all my life, but very much so over the last few years. It has given me the strength and love I have needed to walk my walk and still be standing today with no bitterness, no anger, and no resentment. Well, not towards God at least, but maybe towards more trivial issues such as the well-known high street store, who recently sent my order that I was longing for to an address in Cornwall that doesn't exist rather than mine! Then they blamed me for being useless at understanding their complicated web page.

And I still laugh – quite a lot really – I have some very funny people in my life! One of which is me! I make myself laugh all the time. My dark sense of humour often blurts out 'tourette's style' some very inappropriate comments that lighten my situation and have often stood me in good stead.

So, tempting as it is to take the accolade for all aforementioned achievements, the truth is, it's not me alone that enables me to be a slightly dumpier not so glamorous version of Super Woman. The standing ovation for my life belongs to the Father in Heaven. This is the story of how I'm surviving a terrifying, tragic and traumatic tussle with a silent, deadly illness. I wouldn't have made it without my faith and I'd be misleading you if I didn't own up to that from the start. Without God this would most likely be a 'tale of sound and fury, signifying nothing' (Macbeth). With God it has the potential to be a tale full of love and perseverance signifying everything.

In the Beginning

The story begins with a radical piece of unexpected news that blew our minds. At the time we were an ordinary family of five. I was a stay at home mum. Mark was the Director in a Recruitment Company. We had three girls, Mark's daughter Emma who was seven, Evie two and Josie who was three months old. We had a crazy busy life that revolved around our children and Mark's long working hours. We were involved in a local church, squeezed in exercise because this was important to us and tried to get together with close friends, but outside of this there was not a great deal of space for anything else.

Josie had been born on 26 June earlier that year – 2009 – the third girl in the Simpson clan. She was a scrumptious bundle of loveliness. As far as babies go she was delightful and content, a great addition to my Little Women. We'd had a good summer, vacating in Portugal and a reasonably settled start to the September term.

We loved the girls, we loved being parents, but we found it very difficult too. Josie was our third child and what a leap that felt. You go from a 'child each' to being outnumbered. That was the turning point for Mark and I, we both instinctively knew we were finished with babies.

We weren't 'Mother Earth types'. I definitely didn't want to wrap my new babes into my coat of many crocheted colours and never let go. Co-sleeping? I don't think so. Share my bed with a slurping, snoring, snorting, snuffling creature? I already had Mark.

As for 'feed on demand' – I have something to say about that. I rang the NCT support line (National Childbirth Trust) when Evie was four months old; she had not slept for longer than 40 minutes through the night or the day since she was born. They made the craziest suggestion. They told me to take her into my bed to sleep, and when she woke up, allow her to 'help herself' to my breast whenever she wanted. Apparently, this would comfort her and soothe her back to sleep and we'd both benefit from the closeness. I refrained from challenging them over who was in charge here, Evie or me? In actual fact I have discovered over nine years that it is indeed Evie, it's always been Evie – but that's another story. The idea totally repulsed me, to be woken in the night while someone 'helped themselves' to a part of my body without my consent was not for me. Out came the devil incarnate Gina Ford with her unpopular baby feeding and sleeping routines. I love you, Gina, you saved me from social services.

Yup, the baby stage definitely gives me the jitters. I am genuinely pleased for people who fall pregnant, it is a huge blessing and an amazing experience; but I always have a little tussle inside when parents announce a pregnancy. I know I ought to be delighted, everyone else appears to be, but in all honesty, my initial response is one of sympathy; swiftly followed by a wave of compassion and finally utter, utter relief that I am finished with babies. I want to say 'poor you, you don't know what's coming to you' but of course I say 'wow, congratulations, you must be so pleased'. After all, there is nothing more amazing than the miracle of life. I DO really believe that. If only the miracle extended to babies being permanent smiling angelic cherubs and mothers endlessly as calm and serene as the Halo-adorned Virgin Mary portrayed in Baroque paintings of old.

For me, if you survived the first year it began to feel a little better. I loved it when they could toddle along on their little sausage legs. When they could talk, they could make you laugh which is 300% improvement on the previous stage. When Josie was two and the Health Visitor came for a home development check she was playing tea parties. It was all so idyllic. My toddler completely engaged in creative play, the demon TV switched off (the remote was broken from over-use) and chopped up apple for play food (I'd binned the crisps before she knocked on the door).

The health visitor and I were watching Josie playing delightfully with her little kitchen, and both cooing over her cuteness.

Josie turned around with two red plastic cups in her hand and lisps out:

'Mummy, would you like a cup of tea...or a gin and tonic?'

I have so many memories of those early vocal muddles. Grandma and Grandpa were known as 'Wanker and Wankar'; the clock was called the 'cock' and for about six months Archie was proudly introduced as 'Our baby bugger'. I love those blunders. I loved them then and I love them now.

Toddlerdom was far preferable to babydom, but it by no means transformed me into a perfect paragon of positive parenting. I did not fully shed my cocoon of baby stress and begin to spread my beautiful toddler-embracing wings. I didn't exactly prance to the park, or skip gleefully to Messy Monsters, or dance delightfully to toddler groups; this was sadly not the sort of mummy I was. It is true that I got a lot more out of it, as I said the conversations were hilarious and they really did make me laugh most days. They were more portable, which was a bonus, especially once toilet trained. And I had chosen to ignore the NCT advice of 'breast feeding whenever the child demanded it' and adopted the old school approach to a routine of feeding and sleeping at roughly the same times, I had settled babies who slept well.

However, I began to realise that as a child grows up and enters a new phase, the things you long to be free of in any particular stage are simply replaced with new challenges. Nappies may go and sterilising bottles, but along came toddler tantrums and toys everywhere. Then you foolishly have another baby and sibling fights rear their heads. Before you know it they're screaming they 'hate' you because you introduce 'screen time'; closely followed by exam stress and huge questions about what they want to do with their lives. And all the time there is some annoying parent who's a stage ahead of you informing you 'it doesn't get any easier, you know, wait until you have to pick them up at 1 am from a party and they're sick in your car'. Thanks for that, I can hardly wait.

I wasn't the only one who didn't jump out of bed every weekend longing to entertain our children. I would often find Mark on his laptop attempting to 'work' when he was meant to be 'having fun' with the children; or trying to watch football while playing 'Barbies' and being dressed up like a princess. Watching paint dry would have been more interesting to him than 'girls' make-believe play'. He'd be trying to tap away on the keyboard whilst rocking Josie in the bouncy seat with his foot, Evie clambering on his back adorning him with plastic tiaras, and Emma applying pink lipstick and dressed in his customary Saturday bubble pink tutu.

Soft play was always a winner with Mark. Mark would have paid double so that he could sit with a coffee while they entertained themselves. You wouldn't find him crawling around in delight in the grubby dinginess roaring like a lion as some playful parents seemed to enjoy. He was more of a tie a rope round their middles then let them loose in the unhygienic jungle of brightly coloured inflatables and other kids' snot; if he heard them screaming in the depths of the dirty darkness he could pull them out; rather like removing the high priest in Bible times from the inner temple sanctuary because they'd been killed for an unacceptable offering. That's **IF** he heard them over the tunes on his iPod. We **WANTED** to genuinely enjoy it **ALL**, and deep down much of it did make us coo and burst with pride, but the problem was, **MOST** of it, we simply found mind-numbingly boring.

Looking Back

I was number five of six siblings. Four of those siblings already had enough children to create a new continent. I'd become an Aunty at 17, I'd always volunteered to babysit and take them places, I loved children. I was good with children. I spent three summers as a student working with a walking holiday company, prancing around the National Parks of Great Britain like Peter Pan with a raucous rabble of under 10s. I adored it. I was in my element. Singing as loud as we could, scavenger hunts, games and dancing, some of the best times of my life.

After I graduated from Art School I completed my PGCE and went on to teach 9-10 year olds for 12 years. I had always wanted children of my own. I had always had young children in my life. I gravitated towards opportunities to look after young children. It astounded me when I had my own how difficult I found it. I really did.

Pre-Josie I was set on four children; after Josie I wished I'd stuck at two. I don't know what I was I thinking of. My mind was still stuck in my student days romping through the hills like Julie Andrews with my von Trapp family. I had plans to use flowery curtains and make them into play suits and we could all prance down to Whitley Bay beach singing 'Doe a Deer'. Mark can play the recorder, you know. The reality was that there was little cavorting in home-made clothes and much cleaning, crying and complaining.

Mark kept quiet. I knew he wasn't keen on more, but I was confident I'd wear him down. I was getting on a bit – I'd be 38 by the time Josie was born, I was already classed as a geriatric mother, I'd be an OAP mother if it didn't happen fairly sharpish. I had a few cards up my sleeve to persuade him – perhaps involving dressing up in plastic tiaras and bubble pink tutus, as he'd demonstrated a penchant for such items. Fortunately for him, and for me, I didn't have to play my cards.

Post-Josie I did not want any more babies, done, finished; the end of that chapter. If I'd found it hard with Emma and Evie, it was NOTHING on having a third. We were able to have the 'any-more-children?' chat extremely harmoniously and decided that we were content with our three girls. Yay! Look at us agreeing so easily on such a huge subject whilst still bickering over how Mark made the beds. I was hugely jubilant I had no baby-making persuasions to embark upon because my 'cards' would more than likely have had to involve more than tiaras and tutus. I had a sneaking suspicion that in order to get my own way I would need to rake out the high heels and lacy underwear and, frankly, I was just too knackered.

Troubling tiredness

A huge surprise was about to be handed to us. The first clue was tiredness shortly followed by an even bigger surprise. This is going to be the first of many times I mention the word tired. And before I even start – and this will become easier for you as this tale unravels – I want you to try and eradicate any understanding you currently have of being tired. Even in this chapter, I am not describing tired in the normal sense of the word.

I indulged in fell running when I was a student. I was known to persuade my mum to drive me out into the middle of the Lake District, drop me at the bottom of a sizeable mountain while I ran up it – as fast as I could because I was conscious she was waiting at the bottom in the next valley. Sometimes, if there was plenty of time because I'd run it so fast, I'd hit the valley and run up and down the next one. I felt physically exhausted. That's a type of tiredness.

Evie had been a longed for and much-loved baby, but very challenging. She didn't sleep for the first six months and she cried nearly all day and all night. She was extremely unfriendly to everyone and I found that stressful. She drained and exhausted me to the point I was in tears every day. That's another type of tiredness.

I and my two sisters for a period of time looked after and attended to my mother who died of ovarian cancer. It was very sad, life in limbo and nothing could lift until she had died, but of course you don't want the inevitable to happen. That's a different type of tiredness.

Then there's all the other sorts, a hard day teaching, a fall out with a friend, or a fall out with the husband, and then another one with your husband, and maybe a few more; all those things cause tiredness. So please credit me with having experienced many types of tiredness and being in a good position to be able to compare.

The tiredness I was experiencing post-Josie was something else altogether. I felt weak all the time, unbelievably fatigued. I can remember one specific occasion, my sister Sarah had come over to Whitley Bay to help me out. We had walked into the shopping centre with Evie and Josie; Emma was at school. Sarah was doing nearly all the running around and pram pushing. We sat down on a bench and I nearly passed out. Nearly keeled over on the bench, right where I was sitting. Not a faint, just from pure exhaustion, as if somebody had just sucked every ounce of energy out of my body and thrown it into the atmosphere. At the time I didn't know what was brewing away inside my body that was discreetly and silently responsible for this extreme tiredness. But I did know it wasn't normal. You have to trust me – it was not normal.

But I was breastfeeding Josie and had two other children to run around after and Mark worked a 7 am-7 pm day; tiredness was par for the course. I largely ignored it; tiredness, as I went on to learn, is an impossible thing to explain and a misunderstood reason for not getting on with your life. Mark regularly took the girls out at the weekends so I could have a breather and get on top of household chores. On one particular occasion, I was driving to the supermarket. With no children shouting at me I had a little time to ponder how I was feeling. Something just didn't feel right – I didn't feel myself, I wondered if I might be suffering from post-natal depression. I decided to make an appointment with the doctor the following day. In the meantime, I randomly flung a pregnancy test in the trolley at the supermarket. If you're a woman of child-bearing age, complaining to the doctor about non-specific symptoms, they ALWAYS ask if you could be pregnant. Of course I knew I wasn't – you had to be having bedroom gymnastics for that to happen. (This is obviously just a euphemism – neither Mark nor I have ever donned leotards or indeed any form of shiny lycra in our boudoir.) And we definitely were not engaging in such antics three months after me giving birth.

Life is not a coincidence

You can skip reading the next few paragraphs if you don't want to be faced with a few marriage realities. I have to tell the following just as it was because the gritty truth of this part of the story is also part of the overall story that unfolded and very much a part of how divine providence had a hand in my ENTIRE story.

Josie was born 26-6-09. I was breastfeeding her and she was only months old. The last thing on my mind was sex! We had three young children. I'm afraid, for us – well, maybe it was more me – dilly dallies in the dark was not my number one priority. There was no activity in that area during those summer months – zero, no way, not on your Nelly. Now this is not a miraculous tale of the second spiritual conception – of course there WAS a night, but only the ONE. I'd like to emphasise the number ONE. Got it? ONE. Look into my eyes... ONE-ONE-ONE. This basically amounts to no activity. And I was breastfeeding – I wasn't even having a regular, normal period yet. I blame the darker nights. As the season of mists and mellow fruitfulness drew in, I started to have a few glasses of wine again, and we began to socialise a bit more; there WAS an evening when the event happened. No more detail is needed, other than to say the following: four weeks later we could not remember it at all.

With my groceries all purchased, I arrived back home, unpacked the shopping and did my pregnancy test. The test went on the work bench to do its work and I set to work on lunch for Mark and the girls. Unlike the pregnancy tests for the girls that I had carefully chosen for their reliability and fast acting result, this little stick of plastic had been chosen because it was the cheapest. I have no idea how long it sat there with its dirty little secret just waiting to give me the shock of my life; it was at least as long as it takes to prepare vegetables and a chicken and potatoes for roasting, because that was my priority.

I cannot describe what went through my mind when I noticed the clear blue line confirming I was pregnant. I remember feeling hot all over. And sick. I think I laughed, more out of hysteria than humour. Then my head exploded. Well, not literally or the next nine years wouldn't have happened, would they? But the rushing thoughts and anxieties about how we'd cope. Josie was 3.5 months old! How would we manage? We did not want any more children. We'd had the conversation. We'd decided. This was not in our plan.

Mark arrived home; he did not know what I knew. He was blissfully enjoying living in the world of 'three lovely girls'. He didn't know five would soon be six. The end of nappies and weaning, and potty training and sleepless nights was not one-two years away like he believed when he had left the house hours earlier, it's more like two-four. We would have a one year old and a newborn baby. They would be twelve months apart. Evie would be three, Emma would be eight. I felt for him! I really did. I'd had half an hour to breathe and take it in.

I was sitting on the bar stool, pregnancy test in hand. Mark walked into the kitchen. The children had run away and were playing somewhere. In the background the sounds of young children laughing and playing are ricocheting around our home. Mark's smiling and bouncy – reading his body language it would be fair to deduce that he's had a good time at church. Life must have felt pleasant for Mark at that moment. I felt like a wicked mastermind about to press the button that would blast Mark's happy Sunday into the four dark corners of the universe.

Some very brief 'hello...' followed. I'd never been very good at the whole 'small talk when hubby gets in' scenario. I was far more of the 'launch straight into off-loading the top traumatic tale of MY day' kinda wife. At that moment I was sitting on one heck of a traumatic tale; a whopping piece of news. A blue line was about to rock his whole world.

Gulp, here I go.

'Mark, what's the worst thing that could happen to us right now?'

I had his attention. He looked a bit alarmed, then worried, then mad. When he spoke there was an under-current of anger in his voice. I was quite taken aback. My mild-mannered husband was displaying negative emotions towards me. I didn't sign up to be spoken to like this. Unsure how to manage this rare attitude I stopped speaking.

'You've scratched the car pulling into the drive again?'

I laughed out loud. It's made me laugh out loud today, nine years later. Mark was about to be served a very big lesson on perspective. And I was just so relieved that at least 50% of the mess we were in was HIS fault.

'I'm pregnant.'

The under-current of anger turned into a full blown shout. And wait for it – HE BANGED THE CUPBOARD DOOR! If this was an audio book, I would have screeched that as loud as I could and re-enacted the door banging moment. I could not believe it.

I have to contextualise why Mark's response showed just how mind blowing and upsetting this piece of news was to him. Mark has a fuse that you could wrap around the Earth 20 times. I mean it. He is so patient and gentle and understanding that nothing manages to 'get his goat'. One of the areas in which Mark and I are good for one another is the balance between us. Mark is calm, I am not. Between us this means that he calms me down and I spice him up.

He rarely displays strong emotions such as anger or stress; I blast them out nearly every day. Once in the very early days of being married he did get sort of angry. We'd been out for dinner and had had a couple of glasses of wine; when we returned I demanded a hammer to put pictures up in our new house. Mark didn't really want me to – probably concerned I wouldn't get them straight and then turn the hammer on him – but I insisted I could do it and he got angry with me and wouldn't find the hammer and sent me to bed. That was it, very scary Mark. I know when he's upset or disappointed or irritated, he's not a 'closed man' who chooses not to express himself. He's not a 'walk over'. He's a man who is excellent at staying focused in a crisis and not allowing destructive emotions to confuse the situation.

He lived with a woman who behaved like she was mental most of the time – certainly in those days. I could be like a banshee, a loon and with three lunatic daughters, all equally full of emotion and certainly not afraid to share it, his life was full of opportunity and triggers to retaliate and fight with us. But day in day out, no matter what we threw at him, he would calm us all down and sort it all out. And I was seeing him bang the cupboard door AND shout, at the same time:

'HOW HAS THIS HAPPENED?'

I knew he didn't mean that. He did know how babies were made. And I was confident he knew I wouldn't have had a dalliance with the coal man. The coal man knew what I was like – he'd heard me yelling like a nutter at the kids when he came to the door for his cheque. The coal man hot hoofed it down our drive faster than a whippet from the starting gate. Mark just needed to calm down and we'd get the diary out to prove there had indeed been a forgettable mistake.

It's rather disturbing to find out you're pregnant and neither of you can be certain how you created this new life. It was obvious we had, but the one occasion was such a non-event that we literally did get the diaries out and pinpoint the exact date. We were able to do this because it was one of the very few social evenings we had managed to have since the birth of Josie. When we saw the date, we knew. We knew we were guilty as the little plastic stick charged. No further proof needed. No accusations about coal men, window cleaners or decorators. Sorry, Archie – one day you'll read this and have to face that your life was not planned by two responsible adults who longed desperately for a fourth child and went about having great fun creating you. Rather it began by two exhausted parents behaving like irresponsible teenagers on a night out, having one glass of wine too many and a fumble in the dark that neither could remember later! Bless you, son.

I've debated over whether to include the next paragraph. It's a controversial subject for many. However, I have decided that I have nothing to hide. This is a story about real life, and real people, and real decisions. I want to be honest, I believe my story has impact, because I am exactly that, honest. If you judge anything I reveal, then so be it. God's judgement is the only judgment that matters to me and he knows my heart and my motives. He forgives all my mistakes and loves me unconditionally. This situation was no surprise to him and neither were our reactions.

We seriously discussed abortion. I share that with you because I want to illustrate just how scared we were of another baby. I can already hear the whispers of some peoples 'opinions' and smothered judgment. How could they seriously think about THAT? They have three children, they know what and who they become. Or this one – they are a capable and financially stable couple, what could be so bad for them that they had to consider THAT? Maybe you think this. To get out of the mess that THEY made they were potentially going to do THAT? I don't know. There are probably many variables.

Our defence was that we were really finding life THAT hard. I've tried to illustrate our discovery that we were only just managing how demanding we found the reality of having children. Another baby felt like it would break us apart. The extreme and abnormal tiredness I had been feeling was a part of our panic. Please attempt to see beyond the physical circumstances and connect with how much we were struggling. We did not go down this route. But it was a discussion that reminds us both of how terrifying that news was.

On the positive side, discovering I was pregnant explained, or so we assumed, a whole lot about my exhaustion. And this in itself was a relief. I'd been trying to lose my baby weight through hard exercise and careful dieting. This, whilst being pregnant, had probably contributed to my total loss of energy at times. In previous pregnancies I had all consuming carb cravings constantly. I was like a hoover. Chips, bread, pasta, cakes, I once ate an entire bag of oven chips in the time it took Mark to go to Morrison's for some milk. I would text him on his way back from work to bring me a McDonald's, as a starter before dinner, and I could easily consume a whole loaf of bread and marmite before Homes under the Hammer ended. And I'd been TRYING to survive off spinach leaves and a strict Weight Watchers diet. No wonder I felt so awful. It was a relief to have an answer, and to know the solution: EAT. I waved goodbye to Weight Watchers; 'Come to Mama, you beautiful buns, bagels and baps.'

It took us a while to accept that this was really happening to us. He was planned. Not by his stressed, irresponsible and exhausted parents, who were absolutely never ever having another baby – but by God. God, who is so mind numbingly mighty that he has placed billions of stars in our galaxy and hundreds of billions of galaxies in the universe planned and intended for Archie to be conceived, on that exact night. Mark and I had no choice, we knew this baby was no 'accident' – this baby was here to stay, there was a plan for this baby's life. When you have the power of God behind you, you have a candle for every corner, an anchor in every storm and direction for every turn. We trusted God that we would manage and asked him to show us the direction. So we began to walk forward – straight into the eye of the next storm.

Entering the Valley

The next couple of weeks passed in a bit of a blur. We were unable to tell anyone our 'news'. We were struggling to come to terms with it. Six months previously we had booked a night away in York; Mark's parents were coming to look after the girls. We intended to use the time for Christmas shopping.

As I'm reflecting on the plan we'd made for that particular date, long before we could ever have dreamed we may find out I was pregnant, the more I believe this trip away was not a coincidence. I believe that someone 'up there, in the heavens' knew that **THIS** night away was going to result in a second life changing discovery. What we were about to uncover we probably wouldn't have found if we'd remained in the chaos of our normal situation.

We had to get AWAY from our life in order to stop for long enough to find out what else had been growing in my body aside to a baby. We needed some time together and we needed space to relax. It was the first night away, without children, we'd had.

I have always believed, be it on a relatively shallow level, that our lives and what happens in them are in fact planned. I don't believe in being petty about this, as in it's 'predestined' I'll choose tomato soup for lunch rather than a baked potato. It's more the bigger, potentially life changing stuff, the stuff that can make us or break us; and I can't believe that this predestined 'plan' isn't co-ordinated by a 'something' much larger than little old me.

There is something inside me that can't get away from the facts and the evidence in my own life; and my observations of the world surrounding me and others around me that that this 'something' is guiding or leading, or pulling me in certain ways. The only answer for me that has ever felt completely satisfying is that this 'something' is not a 'something' like a force or a rule of nature but it's a 'person'. A loving, powerful, directive mind, the only answer to the confusion I felt within the world I inhabited. After lots of searching over many years I began to believe that this was God. The more I looked at this, and the way it made me feel inside as I agreed with this, the more I found further evidence to support this as a universal truth. I was not brainwashed or cornered into it, I am not deluded, bullied or in fear; it simply makes sense.

I don't see him as some sweet Grandpa who is very wise, soft hearted and kind, but very, very, very old. Great when he's awake, but has a tendency to doze off when you need him. I believe he is fully switched on, he watches over us, he has a vision for our lives and he knows me as an individual, and knows what I need. He knows how to get me into the right place at the right times. He's not a dictator; I am free to choose which direction I go or what choice I make in any circumstance, but he is with me and offers to guide me. Even if I make a silly choice, he will make good out of it for me.

It's a little like I parent my children; I know that they should scoot down the hill outside our house with care and caution. Do they listen? Not at first, because it's exciting to go fast and feel the wind in your face and beat your little sister or brother. After a few nasty falls and bleeding knees they begin to learn that perhaps you were right and next time they might possibly trust that they should listen to you. That there could be some value in what you say, that maybe you are much more able to see the 'bigger' picture and they slowly start to believe what you say.

Jesus made the boldest claim in history when he said 'I am the way', he knows the jungle that life can be; he knows the pitfalls because he was a man and had to walk it like we do. Jesus isn't a fictional character, by the way, he really did exist; there's a lot wider historical evidence that he was real and actually made the claim that he was God's only son.

Looking back, I'm SO indescribably grateful that I already believed in a Shepherd who knew me and would lead me through the dark valleys that might be ahead of me.

On arrival at our hotel I did what any sane mother with young children would do who had escaped all the sniffling, snotting and screaming for ONE night. I air dived onto the king-sized bed. I rolled around and thumped the duvet in delight, and then settled onto the hundreds of pillows – legs and arms spread starfish-like across the bed so that there was no room for Mark. He seemed happy enough setting up his camping mat and sleeping bag. I was about to fake sleep – I still hadn't quite forgiven Mark for his part in the creation of the fourth Simpson; there would be no 'come to bed eyes' just yet.

That's the moment when I found it. This lovely oasis of an opportunity to spend some time together, had provided a window in which I would lie still for long enough, without a small child jumping on me; and that's when I felt the lump that had been lurking in my left breast.

I didn't immediately think cancer. I was breastfeeding, I had recently had a baby and I was carrying another. All very good reasons for lumpy breasts. Anyway, Mark googled it and Google said hormones were the most likely reason. Good for Google. Just to make sure, I rang the doctor's and took the next available appointment which conveniently happened to be 5pm ish the following night. Perfect timing: we were due back to rescue the haggard grandparents from the grabbing, grasping grubby hands of the children. We weren't worried, Google was very reassuring, and anyway, we had a night out on the town to look forward to. Well, maybe more Juice bar and Joggers than Happy hour and Heels, but it didn't matter. We were child free!

So we forgot all about it.

The Lump

This paragraph is going to be a series of factual information: designed to be read quickly but gives an idea of what happened next. The Friday night GP appointment resulted in a referral to a breast clinic – this is standard routine now for women who find breast lumps. The doctor was reasonably confident it was nothing to worry about. Mark had private medical insurance – a perk of his job – so we drew on this benefit and had an appointment lined up with a breast specialist for Tuesday morning. On Tuesday Mr Griffith, the consultant breast specialist, examined the lump and did a needle biopsy. This removes cells from the lump, which are then analysed, and concludes whether breast cancer cells are present. He was reassuringly positive that he didn't think it was anything to be concerned about. So I wasn't.

There are moments in my story as precise as a specific 10 minute window. I can't tell you the date, as I explained in my opening paragraph – dates and even entire years tend to allude me – but I could use my words to paint the scene with such delicate detail that you'd see it come to life before your own eyes. I could tell you what people were wearing, where they were standing, what they were doing. I could describe the paint colour I had on the walls at the time (plum, if you're interested) or what was in the fruit bowl. I could begin to recall the smells of cooking, or what music was playing on the iPod. Numbers aren't my thing; I'm a creative, visual person and I recall my surroundings with such accuracy because I'm interested in them. The accurate recollection of one's surroundings, the sights, sounds and smells, enable an entire memory to come to life not just in your mind, but in your heart and therefore in your emotions.

The moment I'm about to relate is one such as I've just described. It is indelibly printed on my mind and heart – every single detail. It was

5.30 pm ish (seriously, you didn't think I was going to be as detailed as 5.33, did you? That wouldn't be creative memory that would be insane, OCD at its most extreme). I will spare you ploughing through the detailed descriptions that I have frozen in my mind such as Grandpa was wearing a pale blue V necked sweater – it will have no impact on the story whatsoever and probably make you go to sleep. We were all stood around the island in our kitchen before it was extended and overhauled. Mark's parents, who if you remember had come to visit to allow us a Christmas shopping spree, Mark, Josie was in the bouncy chair on the island and Evie was sat on the edge of the island drinking from a pink plastic feeding cup. My phone rang. It was Mr Griffith, the consultant breast specialist.

I walked into the hallway so that I could hear him properly. He was very matter of fact.

'Mrs Simpson, the results of the biopsy that I took this morning have come back from the lab. I'm afraid it confirms that there are breast cancer cells present.'

My immediate thought was what about my baby.

'What about the baby?'

'We HAVE successfully treated a few people in your situation. I have made an appointment for you to have a scan of your breast tomorrow. And an appointment to meet me at the RVI on Tuesday. By then I will have all the results together and have met with the Breast care team. We will have decided on the best course of treatment for you.'

And that was that. It only took minutes for my life to be blown apart. I'd walked out of the kitchen an ordinary wife and mother, battling the everyday issues that all my mummy friends wrestled with; I walked back in to break the news that I was now a mummy (a pregnant mummy) who was battling something insurmountably bigger than Kiddies, cooking and cleaning. I was battling The Big C. I had breast cancer.

It is so hard to write about that moment and do it justice. I don't think it is a moment that can be described. It's just catastrophic; my memory doesn't recall anything being very sequential. I didn't go through a series of responses; I remember it more like a rushing, tumbling, cascading sensation of many, many thoughts and feelings under which I was drowning. I felt darkness close in around me – rather as if someone had engulfed me and my happy enough life in a heavy black shroud then repeatedly spun me around, I was completely disorientated. In the seconds it took to be told I had cancer I changed. EVERYTHING changed. I knew life was never going to be the same again. I can't describe how devastating that is. I had begun a journey with grief that broke my heart – I had no idea at that point just how painful it was going to be, and how many losses – but I knew deep down that nothing would be the same again.

The battle began

A few things leap out at me about that particular night; they have significance because in many ways they have remained the biggest battles for me. I have a very distinct memory of sitting on the green sofa rocking Josie in my arms and weeping. She was wearing a pale pink babygrow with pale brown flowers on it – it had been Evie's. It was about 6.30 pm, she was full of milk and her cheeks were bright pink, which meant she was tired. I loved her so much. She was a slightly podgy baby, born bigger than Evie she was adorable to snuggle; she just lay there and looked up at you, not wiry and wriggly like Evie had been. I wept hot tears, they rolled down my face silently, and I whispered 'sorry' over and over to her. At that moment I knew nothing much about the outlook on cancer – I just knew that lots of people died from it. Maybe I would be one of those people. And that is why I wept; I couldn't imagine leaving Mark, Emma, Josie and Evie and possibly the unborn life that was growing inside me. They would not be able to live their lives without me. I don't care how dramatic that sounds, I was faced with the real concept that I may die and my carnal, gut mothering instinct was to be frightened for my babies and my husband. My job was to provide, nurture and love them, and nobody could ever do that better than me – yet I was having to consider the possibility that I may let them down and desert them many years before they would be ready to stand on their own two feet. It was unthinkable. I cried for a long time.

My second significant memory from that night was dealing with how other people respond to my diagnosis. This is a very difficult aspect to the disease – in the midst of the trauma of what you are dealing with you have to manage everybody else, and I'm sorry to say this, but most people don't respond very well. My favourite poor response in those early days was the following and I apologise if you are reading this and recognise yourself, maybe a comment like this wouldn't bother someone else, but it bothered me.

'My Great Aunty Mabel (name changed for protection!) was diagnosed with breast cancer aged 70 and she's still going strong after 15 years.'

'My mum's best friend's hairdresser had cancer. She lived a lot longer than they said – eight years from diagnosis to death – it's amazing what they can do now.'

'My mum had cancer – they thought she was cured because she reached the five year marker, but then not long before the 10 years all clear it came back.'

I understood these people were trying to reassure me, trying to 'keep my chin up'. But I was not interested in Great Aunty Mabel or someone's mum's friend's hairdresser who was fortunate enough to live for eight years! They had nothing in common with me apart from brushing with an illness which had the same name. I had three children and one on the way – as far as I could see, that fact alone put me in a camp of one. Frankly, I particularly despised Great Aunty Mabel for her 70 years of life: everyone has to die from something, and she'd had a good innings as far as I could see. I hoped she was grateful for having seen her children and her great grandchildren grow up; I wasn't sure I was going to get that blessing. Why couldn't people empathise with the moment I was in – MY moment, MY tragedy, MY tears? But many couldn't handle it, so they had to deflect from MY tragedy with some story of their own, believing this would make me feel better. It may have made them feel better, but it did not have that effect on me. This was my first brush with loneliness. I very quickly realised that in my time of need most people were going to let me down.

I needed people who were willing to draw close to me – this meant people who were prepared to LISTEN to ME and be led by how I was managing. People who could cry with me, face my worst fears with me, deal with my darkest thoughts as I worked through them. What I more often found was people could not handle this honesty and they shut me down. There are many ways to shut a person down; the minute you STOP listening and empathising and start telling a person what they should be thinking, doing or feeling, or what your experiences are, you've shut them down. And I'm talking about my friends – these comments were not necessarily from the second tier of people in my life, they were from people I expected more from. 'Don't think like that.' 'You can't say that'. 'Don't allow negativity into your mind.' 'We're not having it.' It made me so angry – I'd literally just discovered I had a disease that kills many people – it MIGHT kill me. At this stage anything was possible. How COULD my friends tell me I was not allowed to think about the worst case scenario? Most of THEM worried about a lot less.

I have always been extremely honest. I'm not talking about honesty in the black and white sense; I have definitely told lies in my life. For example, when I was a young and one of my eldest brothers examined my breakfast bowl and asked if I'd had seconds, I said 'no' because we weren't allowed. Sadly, he was older and cleverer than me and could see cornflake debris as well as rice krispie remains. I think I got beaten up. It happened often. It cost me a fortune in counselling. Mark frequently asks me how much the new dress I'm wearing cost – I always knock at least £10 off – I may even tell him it's not new, he just hasn't seen it before. And I've definitely told the children it was Dad who ate the last of their sweets, not me. Obviously, I've told more lies than three – I was just giving a few examples.

I'm talking about honesty in terms of who you are, what you struggle with and being real about the life you have and are CHOOSING to lead. I take responsibility. I face my fears and my worst case scenarios – and I FIGHT them; I rarely run from them, and if I do try, I don't get far. I don't hide behind other distractions or blame others, and I take help and action from any source that's sensible in order to defeat them. They have no secret hold over me; they are not lurking terrors that I wake in the night having sweats over. I'm not frightened of the monster in the closet, I just open the closet door and see what he looks like; if I need to call on God to help me wrestle with it, then bring it on, 'let's do battle'. Then I walk forward and I ask God to show me where to put my feet, which weapons to use, and the Holy spirit to guard my mind and heart from the monster's fiery darts. I realise this is not a trait that is common to all. It's available to all, but few choose to live like this.

I had a serious illness, I faced it, and therefore wasn't scared of it – but other people were. They wanted to deny it. Denial is fear; anything you can't stare in the face and face up to has filled you with fear. Many people are in denial that they're in denial. Some people stayed away from me, some talked about other things, some wouldn't allow me to contemplate or share with them that my life maybe shortened, they said trite and insensitive things like 'don't think like that'. Some people denied the possibility that I may die from it, they told me not to worry, that I would get a miracle. How on earth they knew that I'll never know, they must have one heck of a hotline to God; wasted in a small place like Whitley Bay, surely such a gift of prophecy is worthy of National Ministry if not International! What did they have to say about all the people who clearly don't get these guaranteed miracles? They only wanted to talk about victories and battles already won. God showed me that people were scared of my honesty because there is much they could not be honest about in themselves. In MY mind you're only demonstrating real faith and boldness when you HAVE stared into the abyss and can truly say 'Lord, your will be done, your kingdom come'. And that means even if I die. At this stage I did not respond well to people's denial – just being honest: I actually wanted to smash a few people's faces in. Oops, there's that honesty again.

I'd like to offer some ideas on how to handle people who are going through incredibly difficult circumstances. Firstly, confront your own fears – if you find it scary to talk to someone who has just found out they have cancer, then don't ignore them, ask yourself why? Why do I feel this way? What are YOU scared of? Then deal with it and get on with being a friend to someone who really needs you. Because you're not scared anymore, you can ask them how they are. It's that simple. ASK THEM HOW THEY ARE. If it makes it easier, follow this up with 'you don't need to talk if you don't want to'. Then you LISTEN. You simply LISTEN. I have been blessed enough to find a couple of very lovely new friends out of my situation, simply because they weren't afraid to ask me how I was and they were prepared to face the answer. I would then suggest one or both of the following. If you believe in God offer to pray with the person, and then pray about what you've LISTENED to. If the person has said they're scared, you pray about their fear and anxiety, not what YOU want to pray about. I had countless prayers for my healing, but very few about my anxieties. I wasn't worried about healing – God would take care of that – I was worried about how I was going to take care of the children which leads me to practical assistance. Offer to help, ask them if there's anything you can do to make life a little easier, and mean it.

To balance this up, I have to say that right from the start there were a small number of people who dropped everything and made themselves available to us, 24/7 if we needed it. In reality, these are the right people for the job, and I had to learn to let everyone else go. These people have remained close to us – they have had difficulties in their own lives – but their constancy is to be commended. Their hearts to us have always been to serve and love us in whatever way we need. They didn't just feel our pain, they lived it with us. Sure, others hurt for us, and helped when they could, but these select few gave to us sacrificially on many occasions and still do. It was evident they were heartbroken on our behalf, they entered into our suffering and have been in it for the long haul. I can't name you, but God knows who you are, and I really hope YOU know who you are. Knowing these people as I do, they'll be reading this and thinking 'she won't mean me, I haven't done enough'. So, this is a reminder to me to make sure I tell you – AGAIN – for years now, you've done more than enough. Thank you.

Finally – sleep. It was the beginning of sleep deprivation, the start of many more years where sleep on the whole began to elude me. Sometimes it would be anxiety, sometimes it would be a side effect of treatment. That first night following the news, my head hit the pillow and my mind hit the panic button. The 'whaddifs' and the 'howells', a hideous couple to be saddled with. 'Whaddif the next scan shows it's spread?' 'Howell I cope if they say I've only got a few years left?' 'Whaddif I lose the baby because of all the treatment?' It just went on and on. A horrible sack of worry plonked itself in my life; it also led me to my final significant memory of the night. I KNEW that God was with me, I KNEW he was a loving and good God and I KNEW that this whole situation was in his hands. In my heart I had God's peace. I had the answer to the burden of worry.

God wasn't behind me yelling 'Go this way!' He was ahead of me bidding me to 'Come'. He was in front, clearing the path and guiding me, he would say 'Turn here' or 'Step up here'. He would tell me what I needed to know when I needed to know it. God places himself between us and our needs – he will do the right thing at the right time; I believed this. God's presence engulfed me that night – He told me I had to learn to give him my entire attention and not get worked up about what may or may not happen tomorrow. He would help me deal with whatever hard things came up when the time came. The key I began that night to learn and I have diligently applied in many of the scenarios that have arisen since this night was this: Meet today's problems with today's strength. Don't start tackling tomorrow's problems until tomorrow. You do not have tomorrow's strength yet. You simply have enough for today. Sometimes this has been a very hard principle to live by – and I have by no means mastered it – but I am very grateful that God gave me this as a very personal word all those years ago. It was a revelation straight to my heart and as the road ahead unfolded I was very glad I listened and practised when things were easier. God wasn't going to let me see the distant scene, so I might as well quit asking, looking for it and worrying. He was promising me a lamp to guide my feet, not a crystal ball for my future; he wanted me to trust him. That night he came like a soft spring breeze and whispered to me that he is GOOD. I did not need to know what was going to happen, I just needed to know that God was my Daddy and he was a good God and I could trust him. He was going to lead me and I 'would find grace to help me when I needed it' (Heb. 4:16).

The Black Hole

We had a very heavy few days lined up. The next day I went for an ultrasound scan on my breast to determine the size of the lump. As I lay back in the chair and the Sonographer squirted gel on me and rolled her scanner around I felt it move under my left arm pit. She shouldn't be going under there – I didn't want to be sued by the NHS for her equipment getting tangled up and lost in my rather overgrown armpit hair. She explained she was checking the lymph nodes. THE WHAT!? Of course I'd heard of lymph nodes but I had no concrete idea why she was particularly checking mine out at this moment in time. What did those sneaky little suckers have to do with my breast cancer?

I had done no research on the internet regarding breast cancer, partly because I didn't want to be bamboozled with information, but mainly because most of my experiences of trying to do things on a computer failed miserably. My attempts always resulted in utter frustration that in turn Mark would have to sort out. I did not need to be frustrated by technology at this point in time. I'm a classic technophobe, I just don't 'get it'.

I never lived down my response to a fax machine when I was a teacher. I took some paperwork into the office and asked the secretary to post it to another school. I lay it down on the desk, and she said she could fax it and it would go immediately. She picked it up and started feeding my documents into this piece of machinery (it was the fax machine, of course, but I had never taken any notice of a fax machine or indeed any machine, and had no idea what it was capable of). I shouted 'STOP, DOREEN, I don't have a copy of those letters!' Silence fell in Doreen's office. It was broken by loud laughter, which didn't stop for some time. I had no idea what they were laughing at, but sensed I'd made a bit of a blunder. Alan (the caretaker) – why on earth did he have to be there at that exact moment in time? If a teacher is going to humiliate herself and behave like a total and utter blonde, she does not want to do it in front of the caretaker. He will NEVER let her live it down! – asked me what I thought was going to happen to it. I began to explain that I thought it was being sent into the machine and then transported through the wires and would end up somewhere else – hence my panic over not having copied the original. That made them laugh even more, and of course when forced to give an explanation I too could see that this was not likely. I constantly come up against issues with technology – it bores me and I don't care enough to learn; I just about function without it and life is fine. Have I mentioned that I have an amazing husband called Mark? He CAN do it – thank you, Mark. Anyway, back to the Sonographer.

She started to hover around my lymph node area rather too long for my comfort, and did this whole clicking thing with her handheld slimy mouse; I expect it's got an official name but I'm not going to stress myself out at the moment by trying to Google it. She'd done this on my breast lump and I'd guessed she was measuring it. It made me nervous that she seemed to be measuring something else. So I asked her, and she explained that two of my lymph nodes looked slightly enlarged. I can remember my response.

'That's not good, is it?' Her exact words filled me with dread.

'It would be better if they weren't.'

I cried.

She explained that because my lymph nodes didn't appear normal, I would need to have ultrasounds on my bones, liver and lungs, the favourite destinations when primary breast cancer spreads. If it had got into my lymphatic system it could already have developed secondaries elsewhere in my body. This disease was just getting darker and darker and darker – the lump was problematic enough, but now I had rubbish lymph nodes that had failed me by potentially allowing the demon cancer cells to rampage all over my body at their pleasure. I was sent immediately to the RVI to check out if these silent, sneaky, surreptitious cells had crept into my vital organs. I would have five days of near hell to wait for all the results. The next day things got even darker.

Into the Abyss

We had a midwife appointment – remember, we were still dealing with the very recent news that I was pregnant, we'd processed that we were in actual fact having a baby and any idea of termination was long gone and repented for. We wanted this baby – we had told very few people about it, but in ourselves we were happy with our accident. It had become our 'hope' in a time when everything was looking hopeless. At eight weeks you are given an appointment to register the pregnancy; from this appointment and very early check, the pregnancy is on record and dates for your 12 week and 20 weeks scan begin to be processed. We sat down, she had her paperwork out and began the standard questions. A very early one was 'are you fit and well?'. YES, I wanted to scream. YES, I am, I'm probably fitter and in better health than 80% of 40 year olds, I'm definitely fitter than YOU! (I knew this because she was vertically challenged.) It's NOT FAIR! However, I restrained myself and explained where I was up to and what we knew so far.

She looked at me, she slowly closed her notes, laid down her pen and said:

'I don't think we should register this pregnancy today. I know that some of the treatments they have to give people for cancer are very invasive and definitely not compatible with pregnancy.'

I felt devastated, utterly devastated. The black hole that swirled around me threatened to suck me down further into its fiery smoky depths. She was telling me I may have to decide to have an abortion, that the life inside me may have no future because I had cancer. Mark and I had indeed discussed abortion, and were decided – NO! this child was wanted, it was a God ordained life, there was already a plan and a future for this baby. In the space of a couple of weeks it was a word never before spoken but being bantered around once more. An enormous surge of fight for my baby rose up in me. I looked at her, and I thought three things: you are not an expert on cancer treatment, you are not God, and you are not killing my hope.

I straightened myself up from my defeated and slumped posture; I metaphorically rose like an Amazonian warrior and swiped my imaginary machete towards this imposter.

'I want to register my pregnancy – TODAY,' I said.

I had my first surge of faith. During this journey I can testify to having these power surges particularly in times when I'm being told tragic news. In these early days I'm not sure I would have identified them as Faith. I would have called them my 'will' to survive or my 'mother instinct to fight'. In a way they probably don't feel dissimilar. A feeling that rises up from your gut; a strength and power that pushes you forward, makes you determined to defy the problem that is threatening your life and blocking your goal. Tenacity kicked in and compelled me to kick ass. At the time I would have owned this fighting spirit as part of my personality; my desire to survive. I didn't fully understand that this was God.

You see, I'd found myself in some very deep dark undergrowth, I was totally out of my element. I was wandering into some thick thickets, facing failing health and hospitals, and yet deep within me I had hope. I knew I had someone who knew the way out – God knew the direction. My situation was indeed deep dark undergrowth, and it didn't look like it was set to change – but I could change. I could listen to God who urges us to lift our eyes off our circumstances and look to him. 'Don't shuffle along, eyes to the ground absorbed with what's right in front of you. Look up and see things from God's perspective' (Col 3:2). These truths do not necessarily change how you FEEL. I FELT awful; Faith and feelings are polar opposites. I felt unbelievably terrible. I really did, my body was heavy, my mind was heavy and my heart was heavy. But my Faith had risen within me – my faith didn't cave because my world had caved; it rose up. Faith is not from me – it didn't matter that humanly I was weak because God's spirit within me is strong. When we are weak, he is strong; it wasn't me, it was Christ who lives in me, the Holy Spirit rose up and carried me. On this occasion home, quite literally, as we left her office I could hardly walk, I have never felt so weak and weary as I felt at that moment and it caused me to make one of my most regrettable decisions.

We headed home through Whitley Bay and passed Escape, at the time my favourite shoe shop. They stocked Fly boots – oh yeah, baby, I loved them. I like clothes, and shoes, and boots, and sandals and bags, and accessories. I'm not a 'shopper', I detest just wandering around aimlessly, stopping for coffees and lunch, I'd much rather be out in the mountains than in the malls. But I do like new clothes – I know what style I like and I know what suits me and I know the shops to go to in order to get what I need – erm – want. The actual process of shopping for me is a military procedure. I plan the targeted locations, I plan the route, I plan the time. I want the clothes, I just don't want to shop for the clothes. I catch the Metro to Monument, straight up Northumberland Street, take a right into H&M, 'in-out shake it all about'. Carry on towards Haymarket, take a left into Fenwick's, Top shop, Ted Baker, and Coast – DONE. Then I continue into Eldon Square – practically running now – time's against me. Off to Superdry and Debenhams, no time for the meandering civilians, they part rather like the Red Sea did for Moses as this frenzied woman with a mission in mind forges through. Head down, elbows out, like some mad goose about to take flight. Mission accomplished, Sergeant – 2 hours 20 mins – purchased-1x jeans, 3x tops, 1x jacket, 1x dress: 'look good-feel better'. Best gift Mark could ever give me? That's easy, a lifetime pass to guilt-free clothes shopping.

For a month or so I'd had my eye on a very spiffing pair of knee length black leather boots in Escape with a funky heel and buckle. They'd be a welcome addition to my other boots, join the family so to speak and I'd sure be the bee's knees wearing those in the school yard, cause a bit of envy amongst some other mums. I'd hinted a few times to Mark – I HAD to involve him in a purchase of this amount- –there was no way I'd get away with 'have you bought new boots?' 'erm – yes, but from a charity shop'. Even knocking a £50 off the price wouldn't make it any more acceptable. He had not bitten; he hadn't even suggested getting them for a Christmas present – meany. As we walked silently past Escape on this dismal dark and depressing day Mark said the words I'd longed to hear many times and on many shopping trips. He stopped and turned to me.

'C'mon, let's treat you to those boots.'

I never ever, ever thought I'd respond to an invitation such as this with anything other than running and jumping into his arms shrieking:

'Oh, are you sure, darling? Are you certain you don't want to buy that new drill bit? You are so good to me, I love you, I really love you, let's get jiggy tonight.'

I stood on the street and looked up at him doe eyed and teary and with a very sad heart I said, 'I don't want them.' I felt nothing but blackness.

It's worth mentioning that I have since more than made up for this missed opportunity. I realised as the years rolled by that the cancer card can come in very handy. 'Just remember, Mark, I have cancer' has preceded many requests. Apart from clothes and shoes it's been useful for larger items too such as holidays or weekends away. I think I may actually have swung the renovation of our entire property on the back of a line that went something like this. 'I have always longed to live in a home fully decorated and furnished to my taste, not with some rooms done and others waiting; but I guess that's not an experience that I'm going to be able to have now.'

I know for certain that it was cancer that eventually persuaded him to agree to our hideous green sofa being replaced. We'd bought it in haste in a very reputable furniture shop; I don't know what I was thinking of. From the moment it arrived, I hated it. It was so green, lime green, lurid, lucid, lime green. Green is not one of my colours, I never wear green, I have never decorated anything green, and I have never gone in for bold colours in furnishings, especially not grass coloured green.

Mark loved it. He wailed and gnashed his teeth when I eventually made a full and honest confession to my distaste for it. He promptly told me that we'd have it for at least 20 years given the cost and quality of it, so I'd better do some careful accessorising to make the room more palatable to me. Believe me, there's nothing that makes illuminous green look good. Brown and cream worked the best but turned the room into some sort of 70s throwback and not in a funky way. The green sort of glowed when the sun hit it and cast a sickly green hue onto the cream walls everywhere. It depressed me.

Cancer rescued me from my 20-year prison sentence spent swathed in tones of green. 'Mark, I might get too sick to get up the stairs like my mum did; please don't let me die on this horrendous green sofa.' That was the deal breaker, my lovely, loving, lush fella agreed to the green sofa being banished. I now have a calm haven in shades of grey that when I take my last breath I will be more than happy to recline on.

Healing and Miracles

It's going to be impossible to write my story without inviting you into my world where miracles and healings probably exist in a more prominent place than many other people's worlds. Many Christians pray for miracles when they hear that you're sick. A miracle is an extraordinary event that is not explainable by natural or scientific laws and therefore attributed to a divine agency – for me, that would be God. They are instant occurrences – someone prays and 'ta-da' one's sickness can be gone on the spot. Healing, on the other hand, can take time and often involve medicine and professional intervention.

I am genuinely grateful to all the people who have prayed and are still praying for me and believing that one day I will be completely cancer free. Having said that I find it difficult sometimes when I am almost shut down if I try to explain how I feel about the whole 'shebang', but this is my story, so I'm politely going to attempt to explain now. The first thing I want to clear up is that I haven't had any physical miracles and neither have I had much physical healing yet – I have cancer that keeps spreading at a rate that my consultant would likely say medically was always his prediction. I have not defied any professional prognosis! Strangely I sometimes find myself being told by others that I have had miracles, one of these being when I didn't lose my hair during my first round of chemo. I want to say that it was *not* a miracle that I didn't lose my hair; some people persistently told me it was. The reason I didn't lose my hair was because I endured the frigging awful cold caps! It was not a miracle from the man upstairs, I'll take the credit for that, I'm afraid – not God!

Miracles/healings/slow miracles/slow healings – honestly, I don't know what to say really. Only that, believe me when I tell you that to me they don't matter half as much as they seem to matter to other people, and sometimes I wish people would listen to *me* and what I think becasue I am the one who is sick. I do believe that God can do anything – miraculous healings being one of those things – that's obvious from some of the amazing stories in the Bible. But, quite simply, the pursuit of and certain belief that I *will* receive a complete physical miracle has so little influence on how I cope with and manage everyday life – sometimes I wish people would ask me more about this.

So, for the record, this is how I manage – I simply seek God for who he is, not what he can do for me. I submit it all to God and then just get on with life and this approach has worked very well and enables me to foucs on present realities not future possiblities. I do what I can to make the best of what life has delivered to me. I am (mostly!) daily grateful and choose to focus on all that I have that is worthy of being thankful for. The *rest*, the nasty bits, I aim not to waste my time focusing on *them*. If I put this in a spiritual context – I do what I can, I leave what I can't to God. I trust that this covers off the outcome of my disease – if I die earlier than I would plan to, then so be it. If I defy the medical prediction and live until I'm 80, then this of course would be the miracle that some are convinced of. If that happens you would be extremely fortunate to have me around and I may even afflict you with more poems, rambling books, maybe a film or even my own TV show!

I am not superhuman, I *do* feel scared sometimes of dying prematurely, not so much about the actual concept of being dead, more issues like how the children will cope, and Mark, and all the other people who love me, which of course is hundreds and hundreds! Death can really give me the heebie-jeebies. However, I have learnt a lot from watching my daughter Evie face her fears. She's one of the bravest people I know. She finds new situations and new people very scary. No matter how many times I tell her that 'it will be ok', she is learning that she can't wait for 'fear' to pass before she'll step into the unknown. She steps out in her fear and then discovers it's not that bad after all. I too had to practise this valuable life skill. I often don't know what is going to happen, but I have learnt to step into the day I have, trusting God with what 'might' happen in all my tomorrows.

Carpe diem.

D Day

We arrived at the RVI; it was results day. We would be told all about my disease and what the plan of action would be. All the results would be in and the multi-disciplinary team at the hospital would know everything there was to know about my body's unwanted visitor but nothing about me. I was a faceless NHS number. We actually bumped into my consultant in the main lobby area of the hospital – we'd got a bit lost; his consultation rooms were in a place called The Lodge, which was outside the main hospital but connected by a long corridor. He spotted us and beckoned us to follow him. He had in his hand a wad of notes; I knew they were my results. It was the longest walk of my life. One I will never forget.

What does one do in a situation like this? This man knew what he was going to tell me. He knew how serious it was, what hope I had, what was going to happen to me in the coming months; it was very surreal. I am not a small talk person at the best of times, I was keeping pace with a Mastermind; he held the plan for my future – what on earth DO you talk about? The weather, your next holiday? It was the biggest case of avoiding the elephant in the room that I have ever found myself in. I desperately searched his demeanour for signs of good news or bad news, I wanted to rugby tackle him to the floor and wrench those notes out of his grip. They were MINE; about ME, containing MAMMOTH information. I lessened my pace and chose to walk behind him, time slowed right down and that corridor went on forever.

There's no softly softly when you are given this type of news. It's factual and medical. I had Stage Three Breast cancer, classified as this because it had already spread into my Lymph Nodes. Despite it being only a 1cm lump which confirmed it as being early stage breast cancer, it had already spread; very unfortunate. It was an aggressive HER2 positive and oestrogen receptive tumour. I would require an immediate left breast mastectomy and lymph node clearance and then six sessions of chemotherapy given every three weeks for about six months; followed by 15 sessions of radiotherapy to the chest wall. I would then be given 18 months of Herceptin, a type of protein, given via IV that can be effective in controlling the growth of cancerous cells. In addition I would take a tablet called Tamoxifen which blocks oestrogen from reaching the cancer cells.

What about my baby?

What I was told next, for me, was nothing short of a miracle. Because of the times and dates of my developing pregnancy, alongside the times and dates which were optimum for my treatment to give me the BEST chance possible of clearing out these naughty cells forever, there would be no risk to baby. In other words, I could proceed safely with my pregnancy, and still have ALL the BEST treatment I needed to fight my sickness.

I want to devote a particular paragraph to explaining this more fully. I hope it impacts you as it did me and Mark. I needed to get rid of my infected breast as soon as possible. After this consultation I was set for surgery in two weeks' time. My pregnancy would be 12 weeks at the time of my surgery. They would not have performed it if I was not at that stage. It would have been delayed and I would have had to consider whether I wanted to proceed with the pregnancy at the risk of jeopardizing my own health and therefore increasing the chances of more limited life expectancy for me with my other children. A decision that I had already feared might be forced upon me, was not going to be necessary to make. But ONLY because the date of my baby's conception, which remember had been a 'One Night Wonder', dove tailed perfectly with when I needed to have life-saving surgery.

I would then need chemotherapy. They like to give you a few weeks to recover from surgery BEFORE chemotherapy begins. Some types of chemotherapy are safe to give in pregnancy – the particles in the chemotherapy are too large to get through the placenta; it would be like trying to push sweetcorn through a sieve. Firstly, the best type of chemo to give me was one which is safe in pregnancy. Secondly, although it is safe to give some types of chemo to pregnant ladies, they would never do it before the pregnancy reached 12 weeks and ideally would prefer it to be further on. I would be 15 weeks when chemo would start. Making the foetus safely developed and wonderfully protected in its natural cocoon.

The course of chemo I was going to start would be completed when I was around 36 weeks. Radiotherapy would ordinarily begin a few weeks after chemotherapy is complete, but CAN NOT be done when pregnant. I would be induced at 38 weeks, the baby would be full term and safe to deliver and the radiotherapy would be able to commence within its normal time plan. To summarize, my pregnancy could develop in its normal way. The treatment for my breast cancer could proceed in its normal way. Neither was being compromised.

This baby had been created on ONE night. We could never have known that its life and mine and the future of our family were so utterly dependent on this small window of dates. It blew our minds. It was the first solid feeling of hope that I had felt so far – I believed that this baby was a sign of life to me. All around me was weighted with the possibility of death but my baby was a promise of life. A miracle, an unplanned, unwarranted gift to Mark and I, and a much needed reminder that God was good and with us.

It was a consultation of light and dark. I was overjoyed, almost leaping around the room about the baby. It was the biggest relief. I almost felt wings on my back bud and grow and lift me off my feet so I could swoop freely high into the sky with my baby on board, leaving all the other trivia behind us.

This does not mean that I didn't feel despair and great sadness, and I felt both those things after this consultation. I of course wept. The side of the consultation that was all about my breast cancer had been much worse than I imagined. Words such as 'aggressive' remain with you forever. It's a forceful word, aligned with words like 'attack' and 'violent' associated with actions like 'rage' and 'aggression'. These unwelcome cells had invaded my body, attacked my breast tissue and had violated my lymphatic system. I was a young (ish) fit, healthy, non-smoker, non-drinker. Well perhaps not entirely NON-drinker. The odd swig from the wine bottle in the door of the fridge on the pretence of getting the cheese out whilst trying not to kill my kids at a fraught tea time was purely medicinal AND essential in not causing harm to small people so didn't really count as alcohol intake. The surgeon hoped to clear out my lymph nodes and capture this rogue enemy before it caused havoc in the rest of my body. The statistics for a total cancer-free life after treatment were positive so I committed to the deliberate choice – concentrating on the largely very positive prognosis, I set my mind to fight.

The Angel

An angel was introduced to me in this consultation, in the form of Karen Verrill, a clinical nurse specialist who set up and at the time ran the Northern Breast cancer Support team. This was a group of breast cancer consultants whom she managed and was attached to as the 'middleman' between them and the patient. I think it's safe to say that we clicked immediately; in many ways we're wired the same. We're determined, stubborn, focused, hard workers, compassionate, honest to the point of blunt, organised and perfectionists. I found a kindred spirit in Karen; her diligence and care has been unending, way and above the call of duty.

She has remained my life saver from the very start. She made herself immediately accessible, day or night and has done everything within her power to help me out throughout my journey. We share the same ironic, dark humour bluntly saying what many think but don't feel able to say. I think it was only the second or third meeting when she started telling me about a number of past patients, keeping it anonymous and done only to support me. She told me about women also diagnosed with a breast tumour like mine who even when recovered spent the rest of their lives worrying about dying or what would happen if it came back.

Only to live a long life where in fact in the end it was the husband who unexpectedly died! It really impacted on me the pointlessness of worrying about the future and helped me to face my illness from a place of reality not imagination.

Due to her dedication and commitment to the job and others, we rarely hang out as friends. I think we have managed only two evenings in nearly eight years with a bottle of wine outside hospital settings. But a friend is how I classify her; I hope I live long enough to see her workload lessen, enabling many more visits to the pub. However, I suspect that this awesome lady will still be fighting the cause for cancer sufferers until she takes her last breath. Assisting people to find their wings and fly again; using her angelic supernatural strength to give them hope.

It should be noted that she extends this extraordinary attention to all patients she encounters, it is not just me. Her husband is my oncologist and what a team they are, dedicating their lives to helping women live well with cancer. He is real and truthful but the vibe that emanates from him is compassion and determination to fight with you. I have no idea how they do it. Karen is now centre head of Maggie's in Newcastle; part of a network of drop-in centres which help anyone affected by cancer. This did not exist in 2009 when I first became acquainted with Karen. I will return to the value of the Maggie's centre further on.

Karen is a phenomenal woman; her life is 100% focused on other people. As a friend she has shared with me some of her private life too, particularly caring for both her poorly parents. Often leaving her day in the hospital well after 6 pm and going straight to tend and care for their needs too. There is no bottom to her depth and capacity to show compassion. She has rescued me and many others from the clawing cloak of cancer. As part of the service that came with Karen, was an invitation to come along to a drop-in group once a month called Ladies in Pink Scarves, a support group for women at various stages of living with primary breast cancer. The first time I went I sat next to a lady called Claire; she was a few months ahead of me in the primary treatment plan. She had already had a couple of chemotherapies, had lost her hair and was wearing a wig.

We connected immediately; strangely she lived just five minutes away from me in Whitley Bay, which made it very handy for all the socialising we were to do in the coming years. Attractive, stylish, same age as me, a mum, chatty, funny and understood the lows and mental challenges that follow a diagnosis of cancer. Which, fortunately, my other friends had not experienced, but unfortunately meant they couldn't fully appreciate many of the difficulties I faced daily. It's a friendship that was borne in tragedy but blossomed in the adversity we both faced. Friendship isn't about whom you have known the longest. It's about who came into your life and never left your side. Claire has been that friend to me.

Our friendship bloomed and we have laughed our way through many shadows. Claire is a natural PA. She slid into this role in my life. When our paths separated, she becoming stronger and I weaker, she took on the much valued and essential role of 'friendship events manager'. There are no limits to the adventures Claire has pondered, planned and purposefully made happen. She even provides picnics. One day she may have to push me in a wheelchair. I imagine she's already got some plans up her sleeve.

The most epic journey she has organised was a trip to Downton Abbey, its real name being Highclere Castle. We were both huge fans of the British drama that follows the lives of the Crawley family and its servants living in a beautiful Georgian Manor from 1912 to 1925.

We had to be at a coach station in the centre of Newcastle for 4 am. What an insanely early start. We arrived in the dark to find only one other passenger waiting, a rather random old lady who reminded me of Maggie Smith, the actor who played the main character in The Lady in the Van (and played Dowager Countess Violet Crawley in Downton Abbey). She smelt a little like I imagined the Lady in the Van smelt like too. Not too good I can tell you. Maybe this woman also lived for 15 years in a dilapidated van on someone's driveway. I persuaded Mark to take me to the cinema to see The Lady in the Van. He protested but the lure of an evening eating Pick 'n' Mix was too great for him and he acquiesced.

I love a good British film, especially when it's based around a true story. I can tell you it was definitely an authentic, honest, real life experience that night. After about five minutes I became aware of this horrible stench; I have a very sensitive sense of smell and a very vivid imagination. I wondered if my mind was playing tricks on me; so engrossed was I in the film that I seemed to have conjured up a 4D experience and could actually smell The Lady in the Van right where I sat. I sniffed around a bit like a dog catching the whiff of a rabbit and discovered to my horror that it was in fact the old man sat next to me. Good Lord, he smelt like he had spent 15 years living in a van too. Maybe there was a whole convoy of them come to view their heroine. I spent the rest of the night virtually sitting on Mark's lap while he munched sweets and moaned in my ear about smelly old ladies in vans; I shoved a handful of cola bottles in his mouth and told him I'd go and see the next Star Wars film.

Claire and I went right to the back of the coach like school girls; the eccentric lady thankfully didn't follow. She sat behind the coach driver and took out her sick bags; I hoped she didn't miss and spew down the back of his neck. We baggsed the back row all ready for a sing-song, having ascertained that this was a coach trip in the middle of the week and based on the age and presentation of 'van lady' that nobody else would be wrestling with us for this coveted position.

Voices ready for 'The Wheels on the Bus', we left Newcastle. We were asleep by the time we hit the next stop. Newcastle to Berkshire is about 300 miles; if you drove it would take around five hours. If you go on a coach that stops at every town and city en route and some that didn't even feel like they were en route it takes more like 15 hours. I am not kidding.

I don't want to do Claire's excellent planning skills a disservice, but somewhere between her concoction of this epic trip and her communication of exactly what it entailed, some details had gone awry. It's a number of years now since we went on this expedition, but if my memory serves me correctly I THINK it came as a bit of a surprise to her too! But the wonderful thing about Claire and I is our mutual sense of humour. The journey went on and on and on, but so did our giggles. I don't think it would matter if all we ever did was sit on buses and ride around for we are two ladies who love to laugh and certainly tickle each other. Not in a physical way, of course.

I had only recently had some treatment that had really caused me bowel issues. It wasn't the only time treatment caused this difficulty, but it was very unfortunate to be in a confined space with a non-family member and the need to fart like a trooper every half an hour. They really smelt too. A bus load of old people helped to masquerade my embarrassing problem. I am convinced there was a few of them dropping botty burps because every now and again I'd get a whiff of an alien smell which I didn't recognise as mine. I tried to let them seep out slowly and silently but sometimes the build-up of wind was just too much and a noise would follow. Thankfully the variety of sounds kept poor Claire entertained.

We arrived at Downton Abbey about 12.00 noon the NEXT day! I should mention that we had an overnight stop – it wasn't 30 hours on the coach. And we were still able to laugh at our monumental misunderstanding about what our mini adventure actually entailed. We had roughly 2-3 hours there, which was adequate, and with our usual easily pleased attitudes we got on and revelled in the film set we had finally reached. Nothing was going to quench our passion for walking in the same footsteps as Carson, the stern but dedicated butler to Lord Grantham. We could tangibly feel his presence.

We arrived back in Newcastle at around 3 the following morning having finally, around 9 pm run out of things to say; for the record running it took Claire and I 41, well maybe 34 hours if you allow for going to bed in the hotel, to have no topics left to discuss. That is fairly impressive. If sleep hadn't finally forced us to stop I'm sure we'd have continued until the bitter end.

Groggily we gawked into the darkness from the coach windows expecting to see Newcastle Central Station. Instead our bleary sleep-filled eyes could make out a supermarket carpark that neither of us recognised. Confused and alarmed, we peered down the aisle and were relieved to see that Van Lady was still perched behind the driver's seat amongst her sick bags. Confirming that we had not slept past our stop and ended up goodness knows where.

It turned out that the engine of the coach had begun to overheat. Thankfully for us and Van Lady, the bus driver had managed to get us into an Asda carpark in the small place of Washington (not Washington DC, although NOTHING would have surprised me), on the outskirts of Newcastle. There was no other option apart from phoning a taxi. I'd like it to be noted that we were kind citizens and despite the fear of the sick bags we asked Van Lady if she wanted to share with us. 'Which part of Newcastle do you live?' she asked in a distinctly upper class accent. Her diction did not match her bedraggled, saggy, wrinkled stockings and dishevelled vintage floral corduroy dress. She was an apron, rollers and head scarf away from Hilda Ogden; the working class cleaner in 1970s Soap Opera, Coronation Street's 'Rovers Return' pub. We stammered in surprise 'Whitley Bay'. 'Oh no, darlings' (very luvee amateur dramatics style) 'I'm going to The Grove in Gosforth, wrong direction, dears, but thank you awfully.' Never judge a book by its cover.

Van lady, not waking to the archways of the train station, 50 odd miles on a coach for a three hour whiz around a house, my farts, the whole saga sent us so past ourselves that we laughed and laughed all the way home in the back of a taxi. The taxi driver must have thought we were loons on the loose. I am inclined to agree with him, but I love being a 'loon on the loose' and Claire and I have done it many more times since this incredible journey and plan for many more trips in the future.

HO! HO! HO!

Christmas 2009: surgery was set for after the holidays. I have sat here at my laptop trying to think of how to explain the 2009 Christmas, and I've drawn a big fat blank. I was 11 weeks pregnant, with a six month old, a two year old, a seven year old and a tumour. The existence of half of those was totally unexpected and extremely challenging. My New Year was to begin with my left breast being butchered and six months of poison pumped into me which would make me sick, exhausted and lose my hair. I was to be transformed from a seemingly healthy individual into an extremely poorly one; yeah, right then there was not a lot of festive cheer bouncing around. We'd been hit by a meteor and thrust into the darkest of stratospheres. We had not even begun to land back into reality and were now having to listen to Jingle Bells, rake out our Elf onesies and fight Christmas shopping frenzy to purchase plastic tat for the kids. It would be fair to say that it was a struggle; actually, it was horrendous.

When you are given news like we had been given it may be corny, overused and you've heard it all before; but there really is no other way of saying this, you have immediate PERSPECTIVE! 2009 Christmas became about perspective. Your life comes into sharp focus, you shut down, you prioritise people, activities, materialism, you enter survival mode. This means that anything that might cause the ship to sink gets thrown overboard. You cull. Brutal as that sounds, that is what happens. You don't even do it deliberately, it just happens because you have to give all your energy to surviving. Relationships are the main one to go. I discovered very quickly that many people were a drain. The ones that stayed remained because they GAVE. They focused on us, they saw a need and they responded. They said very little, but in their own unique ways they served a lot.

The small group who did this, of course, were people who were already close to us, lifelong friends so to speak. An experience such as we were facing offers the opportunity to separate the wheat from the chaff; it's interesting seeing how various people react and respond. It's awesome when friends whom you knew were keepers prove to indeed be so, but on a superhuman level. Beth and Richard Brown – 'on it like a bonnet' Browns – before I even thought about what I needed, they had it sorted. The best 'couple' friends a couple could ever hope to have. It was these guys who at the same time were able to stare reality in the face whilst be our 'practical' pioneers; looking at what was going to be essential for survival in the coming year and organising how it could be provided. We had a Nanny in place but what would happen on a Saturday and Sunday. 'On it bonnet Browns' just went ahead and organised a rota of church volunteers to take the children to the park or out to tea, lunch, swimming, anything that would give us a break and a chance to recuperate.

We have such a rich tapestry of experiences and intertwined lives with Betty and Ricardo. Family holidays when their kids were young and ours kept popping out, Portugal, camping, BBQs, skinny dipping (we will never divulge that story – too many suspicious little minds who'd make it into something it really is not). New Year parties together playing dares, Richard, do you remember the window in Armstrong Avenue? We saw the whole of the moon that night, didn't we? Torturing Beth with games such as pass the orange; ignoring her fear of physical contact. Sunday lunches, Saturday night parties, Friday night sofa crashing.

Highs of life, lows of life, Richard's and my constant hilarious life stories about the blunders we make and the scrapes we get into, journeys of spiritual growth, personal challenges achieved and failed, laughter, tears, arguments, disagreements, honesty, maybe wanted but sometimes not, advice given, advice rejected, care, signs of aging, signs of maturity (maybe not in Richard or me), money shared and so much time invested. Underpinning all of this, such love; vast as the ocean, reaching to the skies and digging down to our depths. Such commitment, such faithfulness; I truly believe that there will never be another couple who have loved us and served us like Betty and Dick. I am unable to express or do these two bosom (I can hear the sound of me and Richard giggling over words such as bosom) buddies justice. I could write a whole book simply on the lives the four of us have shared. No one would be interested so it would be a complete flop, but a foursome as awesome as ours deserves one.

Dawn Foss, a girl I rented with in university days. Her bedroom was next to mine and on summer nights we would hang out of our windows and put the world and each other to rights. She's in Cornwall now but even from that distance she's found many ways to bless me and support me; our phone calls are legendary. They start with 'hi darlin' then cut to the deepest part of soul bearing; always ending with 'I love and miss you so much'.

She is such a testimony to the fact that distance and physical time are not the main ingredients for close, solid, dedicated friendship. This woman unceasingly searches for little, personal ways to demonstrate her affection for me; to remind me that although she is not round the corner anymore I am always in her heart. Cards, letters, wee gifts in the post, subscriptions to magazines, trips to meet me, trains, planes, or automobiles. She's hilarious too and such a spectacular laugh. She opens her mouth really wide, like she's going to swallow me whole, and shrieks; it's contagious.

To be honest, if she still lived locally I'd probably have divorced Mark and moved her in. What do you think, Dawn? Shall we start planning our nursing home? Mark told me the other day that if he died I'd have a lot of money. 'These things can be arranged,' I told him. I love the thought of us growing old together, pair of old dears in slippers, drinking tea, still putting the world to rights, toothless and carefree? I reckon that pesky younger sister of mine would have to be included too; there's always a cloud on the edge of a silver lining.

Then there's Jackie and Alan; my Geordie Mam and Da. Anything I ask they try and do, such love for me and so faithful in prayer and practical support. On the surface Jackie and I are unlikely friends. Different backgrounds, different education, different type of family, different heights (this isn't difficult because Jackie's the size of a small child), different styles, humanly very different. But as we grew in friendship we discovered that we actually have a lot in common.

We love trashy TV, musicals, humour, time keeping, organisation, 'plans' and we both make huge typo blunders in texts. Our mutual love of London is a biggy; we are the most excited tourists you will ever see. Shrieking 'It's Big Ben, get a selfie quick, it's just like it is on the telly'; trawling Covent Garden and Oxford Street hoping to spot a famous person. One such trip holds one of my favourite memories. We were in a café just near the British Museum and she sent a typo error in a text to a lady in the church. Rather than start the text with 'hello Fiona' she'd put 'hello dirty'; I have no idea how she'd got from Fiona to Dirty, but it really tickled us. We both laughed until we cried, like silly schoolgirls, but that's me and Jackie. You had to be there really.

She is, aside from all the laughs, a very constant friend in my life and was amongst the first couple of people I rang when I discovered I had cancer. She was shopping in the Metro Centre when I called with the news that not only had it just been confirmed that I had breast cancer, but that I was 6 weeks unexpectedly pregnant. Before that day Jackie and I had not really been friends as such, but from that moment it has grown and grown and become deeper and deeper. She has referred to me like the 'daughter' she didn't have and I feel hugely honoured. But to be honest, although I can think of no greater compliment from anyone, for me, although there IS an element of 'parenting' in our friendship, mainly I see her as one of my best friends.

These are the people who took the un-cut version of who I am. Through tears and snot, they cried with me, they comforted me, not by words but by companionship. They had hope on my behalf, they stood in the gap for me when my grief became too much to bear, they didn't run from me or were uncomfortable with my raw emotions, but they felt the same. Friendship isn't necessarily about whom you've known the longest. It's more about who's walked into your life and proved they're there for you in all circumstances; always seeking to meet your needs in small or big ways. These people are still doing this today.

My closest friend Sarah, my little sister; my whole life she's been involved in everything I do. I have no memories of life without her. Born 18 months apart, we have shared and supported each other; my bezzie mate above all others. Always stepping up to the mark when life has given me a bum deal; always cheering me on when there's cause for celebration. I guess we've shared all of life together and that cannot be matched by any other person. I am unable to reference any particular event or experience as being the reason I love her so much. She understands who I am and why I am who I am, because we have no memories that do not involve each other. I have written a poem about Sarah; it sums me and her up.

Sarah

You have never known life without me
I had only 18 months of life without you
Sliding, careering,
Meandering, flying
Dipping, diving
Weaving and wandering
Pulling each other through
To THIS – our Middle Ages.

Early memories are distant and few
Down in the allotment summery days
Amongst the daisies, daffodils, sweet peas
We sat side by side smiling
In matching summer flowery dresses
And heated haze
Cabbage patch kids
With sweet little faces
That was me and you

The Baptist Church bluebell picking
Swathes of indigo under dappled trees
Bonfires, dunking apples so carefee
Mrs Baxter's sticky treacle toffee
Easter singing with Harry on the organ
'Up from the Grave He Arose
With a mighty triumph o'er his foes'
You were always singing with me

Keswick-camping – giggling
In our bags at night
Made up games of Wonky Donkey
I can still feel you riding on my back
Practising kissing on each other
And daring each other to 'touch tongues'
Nipping, fighting some vicious attacks

Sibling threats and throw away hurts
But a loyal indestructible love lies
Between You and me

Rain or shine the lakeside mountains
Mummy beckoned us and called
Up Helvellyn, High street, Blencathra
Fog, gales, snow
Sun, vertical rain – all seasons
Windy photographs on blustery peaks
We reached the heights of
Many mountain tops
Always conquered with you and me

The dam at Braithwaite
A favourite location
Dinghies and diving
Ducking and delight
Hours spent in mountain streams' water
Straight from freezing springs
Slate houses, pooh sticks under little stone bridges
Summers passed in glorious hue
And none of them spent without you

Christmas Mummy's favourite time
Gifts of dolls and home-made clothes from her capable hand
Tiny tears, teeny tiny tears
Teeny weeny tiny tears where would the line end
Mini micro Itsy bitsy teeny weeny tiny tears?
Hours we spent with our dollies so dear
Just like us our Tiny Tears, we cried real tears
We were make believe mothers
With babies to love and rear
Childish nurturers were you and me.

Love and Marriage
Longed for – found – re found and lost
Babies yearned and desired for brought joy

But unexpected cost
In sickness and in health
We've done it all together
Down to the depths and on mountain tops too
There is NO ONE in my life
Remotely like YOU

Sarah – I could go on and on
There's nothing we haven't gone through
Separation
Misinterpretation
Fights and fall outs
Disappointments, depression
Death of both parents before we were due
Rejection, dejection, disconnection
But always, always and forever supported by you

Life can be a battle we both know
But we'll stand side by side
Into the next fight we go
Shields to each other offering protection
Loyal, faithful 'Brave Hearts' are we
Our Blood runs deep with devoted affection
Sarah, dear Sarah, I want you to see
That there will never be a time without a you and a me.

Rebekah Simpson

Because of such people we were able to navigate the tat, tangerines and tinsel, and focus on the gifts of family and friends. Humour is big between my siblings, sometimes it's a little dark and maybe others wouldn't be so direct, but I love it. We landed at my elder sister Ruth's and were greeted with a 'nipple tipple'. A champagne cocktail with a red maraschino cherry bobbing around in the top, a tribute to the nipple that was due to be discarded. I loved it: nine members of my family all raising our nipple tipples and able to laugh and joke despite our broken hearts.

Mummy

We were so blessed with our children and an unexpected one on the way. Perspective helps you get the wrong things in the right place and the right things in an even better place; in many ways I am very grateful that cancer brought that mindset into a daily reality for me. I faced the possibility of death, based on the doctor's prognosis; I felt its icy grip wrap around my heart and this experience, I know now, never quite leaves you. It changed me as a mother.

My relationship with my own mum had been far from plain sailing. She did love me, she prepared meals, not necessarily ones I liked, such as sausage meat Shepherd's pie, or liver with tubes in. Due to finances it was always cheap meat like sausages which my brothers took great delight in extracting the gristly bits from and waggling them in front of my face while she was back in the kitchen. I'd cry and not be able to eat the disgusting thing, then I'd get told off and made to sit at the dining room table alone facing the cold, fatty, grisly meal until I'd finished. The best thing that happened in our house was getting our first dog Scamp; I quickly realised that she was more than willing to wolf down sausage scraps that I threw off my plate under the table. Even my brothers didn't cop onto that one and tell on me.

She provided clothes, if I'm honest, a little more HER taste than mine; she had a very perverse desire to only ever get you the clothes that were in fashion, but when they were definitely no longer in fashion. This was torturous for me; I have always had in interest in clothes and fashion, which was in direct conflict to anything she was interested in. I have lots of tales of changing down back lanes and in public toilets, removing the oversized unflattering outfits and replacing them with clothing much more in keeping with my peers.

She supported us educationally, to work hard, do our best and focus on our talents and gifts. This area was her greatest success as a parent. I knew what I was good at and I was free to enjoy this aspect of who I was. She was in awe of my creativity and very proud of anything I achieved. She believed in commitment and doing your best, not giving in at the first sign of difficulty. I have been able to turn to those deeply entrenched values many times in my life and am convinced that it is largely down to this that I have survived so well the situation I am currently in.

The most important thing: she believed in God, and this has, overall, been of tremendous importance in the person I became and am today. I can never remember a time when God was not in existence within our family; he was not always 'healthily' demonstrated but there was enough truth and positive experience to have an impact on choices I ultimately made as I grew up.

Her own emotional love for me was sadly lacking. I have no memory of her ever telling me she loved me or ever cuddling me. She praised my achievements but never affirmed who I was as a person. I do believe she didn't really like me much; she loved me, in the sense that she was not a cruel woman and she had a carnal love for me; but I never felt she liked me. She was dictatorial, needed to be in control and if she couldn't get control verbally, she would hit you. Not in a way that would have warranted outside intervention, but it was undeserved, definitely out of control, and produced nothing but anger and hurt. This greatly affected my confidence, and my sense of being loved, accepted and secure.

Long ago, thankfully when she was still alive, I forgave her and worked hard at building a relationship with her in my later 20s. I never received an apology from her or a declaration of love. We did achieve a relationship of sorts but how I wish I didn't have the memories I have or the lost years to grieve over. I would love to have heard, just once, 'I love you, Rebekah'. People are complicated, she was complicated; I'm glad I felt driven enough to continue seeking and pursuing her. As time has gone by I've been able to focus less on the faults and allow the pleasant memories to surface.

When I had my own children, the first thing that hit me was how much I loved them. Not in a distant, removed fashion, but in a deep and totally natural fashion. I found the practicalities difficult as I explained earlier in my story, but from my heart, I adored them. From the first time I saw them I was enraptured and despite all my difficulties in actually raising them, I still daily feel that way. Just this morning, Josie was reading her school book to me. I wasn't focused at all on what she was reading because I was having a moment. A moment is when I feel utter love for them. I looked at her beautiful face, straining in concentration over some word or other, and watched her little mouth try to sound out the words and I just felt love for her. And I had to tell her, I leant over and stroked her little soft freckled cheek and said, 'Josie, I love you so much, you're adorable. How did I get to be so blessed with you? I'm so grateful you are mine and didn't go to another mummy.' Some of you may be reading that and feeling a little queasy; it does read like a paragraph out of some Mills and Boon novel, but it's the truth, I really feel that way and I really express it to them, all of them.

Now please don't get this out of perspective; I lose the plot all the time. My all-time low was chasing one of them round the pool table. I like the last word, so do all of my children – this causes problems, many problems. On this particular occasion I had gotten into a very enraged and feisty argument with one of them. Arguing with young children is a pointless activity which I frequently used to give into. Out goes my 40 something year old maturity and I'm back in the playground again.

The root of everything they say is motivated by something they want and a reaction to you saying no. They are relentless, and they scream and cry and get really cruel when they don't think you're going to cave. This particular child would call me horrible names like 'rat face' – oooooooo, that hurt, being told you had a face like a rodent was just nasty. Or 'fat head'; I resented any reference to 'fat' – I worked really hard at weight watchers – and the worst was 'big bum'. Never, ever, tell a woman she has a big bum; they might just chase you round a pool table, or any table, or just chase you. Which is what I did. The child was too fast for me, I pulled a muscle in my back trying to take the corners of the table too sharply. When I eventually caught up with her in the hall I decked her and we both rolled around like that until our eldest child separated us.

This was not one of my finest moments. Many of these scenes and the lack of control I demonstrated were a direct product of my own experiences as a child. I was in danger of turning into my mother. I maybe told my children I loved them, which I prided myself over because my mother never achieved this; but I needed to be in control and definitely struggled to stay calm in the face of the storm, especially if my bottom was under criticism. Cancer was instrumental in eventually changing my perspective and my behaviour in all aspects of my parenting.

If it hadn't been for the perspective that having a life-threatening illness brought to me, I am certain incidents like I describe above would have continued to happen. I was parented in a harsh way, and although I adored my children I knew that I was in danger of repeating the same scenarios that I had grown up with. When I got diagnosed with cancer, I had a huge awakening. I loved my family, I didn't want a household that was amazing sometimes and like a war zone at others. I knew at times that I overstepped the mark, and having the reality of potentially being removed from my children's life prematurely and never having the luxury of addressing issues with them in their late 20s as I had, made me begin a journey of improving MY behaviour before it was too late. I was given a fresh chance, a chance to love even more.

In a strange way, I am very grateful. There's nothing like the reality of death to make you re-think your attitudes and actions. To choose to behave differently; kindness over justice, joy over misery, peace over conflict, patience over irritation, goodness over bitterness, faithfulness over inconstancy, gentleness over harshness, self-control over control and Love over everything. I have in no way mastered living this way, but I know that I may never have even made any of the small changes I've made if it weren't for Cancer.

The Nanny State

Have I told you before that I have an amazing husband? Just to hammer the message home: I have an amazing husband. He has a rational, compromising, calming, compliant personality, the perfect balance to my more irrational, stubborn, feisty, challenging character. He calms me down and speaks perspective to me; I rarely listen immediately, but he never gives up on me. He'll watch me spark off, fly around the house like a banshee banging doors and slamming pots and spitting foam, and then I hunt him down, seeking his soothing persona and all is well. I fire him up a bit, my dramatics turn him from a korma to a Dansak; the pepper to his salt, the storm in his teacup, the fire in his otherwise stable, logical, reasoned world. He says he actually quite likes this and it was one of the things that really attracted him to me.

As much as we may differ in personality, we are fundamentally similar in our attitudes to life. We have the same beliefs and morals, and very similar goals, aspirations and priorities in regards to key areas such as money, kids and family. We have enough in common to enjoy sharing leisure time together and in essence we're the best of friends.

We sit together most evenings watching TV and Mark massages my feet. This is an institution in our home. It started during some gruelling treatment, to give me relief, and it has never been allowed to stop! Uh Uh, no way; it is an essential part of marital harmony now. Mark tried a few times to 'reduce' massaging my feet and I was forced to pull the 'cancer card'. The cancer card can be a very useful tool. I am not proud of this weapon, did you hear me? NOT PROUD, but as this is an autobiography based on total honesty, then I am willing to share. It goes a bit like this. I see some item of clothing or footwear that I'd like to have but it doesn't pass Mark's 'Ok to Purchase Test', which is basically 'Do you need it?'.

Well of course I don't NEED it, not in the great scheme of things I don't. My life doesn't depend on the latest pair of Birkenstock sandals – which woman's really does? I just WANT them, they'll give me a little spring in my step and a splash of happiness in my world of domesticity. I know women who have entire rooms for their clothes and shoes; I'm not one of these blessed females, but I know of them. Mark needs to work on his perspective in this area, and remember the advantages to himself when he says 'yes', say no more, wink wink.

Pulling the cancer card means all I have to say is: 'Can I buy a new pair of Birkenstocks? Just remember, I have cancer, I might not be here much longer.' It works every time. Please don't judge me – if you had trawled your way through the removal of part of your essential gender definition, had suffered much sickness, lived in constant pain and discomfort, watched all your children distressed and scared about Mummy being ill and observed 'normal' life largely slide right past you, you'd probably resort at times to the odd bit of manipulation. Cash in on the benefits so to speak. Keep it real, ok?

The cancer card had to be pulled over Mark's attempt to reduce 'foot massage time'. It just had to be. I couldn't get through my challenging day without looking forward to this time of connection with my Super Man. It is now an integrated part of our life and has been for years; we even named the moves. The Yank, the Twist, and the Crack Rub (which is my personal favourite). I'll leave the details to your imagination.

The one of the most amazing things my husband does is manage our finances exceptionally well. I am a kept woman. I mean this in a healthy balanced way; he's very good at it and I am good at other things. One of which is seeing his faults and making sure he knows about them in case he gets too arrogant – who'd want an arrogant husband? Not me. It's a vitally important and very loving trait of mine. It keeps Mark's character finely tuned. As I write this I'm realising that perhaps Mark does not appreciate my life coach skills; he can at times be a tad ungrateful for my correctional skills. I'd better do the loving thing tonight and tell him that his attitude needs sharpening up a bit.

Mark has always worked hard and earned enough to meet all our needs; he saves and invests wisely and he gives generously out of the wages that he earns. We are very blessed. When I gave up work to have Evie, un-known to me, he took out a life insurance to cover me if I was ever to become too ill to work. With my wage going, and no family locally, if I got too sick to look after the children we would be in a lot of trouble. In the midst of Christmas 2009, Amazing Mark shared with me that our biggest concern, looking after Emma, Evie and Josie following my mastectomy and throughout six months of chemo whilst pregnant, followed by radiotherapy, was taken care of. The insurance would pay out and we would employ a Nanny to help me.

We started the process immediately. Interviewing nannies was certainly not a position either of us ever expected to find ourselves in. Attila the Hun was out straight away. I was sure she'd keep them in line – her facial hair alone would be enough to silence them; they'd be able to twirl it round their plump little fingers and giggle at its wiry feel. Even MY knees were knocking underneath the table from her terrifying stare.

Mary Poppins was very sweet, but a spoonful of sugar one too many for my liking. The Big Momma was awesome, she promised us home-made pasta, meltingly good pizza and gelato. I could feel my thighs getting larger with each calorific laden description. I imagined me and the Momma swigging glasses of red wine in the kitchen over the large pan of rich bubbling Bolognese singing 'That's Amore' while the 'bambinos' snoozed. I couldn't take my eyes off her enormous bazookas. I don't know so much about the moon hitting my eye, probably more likely her very soft swinging breasts – the idea of my Friday evenings slurring after too much wine was certainly 'amore' to me, but it would be a situation that ended in tears. I would end up like an oversized piece of pale, dumpy Gnocchi. For health reasons alone she didn't get a second interview.

Then there was the pretty princess, absolutely beautiful blonde petite girl, perfect skin, perfect body. But there was no way I was going to be accompanied anywhere with her. It would be like Mr Blobby hanging out with Taylor Swift. As my pregnant body enlarged and ballooned over the coming seven months this tiny, miniscule little doll dressed in skin tight jeggings and itsy bitsy teeny weeny tops that looked like she'd borrowed them off a Barbie Doll, would be lost forever in yards of fabric from my voluminous tent-like Mothercare Maxi Maternity dresses. I was capable of becoming so depressed and green eyed about this imbalance that it was not beyond the realms of my imagination that one day, under the pressure of pregnancy hormones and chemotherapy sickness, I'd lose it big time. Simply launch myself at her like a hippopotamus might, unprovoked, but threatened by her sheer perfectness. Flattening her underneath my huge stomach and swinging breasts. In the interests of saving her life, she would not be employed.

We did find our girl. She had been a Nursery Nurse for a couple of years. She was also pretty, tall, and blonde, but she had an eye that looked the wrong way and somehow this made her more human. I found out in the coming months that this was down to having come into contact with cat faeces as a baby; she'd contracted Toxoplasmosis and subsequently lost her sight in one eye. She was real, open and had an excellent sense of humour; very sharp and able to make fun of herself.

The One Eyed Nanny; I loved that we could connect like that; both Mark and I felt she was the one for us. Her references were outstanding; she had no experience of being a Nanny, but this was perfect too. She brought no comparisons with her of other children she'd nannied, or other bosses; we'd all be learning together how to make this strange scenario work. She lived down the road, had a wonderfully supportive family and due to her age, 17, we were confident she wouldn't be bailing out on us in six months to get married or have babies of her own. The job was hers.

Hannah Burridge, an angel, still in our lives today. Nine years of service and devotion and the biggest heart ever. No longer classified as a Nanny, she's part of the family, I love her very much. She walked the journey with us in those early months and what became years, in a more intimate way than anyone else in our lives. Nothing was too much for her: at one point she sustained 10-hour days, six days a week. She looked after Emma, Evie and Josie and of course Archie when he arrived, with the tenderness and love that you would give to your own. She cared for me too, food, shopping, laundry, cooking, washing, even gardening. Nothing was too much for her. From the start her heart was unselfishly for us, her work ethic was exemplary and her attitude unfailingly consistent. And she continued to make me laugh, even in the darkest of days.

Hannah, do you remember that time in Evie's bedroom, she was about to topple off the chair across the other side of the room? She could only have been about two and a half; you and I were stood by the door. We both reacted at exactly the same time and half raised our arms, putting our hands into a grabbing position in order to rush across the room and stop her from toppling over. But because we were BOTH there we paused before taking the steps to move, uncertain as to who should go. We then looked at each other, still uncertain on whose responsibility it was to rescue Evie. It tripped off your tongue: 'look at us, we're like two dancers from the Michael Jackson 'Thrilller' video'. It cracked me up, we laughed until we cried. It was so quick and such an accurate illustration of the positions we were holding. Sometimes a sense of humour is the tonic you need, and Hannah had oodles of it.

Equally, she cried over any bad news I ever got. I know she found it really hard at times to watch me so up close and personal going through all the illness and struggles that I had. She was really living it out with us, she saw it all. She lived the reality of us trying to remain a normal family, having to find the courage and the energy to face each day in the face of tremendous physical weakness. She understood my pain as I became too unwell to be the mother that I wanted to be to the children and how much that grieved me. She worked so hard at being sensitive to me over this issue, always handing me the ultimate role of being their mum, even when she was around. Recognising when I'd had enough and needed her to take over; it was a match made in heaven, quite literally. I can't imagine anybody more suitable for us – God had his hand in every part of our situation.

The Booby Prize

Christmas went, I don't really remember where, but it went. Nanny was employed, New Year had happened and I was in hospital being prepped for surgery. It was all still so hard to take in. Despite the fact that this has taken me about 17,000 words to get this far, in reality we had only found the lump five weeks ago. So much had happened, mentally, emotionally and now physically.

My biggest fear was that I would not come round from the anaesthetic. I directly asked the anaesthetist if this was likely to happen. It's rather a stupid question really because he's unlikely to say yes to the pale faced patient sitting in front of him. He knew and I knew that if I didn't have this surgery I'd most likely die anyway so even if he said that it WAS likely I would not wake up, I was going to take that risk. I'd written all my goodbye letters, I really had, and I'd told Mark where they were. Top drawer in the cabinet I'd inherited from my mum in our bedroom; so although I was scared, I was prepared. You can take the girl out of the Girl Guide but you'll never take the Guide out of the girl: be prepared, it was a motto I held dear.

I signed the forms that the surgeon handed me agreeing to my left breast being removed and lymph node clearance. He used his purple pen to draw some dots and dashes for his scalpel but he would not allow ME to borrow said pen and write HIM a personal message. One that he could read before he butchered me, remind him I was a real person and not just a lump of meat. Something simple like 'It is essential to me that you cut on the dotted line' or maybe pander to his ego, just to ensure he did a good job. 'I love a man in a mask'; 'what great knife skills you have', or this might do it, 'imagine I'm your sister'. He just laughed at me and walked out. So I donned my open backed surgical dressing gown, which graciously provided perfect viewing of my comfortable maternity pants covering my ample, dimpled pregnant lady bottom and then set about putting my surgical stockings on.

Compression stockings are a nightmare. They are designed to apply pressure to your lower legs, helping to maintain blood flow and reduce swelling which may be caused by surgery. They do exactly what they say, they apply compression, they are tight, hot, and decidedly unattractive. I have one particular internal tape that plays constantly in my head 'look good – feel better' and it has never let me down. If you make an effort to look good, you feel better; it always works for me.

It is an extremely rare situation that you would find me not wearing even the tiniest smattering of makeup. I favour the natural look – we're not talking caked-orange oompa loompa foundation, fake eyelashes and trout pout. Just a flick of mascara, a brushing of blush, and a tad of light coloured luscious lippy and I'm good to go and feel better. I do believe that beauty is from within and it's your character that is your real beauty; but there is no harm whatsoever in enhancing your features so that one does not scare small children with one's sickly coloured skin and piggy eyes.

The same could be said for what I wear: I'm a dressed down kind of girl, converse, skinny jeans and hoodies usually. But it takes no extra time to make sure things match up and for me, personally, are vaguely fashionable, in a 'cool older mum' kind of way. Compression stockings with backless gowns were NOT a look I would recommend. And getting the darn things on is nothing short of hilarious. I was given some super small ones. I'd like to think this was because despite my being at that point in pregnancy where 'you MIGHT be pregnant, but you MIGHT just have eaten too many pies' stage they had viewed me as a reasonably petite lady. I liked this.

They were so small that I couldn't imagine them even stretching over a small dog's leg never mind my 5 foot 4 and a half woman's leg but it had to be done. It was exhausting; I sat on the side of the bed while Mark rolled them up, rather like putting socks on a kid. He fed the white stretchy tunnel over my foot and then we both heaved and wriggled and pulled the thing up and over my knees which was like squeezing a football into the arm of a jumper. I writhed and jumped up and down whilst heaving and pulling these necessities onto both legs. It remained to be seen once they were on whether I would actually just burst out of them like a sausage from its cooked skin.

I made Mark laugh as I strutted around my hospital room in my strange garb, like an escaped mental patient. With a flapping gown, big knickers and thick white stockings that pushed every ounce of fat and tissue onwards and upwards from my calves and thighs to spill over the top in my crotch area. I've never worn tummy and thigh control underwear and after this experience I don't intend to try. I get the concept, but I fail to see how such items REALLY hide your fat – it HAS to go somewhere. My logical brain says it will spill out when it gets the chance to be released, and these compression stockings proved my theory. A small tyre of fat now circulated my leg at the top of the stocking. Nice, and so HOT – not in a sexy way, but in a perspiring, sweaty, greasy way. I had to lie down on the bed and be fanned by Mark. It was a great relief when the door opened, my trolley awaited me, and I embarked on the ride of my life.

First stop, ultrasound to see the baby; a scan would be taken before the operation and another the morning following the operation. These scans were to be the silver lining to our cloud; we would have growth scans every month for the duration of time I would be having chemo until the baby was born. They would reassure us that our baby was developing normally and that the chemo was not passing through the placenta. The best bit was that we got to see our baby regularly, our essential reminder of 'life' amongst the anxiety surrounding 'death and sickness'.

Archie was 11.2 weeks old when we first saw him. I took one look at the significantly sizeable lump between his uninhibited splayed legs and knew it was a boy. I asked the sonographer what he thought but he refused to be drawn and said it was too soon to say. I knew he was technically correct, but I'd seen all the scans of the girls at around 12 weeks and NONE of them had such a swelling between their legs. It was our first son, a miracle baby, a life that gave us Hope. Surely God would not have given us this miracle of life if he had planned for the tragedy of my death. I don't know if there's any theology around this view, but it certainly helped me keep hope alive.

As we looked at the image on the screen I was reminded of how miraculous the creation of life is. Even at 11 weeks our baby-to-be's brain and spinal cord was already developed. The Cerebrum had formed – this is the area responsible for thinking, remembering and feeling. The

Brain Stem was in place, the engine that would drive most of our baby's most vital functions, such as heart rate and breathing. The cerebellum, pituitary gland and hypothalamus are developed and therefore baby is able to grow and move and experience hunger and thirst, sleep and emotions. By now our baby could wiggle around, curl into the foetal position, have its own little party in there and even had a sense of touch.

At 11 weeks it is around 1.5 inches, the size of a fig and almost fully formed. And when I consider all the intricacies involved with this new life growing I cannot rationally attach it to anything other than the conscious and direct involvement of an active, guiding and HIGHLY intelligent force; I call that force God. And I was greatly encouraged that such an intelligent force was involved in my life.

Next stop, theatre; no, sadly not to sit with a box of popcorn cocooned in the rich red velvety darkness while spotlit people pranced about for entertainment. This was more the Theatre of Horror, a place where masked professionals wear the same muted amorphous costumes and perform macabre scenes of gruesome bloody barbarity encased in a room of white. Their props glint menacingly under the clinical lights and no laughter or clapping is heard when the curtain comes down and the scene is complete.

A more sombre mood had descended on us. Mark walked down as far as he was permitted and I passed through the double doors to the unknown. Surgery took about an hour – it was all over in the blink of an eye. When I came round in recovery the first thing I did was check that my left breast really had been removed. Even on awakening in the reality of the recovery room with medics around and the startling hospital lights, I think there was a tiny part of me that had hoped it had all just been a terrible dream. Perhaps when they'd been about to lop off the infected body part they had realised there was no tumour and left me intact. Hope is a powerful weapon, but sometimes it melts into fantasy and Never Never Lands that exist only over rainbows. I viewed the bandaged area and cried, silent, hot tears. It wasn't because I particularly loved my breasts, it was because the removal of one was physical evidence that I did indeed have cancer. I was forever going to have to see that scar and it would remind me of the disease I was fighting.

Moving on

The first few weeks following the surgery were difficult. I had limited movement on the left side and most of my left arm was numb from the lymph node clearance but very tender deep inside. Simple tasks such as getting dressed were achievable but slow and frustrating. I was determined not to involve anyone else; I wanted to be independent. Then one morning, I grew a new boob, and for a few blissful hours my existing reality took on a whole new shape.

The product of being a technophobe, as already illustrated through the extremely 'blonde' Fax story is that I rarely use the computer for anything, even Google. Mark has used it to find information and I am just told what I need to know. But for me personally, I don't run to Google to research anything to do with breast cancer and I have never joined any online chat groups. I just couldn't stand the additional stress. It's not because reading information about cancer and how it's affected people's lives is too much for me, it's using the flipping computer that's too much for me. The fear of pressing the wrong buttons and potentially 'agreeing' to something that I should not have 'agreed' to or deleting entire files that are the bedrock of all Mark's carefully stored accounts is just too frightening. I don't seem to be able to touch the darn thing without getting into trouble. The other day I attempted to print out a document and the printer just didn't respond. At some point in my aggressive and relentless button pressing which almost caused a small blister to appear, this thing popped up on the screen telling me the printer was having an 'Error'.

I did my usual troubleshooting solution – switch it all off, reset it, press all the buttons again – and it just kept happening. After a number of attempts I shouted for Mark, who rather impatiently came to investigate. He spent the next hour having to work out what I'd done, only to discover that I simply hadn't had the patience to wait for my document to come out. I had pressed print so many times that the printer had simply shut down, refused to respond; it clenched its little printing mechanisms in defiance at being treated in such a demanding fashion. How dare it, and now we had hundreds of pages waiting to be spat out in disgust at my stupidity. It was easily sorted but my point is that even the simplest of activities regularly ends in war between me and the machine. So, I avoid it, hence I've walked my cancer walk with very little information about what you may expect as a side effect of surgery or drugs.

This particular morning, I woke and did my customary check under the covers to see if my breast really had gone. This was part of my early hours routine, wake, covers up, check breast still missing; feel blue, get perspective – 'it could have been both legs and both arms, it's only a breast, get over it, Rebekah'. Shower and wrestle with my clothes and into the day. But that day was different; when I got to the 'lift covers up, check if breast still missing' to my immense shock I saw what I can only describe as a small breast in place of the one I'd lost!

I was elated, I really was. I thought I'd had a miracle. It wasn't very big and certainly did not match my gargantuan pregnancy breast on the right, but it was a start. I was sure with a bit of massage and some tender loving care my mini boob would grow nicely. Mature into a perfect match for its currently larger twin. I surveyed my pubescent beginnings with great pride and almost sent it round the prayer chain but decided I'd better show Mark first. He found it interesting but wasn't really embracing my miracle theory and sensibly suggested I ring my clinical nurse specialist and tell her of my discovery.

In all honesty I think I knew from Mark's response that there was going to be a rational explanation so I wasn't too disappointed when Karen explained that it was a seroma. A seroma is a pocket of clear fluid that sometimes develops in the body after surgery. When small blood vessels have been ruptured, blood plasm can seep out and accumulate, causing physical swelling. You can press them and feel the fluid moving around inside. I laughed about it, and was extremely relieved that I hadn't posted my 'miracle breast story' on the church Facebook page.

And then there were the conversations with the children. I was showering one day and Evie came in; she played around a bit but while I was trying to dry myself I noticed her stood watching me. She said, 'Where's your boob gone?' Mark and I had decided from the outset that we would be open and honest with the children about cancer. They had already been told that I had it, and that I was going to hospital to have the 'poorly' breast taken away. They were so young that they accepted these simple facts. I told her that my breast had been removed because of the naughty cancer cells and hopefully the doctors had made me better. She was happy with that and probably went on to ask me if she could have some sweets or some other equally mundane and irrelevant question.

People often ask me how the children cope with me having cancer, how it has affected them. This is a question that of course I ask myself often and at times Mark and I have discussed at length. It is a relatively futile question because of course I can't really know, and probably won't know until they are old enough to reflect and express their own views about what they remember. They will undoubtedly at some point have some issues related to the experience; but many of us have some issues with our parents or the way we were brought up that affect us as we mature into who we are as adults. Philip Larkin describes this 'view' very well. I remember the first time I heard 'This be the verse' by Larkin. I was maybe about 17, at the beginning of A Level English. At that age, I felt an affinity with his sentiment, an identification with his view about your parents messing you up, but only because they were messed up by their parents, and on and on the cycle goes. Now I have kids, I realise that you just love them – if we mess them up it's rarely pre-meditated or deliberate, it just happens; we don't mean it to.

My issues with my mother would probably fill a whole library and could maybe even be the foundation of a rather depressing soap opera. In the end it all comes down to accepting that life is not 'fair' and that not one of us is perfect and therefore bad things happen to good people and even people who love you will hurt you. Ultimately, in my opinion, to forgive is the answer and then choose to take who you are and the hand life has dealt you and make the most out of it.

Despite believing this, it's extremely hard to see in the present the pain and the difficulties that my cancer caused the children. Emma didn't really ask or say much, but this is entirely in keeping with her personality. She takes things in her stride and is not really a worrier or particularly expressive about how she feels. Evie, on the other hand, is opposite to the extreme: whatever Evie feels, we all know about it. As she was the oldest of my three at the time of this all beginning and the most vocal, it wasn't long before I did have some upsetting conversations with her.

Evie brought up the death issue on a number of occasions. I remember one night putting Evie to bed and her telling me outright that she was scared I was going to die. She was very specific, it wasn't just a generic conversation with a young child about life and death and all that jazz; she told me she was worried that the doctors might not have taken all my naughty cancer cells away and that maybe I'd get poorly again and die.

I had never talked about death to the children, but cancer is common enough that the children from an early age will have been exposed to stories about so and so's Grandma dying of cancer; or TV adverts and even kids' shows where the subject of cancer will have infiltrated their thinking and lain dormant. I have always placed honesty extremely highly, and at the time the information I had was that about 95% of women who were diagnosed as early stage breast cancer would reach the ten year all-clear mark and be deemed cancer free. Women could get on with their lives as everyone else does having experienced a horrible health blip, but dying from cancer was no more likely for them that it was for anyone else.

But 95% is not 100%, so I had to painfully tell her that this was of course possible. Death is part of life; it's the one thing we can all be certain of. This was the approach I have taken to these conversations, I am going to die, so are they; all living things die. I MIGHT die of cancer, BUT, I might die of something else. At that moment in time with a 95% chance of total recovery, it was truthful to tell her that it was unlikely to be cancer.

Of course, what she went on to say was the real problem; and has remained the problem throughout this entire journey. The children have been accepting enough of the facts related to living things dying and facts about treatments for cancer and surgery. Their real issue, however, which has arisen out of a connection between cancer and death, is the concept of permanent separation from me. Separation had even happened before I died in the form of a nanny and many hospital trips that took me away from them; or treatments that took me to bed. They did not like this and this experience prematurely gave rise to the idea that one day they would be permanently separated from me.

Cancer is synonymous with death; on some level they knew that and I certainly did. 'But Mummy, we won't see each other every day, and I'd miss you.' I am not shallow enough to try and appease that plea with 'don't you worry about such things, go to sleep' or maybe worse 'oh darling, we'll meet again in heaven. I'll be an angel that watches over you, I'll always be here by your side'. I don't even think that's true, the bit about me being an angel by her side or a star in the sky watching over all of them. Staying true to myself I have had to attempt to tell her the truth as I believe it to be, in a factual, hopeful but 'real' way.

I firstly agreed with her that it is unthinkably painful at the moment to imagine us not seeing each other every day. We faced the truth and I empathised with her. I reassured her that when this happens she will have other people around her, so would Emma, Josie and the new baby too, that love them and will take care of them. We talked about which type of people that might be, depending on the stage of life they could be at when I eventually die. And finally I tell them that I believe in Jesus and this assures me of a life in heaven with him where I will meet with all the other people who believe in him who died before me.

Certainly at that stage she appeared to accept this information and thankfully at the time of writing this has not yet challenged me over what happens if you don't believe in Jesus! The conversation probably disintegrated into a random set of questions about heaven such as 'Will there be Barbie Houses there?' I was unable to answer such ramblings; and by this point the Mummy who had not been duped emotionally by such devious 'lights off delay tactics' had wised up. She wanted to extract herself from the headlock type hug and leave the bedroom for a pregnancy-friendly gin and tonic; which is basically just tonic but can dupe the mind into believing there's gin in there.

Poison

Chemotherapy began a couple of weeks after surgery. We had a consultation confirming that surgery was able to support the advice that a mastectomy, as opposed to a lumpectomy had been the right route of action, due to the tumour being slightly bigger than they'd been able to see from the ultrasounds. They also confirmed that after pathology had examined my extracted lymph nodes they had found breast cancer cells in a number of them. This is called a metastasis; I had breast cancer but some of the cells had broken away and travelled through the lymphatic system to my lymph nodes. It meant that chemotherapy was not just a precautionary measure but it was essential for flooding my body with a medicine that would kill the rogue cells that may have already invaded my body.

Chemotherapy kills cells as they are in the normal process of splitting into two new cells. Cancer cells keep on splitting until there is a mass of cells and these become a lump or a tumour. Because they divide more quickly than healthy cells they are more likely to be killed by the anti-cancer drugs (in the form of chemo) because the group of drugs developed and used in chemo are attracted by dividing cells. Cells that are at rest are less likely to be affected. In some body tissues such as skin, hair and lining of the digestive system, cells are always growing and renewing themselves and therefore dividing quickly; these are also affected by the cancer drug. It doesn't distinguish between fast multiplying cancer cells and fast multiplying healthy cells. Which is why your hair falls out, your nails get trashed and you feel sick. Normal cells will, in time, repair and replace the healthy cells damaged by chemotherapy once treatment has ended.

Being told you're going to lose your hair is quite traumatic. I have heard a very small percentage of women who have been faced with this reality say that they were not that bothered; but most found this aspect of it initially very distressing. I have also heard other ladies who have not had any experience of cancer, or being told they'd lose their hair, confidently express how they wouldn't mind. Interestingly there are also women who have not experienced losing a breast who exclaim that 'it wouldn't bother them, they'd just want the THING gone so they could get on with it'.

As I said early on, one of the most difficult things I've had to manage has been the ridiculous, insensitive, two dimensional, throwaway comments based on absolutely no experience whatsoever, which is often followed by the complete unwillingness to engage in any enlightenment that may offer an insight into the gut wrenching reality of losing significant parts of what define you as a female. As I am fairly confident that such women would probably have shut this book by now due to its deep, honest and sometimes brutal truth. I want to say something to these ladies that perhaps you could pass on in a more sensitive manner if you have the misfortune to come across one:

'I have a particular set of skills, skills that I have acquired over a very long fight with the Big C. Skills that could make me a nightmare for an insensitive loose lipped blabbermouth like you. If you learn to be a bit more thoughtful before you shout your mouth off, I will not pursue you, but if I hear of you saying such stuff to some other vulnerable females, I will look for you, I will find you and I will gag you.'

(adapted from Liam Neeson in the film Taken)

No one who has not had to experience amputation due to a serious disease has the right to flippantly throw out to someone who has, what they would do if it happened to them. You have no idea what you would do until it happens to you; and I truly hope it never does.

My hair meant a lot to me, in fact I'd say it was the only one of my outward attributes that I was confident about. There are, of course, parts of my body and face that cause me no offence, such as my ears or toes. Although, actually, now I think about it I'd prefer if my toes were not so long and finger-like; I think God made a mistake and gave me 20 fingers and had to decide to put 10 of them on my feet. And I unfortunately inherited flat foot from my father, though they like to call it fallen arch these days, which sounds quite elegant. Flat foot describes it better though. It means that the foot loses the gently curving arch on the inner side of the sole, just at the front of the heel. I am not at the bottom of the class for flat foot – because MINE is only flat when I stand.

When my foot is lifted off the ground, it returns to its more attractive position. To be completely accurate I have flexible pes panus, which simply means, flexible flat foot. Got it? If it was acceptable to bum shuffle everywhere then my flat foot would not be a problem as I'd be able to hold my foot high above the ground to keep it intact and very much elegantly arched. However, I would then suffer from posterior blisters and a permanent dirty ass which would be worse than flat foot, so I just have to accept it.

The difficulty with my flat foot is that it has made me slightly knock kneed; in other words my knees turn inwards. If I try to straighten my knock knees, or my 'Genu Valgum' as it's properly called, then my feet turn outwards like a penguin. Are you beginning to see what a problem this is? It begins with what seems a small issue but then it continues up my legs and has eventually caused me chronic pain in my lower back. Not only that but I also suffer from joint hypermobility, which means I have an unusually large range of movement. This is great if I wanted to do the splits or go from a standing position into a backwards crab, but strangely enough I don't often have the desire to perform such acrobatics. Hypermobility in conjunction with flat foot is not a good combination.

The result for me has been that flat foot has put a strain on my large toe joint and my hypermobility meant that the joint has loosened to such an extent that it sticks out permanently, like a bunion. Mine is NOT a bunion – bunions are mostly caused by wearing shoes that put strain on the bones and muscles in your feet. When I was 17 the diagnosis of 'flexible pes panus Genu valgum' (*Flexible flat foot knock Knee syndrome – I don't think this is an official name*) meant I had to have specially made insoles for my shoes. These cost a fortune and totally prevented me from ever wearing lovely little ballet pump type shoes or high heels.

Over the years I have on occasions endured them, but there is never a happy ending. The pressure that the high heel puts onto the ball of my foot causes the hyperflexible joint to be pushed out of line and the pain is excruciating. The shoes have to be kicked off before the end of the night and I spend the rest of it in my stockinged or bare feet trying not to get my toes trodden on or step in spilt alcohol or glass. Mark has to piggy back me out of the public arena, either to taxi or car, piggy back me to the house and up the stairs to bed. Which I assure you after all that does not end in passion; it ends with ibuprofen, a cup of tea and a famous Marky foot massage.

Gosh, that was a description of a body part that I don't particularly have an issue with. I haven't got started on the parts of my body that I actually don't like. I could probably spend the next 30,000 words on them all. The point I was trying to make was that my hair was the one thing that I could pick no fault with. Actually, that's not fully true, it did annoy me that it couldn't be decisively straight, or utterly obviously curly. And the issue with this was that when straight styles were the fashion, I had to straighten, and when curly was the fashion, I had to have a perm (yes, this was fashionable in the 80s).

At the time when I was facing complete hair loss it had finally become fashionable to allow long hair (which I had) to be scrunched and very naturally wavy, which would have been perfect for me. I would have been the envy of everyone and saved a fortune on hairdressers and hair equipment, but no, I was going to be losing my hair, that's just typical.

All in all, I have been complimented on my hair my entire life; it was thick, in great condition and although the 'not quite straight – not quite curly' was annoying sometimes it did mean I had great texture to my hair and could more or less get it to do anything I wanted. It could be adaptable to many different styles which as the decades of changing hair fashion rolled by, allowed me to have good fun with my hair and always be part of the 'scene'.

I was even a hair model I'll have you know. Christine Thomlinson as she was then when I was aged 16-18, a spectacular trainee hairdresser in Carlisle, asked me to be her model as she passed through the various stages of her training programme. We created some fabulous styles and hair colours together and it was Christine who said to my mother, 'She's got 'it', Cynth (Cynthia), whatever it is, Rebekah Mells (maiden name) has got 'it'.' My mother actually told me this compliment, which is probably why I've never forgotten because my mum rarely, if ever, said anything encouraging to me at all.

I never actually asked what 'it' was, I think 'It' was a compliment, it was presented as such by my mother – but it seemed too arrogant to go back to Christine and fish for expansion so I left it like that. I asked Mark once what he thought about it and he looked at me and smiled softly (which sounds lovely, but I struggle a bit with soppiness and get a bit squirmy and want to run away or laugh or make a rude joke, I know, I'm screwed up, I'm working on it) and said 'the 'It' is sass, you have sass', lively, bold, full of spirit and a bit cheeky. I like that, that's why I'm telling you, I'm sassy.

It turned out as we got further into the detail of what side effects this chemotherapy was going to have, that there was an option for me to wear something called a cold cap, which can have a significant impact on reducing hair loss. They hardly needed to tell me the details; I was going to do it, I'd made up my mind immediately. The revelation of this option was quickly followed by explaining that they're not widely used by many women for two main reasons. Firstly, that many women, although upset about losing their hair, accept quite quickly that it is a foregone conclusion and therefore didn't want to go through the faff. The second reason is connected to the explanation of what they do and how they do it, and when faced with this, they don't want to have extra discomfort that could be avoided when having to endure other side effects that can't be avoided. In other words, enough is enough, one can only take so much.

I was going to be having my chemotherapy at home; it was a perk of the private medicine. The nurse would come to my home and administer the chemotherapy rather than me having to trail into hospital and be treated on the ward as a day patient. For those who may be feeling politically challenged here regarding private medicine then I suggest you get over it. I used to feel that way until I was seriously ill and pregnant, with other young children at home and no family to help. Believe me, political leanings stand for nothing in that situation – you take any opportunity you are offered that enables you to simply cope and survive.

A cold cap essentially cools your scalp and can reduce hair loss caused by chemotherapy. It works by freezing the follicle, which minimises the amount of drug that can damage the follicle and so cause less hair to fall out. There's no guarantee on how effective it will be which puts people off trying.

There are two methods, a refrigerated cooling system that pumps liquid coolant through a cap, or a cold cap which is a special cap filled with cold gel. I would be having this type because I was having it at home. They look exactly like a tight-fitting swimming cap made out of fabric similar to a wetsuit and have velcro that tightens under your chin to make the fit as close as possible. They need changed throughout the treatment to ensure a steady freezing temperature. So in total you'll be wearing it for about three hours. You place all three in the freezer the day before treatment so that the coolant is fully frozen ready to save your follicles. The consultant had begun to emphasise how difficult they were to endure – they're heavy and uncomfortable, they reduce your body temperature which can make you feel tired and sick, they'll almost certainly give you an 'ice cream' headache and –the 'red rag to bull' comment – they're so difficult to endure that even those who start them rarely continue.

I LOVE a challenge, and I'd just been offered one. I only need to be faced with a glimpse of a brick wall and I see it not as something to keep me out but as a chance to show how badly I want something. I see the brick walls as being there to stop people who don't want something badly enough. I did not want to lose my hair, and to me this cold cap torture was a challenge. The challenge I wanted to take to save my hair. I'm a sucker for a bit of competition; if most other women had tried and failed, then the competitor in me felt attracted by the concept of attaining a goal that many others had been unable to achieve. Having a competitive edge to your personality tends to mean you persevere until you reach the end goal. I don't give up easily and I also look to people who are better than me and set them as an example of what is possible. I don't see problems, I tend to see opportunities; obstacles usually just enable me to learn how to do something better or be better in an area than I was in the previous day/week/year. To be accurate, I think I'm actually a competitive perfectionist; this is a very tricky personality to navigate. I see the tiniest faults in everything and will not settle until I have pushed beyond limits, capacities and boundaries in order to either correct that 'fault' or beat my target. My favourite activity is writing a list of things to be done, setting a time limit for when they're done and then BEATING my own list so that I've achieved the goals in half the time or surpassed them completely.

There are of course disadvantages to being wired like this: I'm 'picky' and praise can stick in my throat. If I've spotted a defect I could choke on words such as 'well done it's excellent' because all I can see is the little bit that's imperfect. I'm not very flexible, and probably carry a generalized level of anxiety related to not having achieved my best in some area or another, or feeling frustrated and disappointed in the flaws of others. I was definitely the kid who couldn't lose at games when they were small because I was so wired to want to beat everyone else. In a family of six, where most of your siblings are a bit like that too and most of them more capable than you, I had a tough but probably vital start in life teaching me how to lose and get over it.

I would have been about 15 weeks pregnant when chemo started; Emma was seven, Evie two and Josie six months. It's impossible to describe what a difficult circumstance we were in. Six treatments, one every three weeks, 18 weeks was the finish line – of this chapter anyway. The cold caps were indeed as horrific as explained to me. Head squeezed into the freezing cap, strapped tightly under my chin with velcro; wrapped up in bed to stay warm with an IV drug dripping into a vein in my hand for around three hours of brain freeze. The cap would be peeled off my head 45 minutes after treatment ended and there would be icicles and frost on my hair. I did not give up; I endured the torture for 18-20 hours in total and my crowning glory was that I kept ALL my hair. Not even the tiniest bald patch or thinning: mission accomplished.

With each treatment that passed I became virtually bed bound from utter exhaustion. You are given anti-sickness medicine to help settle the nausea, but it doesn't take it away completely. One of the side effects of the anti-sickness drug was severe constipation probably made worse by my pregnancy. I am not going to describe what I had to do to relieve this problem, I can hardly believe I had to go to such lengths; but at times I was in agony and would have done anything.

I broke out in a case of acne rosacea, facial blood vessels that enlarged and cause redness; small vessels in the skin became visible and spots and pustules appeared, it burnt and at times stung. I hated it. This issue, alongside the constipation, low level sickness, fatigue and pregnancy put real strain on my ability to engage with normal life. It was like living with a permanent hangover, but with no tales of all night partying frolics to regale. That period of time is a blur, a total blur. I mainly existed in my bedroom and didn't really want to go out because of my skin. And all the time there was the pressure of trying to maintain life; making sure the kids had fun, experienced normal activities and continued to feel love and security amongst the intensity that cancer had brought to our lives. It was so hard.

Knockers and Nannies

There are a two tales that belong to this part of the story that are worth sharing. The first is a short one but caused some entertainment for myself and Karen Verrill (clinical nurse specialist). Until such a time that I could have reconstruction surgery on my left breast, I wore a prosthetic. A fleshy coloured, spongey, breast shaped falsey; it sat inside my bra so that at least when I was clothed I looked normal. This is usually a simple case of being fitted immediately after surgery and then sticking the thing in whenever you want to.

Because I was pregnant it was a slightly more complicated process. Whenever I have been pregnant my boobs have grown to a gargantuan size. Seriously, I'm a reasonably petite lady, who didn't naturally carry around two enormous jugs of joy on her chest; but it was as if some metamorphic process took place and as my body accommodated pregnancy then my normal proportioned mammary glands got overtaken by what can only be described as two bouncy castles. They literally became the size of my head, and I know this because very maturely one day I strapped one of the bra cups underneath my chin to demonstrate to Mark just how massive they were.

The issue with this was the growth rate – it would have been easier if they'd gone from small to unleashed overnight; but of course every few weeks as my baby bump grew so did the remaining bazooka. Roald Dahl could have written a sequel to James and the Giant Peach – Rebekah and her Giant Melon. I'd have to ring Karen and she'd come with her bag of boobs and we'd attempt to find a prosthetic that matched the other monster. It was funny until I reached about seven months and then I'd surpassed the biggest prosthetic she had and we had to discuss having one specially made. In the end I decided to be lopsided; I knew it was only going to grow larger again when I had the baby and my milk came in – it was time to stop. In my unbalanced state toppling over was a potential issue, I had to tread carefully, I eventually resorted to stuffing socks down my bra just to balance myself up.

The other story is more complicated and not funny at all so brace yourself for a depressing read (you might need a bottle of wine for this bit). It was the Nanny. Hannah was amazing, as I have mentioned before; she fitted like a hand fits a glove. She'd work any hours we needed, clearly loved the children and had great compassion for me and Mark. There was NOTHING she wouldn't do to make our lives easier; her attitude was exemplary. If my children grow up to be like Hannah I will be ecstatic. However, over this period of time there was a lot of adjustment going on; I'd had a huge shock over the pregnancy, the cancer and the removal of my breast. Chemotherapy in conjunction with pregnancy and the rest of the young children was making life almost unmanageable practically.

Hannah was taking the load of most of the childcare and chores around the house and I was extremely grateful; but she was also the reason that I began to feel helpless and utterly redundant. I didn't exactly miss the household jobs, I mean, come on, what woman hasn't watched a costume drama and fantasised about being the lady of the manor simply socialising, choosing dresses and pressing flowers? Servants for everything, laundry, cleaning, cooking, gardening, everyone at your beck and call; I defy you ladies to say you haven't at some time even briefly imagined life like this.

When I watch these historic programmes and sneak a jealous peek into their grand lives and seemingly unlimited practical provision, the one negative for me has always been how the children existed in the family. They may have been spoiled with whatever pampering, ponies and poodles they wanted, but they generally seemed to live a sad, redundant and affection-less existence. They were raised by a nanny and rarely communicated with their parents except for a specific time each day. Winston Churchill once said that he could 'count the times he had been hugged by his mother as a child'. (Mind you, so could I and we certainly didn't have a Nanny). Parents would instruct the nannies with what they wanted to be instilled in their children, such as manners, education, clothes, food and so on.

In effect the nanny was a substitute parent. This part of being a wealthy Victorian did not appeal to me at all. The outcome, as far as I could see, were children living without the love they deserved. If I'd been a wealthy Victorian lady, I would have gladly handed over the running of the house, but I couldn't imagine handing over the running of my children; and that's from a mum who finds her children hard work. This was my major problem with having a nanny – I was so sick that I had to instruct Hannah on how I wanted HER to raise my children, like the ladies in Victorian times; this was hugely painful for me. I had given up work to stay at home and look after my children; it was all I had ever really wanted to do.

I didn't get married until I was 35 and had my first child when I was 36. I'd only ever wanted to be a wife and a mother. I had always imagined I would be married in my early 20s on leaving university and go on to have babies in my mid 20s. This plan had effectively been delayed by over a decade and it had caused me some great pain along the way. I watched all my friends settle down with people and have children. I'd had to increase the average age of my social group a number of times as more and more people dropped out of my life for partners and babes.

It caused me bouts of depression and debilitating periods of anxiety as the years slipped away and my Knight in Shining Armour never appeared riding over the hill to rescue me, brandishing his sword and sweeping me off my feet to gallop off together into the sunset to make babies – with a wedding first, of course. The wedding dress had been in a box under my bed for years – JOKING – but at times in that period of my life I wasn't far off such madness. I was not career driven, I was marriage and babies driven. All I had ever desired was to be married and make a home, and despite all the difficulties that I have already described, I was actually the most content I had ever been. A housewife was the life for me.

To cope with the separation difficulties that being poorly and needing a nanny had placed on me I made a choice I deeply regret and believe I have seen the negative effects of this choice in the years that have followed. Emma was at school, and eight years old, so least affected by what I decided during that time. Josie was six months – as long as someone fed her, cleaned her, cuddled her and entertained her she was happy and therefore adapted without any obvious distress to someone else looking after her. Both Josie and Emma are quite chilled, laid back characters, easily pleased and happy in their dispositions.

Evie was quite a different character altogether, very sensitive and particular. I tell the children a funny story about how Evie turned orange when she was being weaned. She was very resistant to solids unless they were orange coloured, and eventually she'd only consume mashed carrots and butternut squash. The effect of this was that her body became overloaded with Beta Carotene and her skin turned orange.

To be honest I didn't notice; it was brought to my attention in a somewhat embarrassing fashion. I was round at the weekly gathering of NCT mums, ladies who were all first-time mothers. We had met during the NCT classes (National Childbirth Trust) whilst learning all about having a baby and the how to manage the first few months. We supported each other through the adjustment period of that first year and I remain great friends with a couple of those ladies to this day. We were discussing the latest trauma, weaning, and one of the ladies started sharing some related information. She'd heard about babies being fed too much orange-coloured food which in time actually turned them orange.

People reacted in a variety of ways: incredulous, disbelief at such a ridiculous tale 'How could you turn orange from orange food?!' Could you turn green from too much green food? But as was always the outcome of these types of tale we all sneaked a fearful look at our babies just to make sure our bundle of perfection wasn't turning into a tangerine. This was followed by sighs of relief from all the 'other mothers' who were reassured that their baby had a healthy pink colour; and they were able to plant themselves solidly in the 'good mother camp'; for that day at least.

Sly sideways glances then ensued at all the other babies to see if a 'bad' mother was carting around the produce of a common fruit bowl. I was still staring at Evie; I looked up and all eyes were fleetingly paused on my bundle of orange. Embarrassed, they put on fake smiles and averted their attention with more tea and cake; the subject changed to the latest news on Mothercare offers, broken sleep, and cracked nipples.

I'm not stupid; I realised in that moment that this particular lady had probably brought this up deliberately as a way of indirectly confronting the obvious colour defect of Evie. If that happened to me now I would probably make an instant joke out of it, confront the revelation head on. 'Oh my Lord, Evie's orange and I hadn't even noticed. What should I do? I feel like a terrible mummy.' They were a lovely gang and I know they'd have reassured me it was all going to be ok. Given me tips on how to distract her preference and so on. But I wasn't so confident then, I felt panic stricken. I hung around for a few more minutes and then made some excuse to leave. I ran through the streets with my fruity baby, wrapped up to her eyes so no one could see her glow; I headed straight to the Health Visitors' drop in centre.

The health visitor asked me if I'd been putting fake tan on her. I was very insulted and said of course not, who'd do that to a baby!? She ensured me that people did and that was why she'd asked – well that was a bit of social education for me. The preference for only orange food was found to be the reason. I was hugely relieved, and grateful for this other mother drawing my attention to it. I was helped with some tips on how to break this somewhat intense and OCD like behaviour that Evie had displayed. That weekend, having seen the funny side of this tale, I asked a few friends if they had noticed Evie's colour. They had.

Food wasn't the only challenge where Evie was concerned. She was the most difficult of all the children to develop good sleep patterns, come off the breast, come off a bottle, get into a car seat, the pram, the high chair, dress, the list is endless and it is still the way she is today.

I see now that she has a personality that leans towards anxiety. Lots of things that are not a problem for most children are a huge problem to Evie. I'm not talking about temper tantrums that if ignored stop, or with distraction, or a cuddle can be appeased. Some of it of course IS developmental and age appropriate, but I'm not talking about the normal paddies and pet lips. I'm talking about fear, gut knotting anxiety that makes her freeze or refuse and dig her heels in.

She hated going in the car seat, and she would scream for the entire journey there and back. People reassured me that this was normal and she'd get used to it; these people had all shut up when three years later she was still doing it. We had to listen to everyone's advice and ideas all trying to take over and believe they wouldn't have that problem if it was their child, blah blah blah. A certain couple who had been very vocal about how to manage Evie took her off in their car one day; when they came back they admitted they hadn't been able to strap her in her seat at all because she'd been so upset. They'd allowed her, at two, to sit in the back of the car outside her seat and hadn't even managed to get the seat belt on her. They felt terrible, but had no other way of getting her home. They'd given her a bag of sweets and she'd sat untethered in the back with the female adult next to her because she refused to sit on her knee. She'd writhed and arched her back, screaming until she was wretched.

This was an older couple who'd raised their own children and probably believed it was myself and Mark's poor parenting. Ha ha ha, this experience silenced them. As time has gone by we have learnt and others have witnessed it's not a phase that Evie's going through, and it's not simply defiance or spoilt behaviour. She IS strong willed and she DOES like a fight, which does not help at all, but it's stress that is the main root of the problem. Anything that brings change is stressful for her and causes her to go ballistic.

At the time of getting a nanny she was two and half and had only ever known life with me tending to her every need, she was old enough to be aware that life had changed and she did not like change. She'd already had to accept Josie into her world, which hadn't gone well. The day Josie came home she lay on the kitchen floor and banged her head on the tiles repeatedly and SCREAMED.

For a nanny to come along and start doing all the things Mummy did, to a child such as Evie must have been catastrophic. I had intentioned that a nanny would be there to 'support' me while I largely carried on being the key person. She would do many of the practical chores and I would get to be lady of the manor and simply play with the children. I had not bargained for being physically incapable of this arrangement and having to allow the nanny to take over my role in entirety. Victorian times had returned to Marine Avenue.

It quickly became clear that Evie was having none of the nanny, and with the same expressive, persistent and fear-filled manner with which she'd fought change many times. She fought this one with such power that I couldn't bear it. I was so sick and at the time didn't understand Evie and what made her be this way that I made a decision which I wish above anything else I could undo.

I decided that I would not be around at all when Hannah was there. I would make sure Evie was distracted and then sneak out of the room. Hannah would swoop in and entertain Evie, take her out a lot and basically use distraction so that she forgot about me. We planned the day so that Hannah would be out parts of every morning and afternoon so that I wasn't entirely confined to hiding in the bedroom. If they were in and I was upstairs I would creep to the bathroom so she didn't hear me; if I needed to be somewhere and they were in, I would text Hannah from the bedroom and let her know I needed to get down the stairs and out of the front door.

Hannah would put 'operation diversion' in place and whisk Evie off to a room from which she wouldn't see me leaving. I told myself that this was better for Evie – she wouldn't be so distressed at seeing me and then separating from me. When I look back I realise what a foolish and truthfully selfish thing this was to do. Evie did scream and she did refuse to allow Hannah to do anything for her when I was there too, but the solution to this was not to desert Evie.

Little Evie, who struggled with change anyway and had only ever had MY undivided time and attention, needed ME more than anything and I chose to effectively walk away, telling myself it was for the best. To be there one minute playing with her, but then when Hannah arrived at 8 am beckoning her to come and take over while I tip toed out of the room not even saying goodbye and not seeing her again for the rest of the day is nothing short of cruel. I made this decision for ME, I couldn't stand her crying, it upset ME too much, it made MY day sad seeing her like that, it was better for ME, not Evie.

One of the reasons that year is a blur is because of this decision. I think in order to carry out my choice I had to shut down to what I'd done. I didn't have the ability or the capacity to change the decision; the result of it was that I felt guilty the entire six months. As I stood by my choice I had to listen to cries for Mummy, a mummy who to Evie had disappeared and abandoned her to be cared for by a stranger. This Mummy had not returned to work; she was often just in the bedroom crying, wishing she was not sick and then she could be looking after her daughter as was her right.

I always explained to Evie that I was ill, and unable to take care of her and that was why we had Hannah. I loved her and didn't want someone else to have to look after her, but I'd be better soon and then it would be me and Evie again. Sometimes this helps me appease what I did because at least I had given Evie some explanation, but in all honesty it was the wrong choice to make. In Evie's little micro universe, for years the face she saw the most of was mine, most of the food she ate and had fed to her, was from my hand. Any trips out she had in the car it was me who strapped her into her seat, jaunts in the pushchair to ogle at the sea or play on the swings were pushed by me, and toddles on foot were guided by the feel of her mummy's fingers intertwined with hers. It was safe, secure and satisfying.

Within the space of a couple of weeks I'd all but disappeared. Hannah would arrive at 8 am and leave at 6 pm and Evie would not see me for most of that time. And I didn't even say goodbye, I just silently sidled away from the scene like a thief in the night and left the tears and comforting to a complete stranger. I abandoned her, deserted her, virtually ceased to look after her. She lost the most familiar person in her little life, and I really believe that she would have experienced a sense of fear as a result of this.

An experience such as this for a very young child gives them the painful message that they are not important or of value. I believe throughout Evie's life I have seen the results of this decision in the form of anxiety separation. It is natural for young children to experience this at some point in their young lives when you say goodbye or leave them in an unfamiliar situation such as Nursery school. It's a normal stage of development and fades as children get older. Evie's anxieties intensified as she got older and got in the way of school and other activities. At times she expressed concerns about me getting sick whilst she was at school, and she would relentlessly go on about not wanting to go to school; up in the night worrying about the next day, headaches, stomach aches and clinging to me at the point when she knew the separation was coming.

One of the key directives for dealing with children who have such issues is to keep consistent patterns for the day. Be predictable and discuss changes and separations with the child to prepare them for the inevitable disappearance, but I did the opposite and all because I didn't want to be upset or stressed at hearing Evie cry. What a coward.

If I'd put Evie first I would have endured the crying as I left the room for a rest – it would have stopped eventually. I would have taught her over time that Hannah WAS putting her shoes on that day, NOT Mummy, and Evie would have adapted to this. I would have therefore been able to spend more time with her while she adjusted to such a massive change in her life.

Time is the currency of love: you can love somebody and not spend time with them, but time is the value you place on what you love and the only real way to demonstrate love. Time is finite; we only have so much of it and how we choose to spend that time shows us how much value we place on something. I chose to spend my time selfishly, I know many of you will be reading this and thinking 'don't beat yourself up, it was very hard, who knows what any of us would do in that situation'. This is true, but it was still the wrong thing to do, and sometimes we just have to face that and take the consequences. If we deny that we make mistakes we are in more danger of repeating that mistake – best to accept that you really are capable of some horrible and selfish behaviour and work on maturing and developing your character so that next time you have a chance of making a different choice.

There were other options I could have looked at if I'd perhaps asked someone else for their advice that would have safeguarded her rocked world and minimised the (probably) lifetime effects of that period. But I was so convinced that this was for the best that I shared with no one how it was playing out at home, that I hid in my room and let Hannah do everything to save myself from the screaming. As far as anyone else was concerned, I had very legitimate reasons for a nanny and no one ever questioned how I was making it work behind closed doors. Perhaps if they had I might have had a light bulb moment and looked at it differently. Who knows?

As a result of this choice, Hannah became very recognised at the local toddler groups and by all my yummy mummy friends. They spoke of her highly and recognised how capable she was and loving towards my children. Hannah had previously worked in a local nursery and had wanted to be a nanny for some time before her break came. It was playing with the children and taking them swimming and to the park that she loved the most. Activities such as these she'd been unable to do under the restrictions of a Nursery. She loved caring for only a couple of children rather than masses – it was the cuddling and having fun with them that was what Hannah did best. So well in fact that it became a problem for me – she was better than me.

She was a model of parenting, frequently demonstrating virtually perfect ways of handling children. They definitely got 'Hannah time'; she would efficiently whiz through any chores and then focus her entire attention on playing with them, 90% connecting, only 10% correcting. This was very different to my 90% correcting, complaining or crying, the other 10% consuming large carafes of wine. She was always in control of her emotions, able to face the present toddler tantrum or baby meltdown with such a calm persona that they were playdough in her hands. The only playdough in my hands was small balls of the stuff that I'd allowed to harden so that I could throw at them when they defied me.

And the crying, it stressed me out so much; my own mum didn't respond well to me crying. I can remember her reacting in such an exasperated fashion when I cried, unable to allow me to be comforted in the safety of her arms. I found it so hard to not repeat this behaviour.

The minute I felt them getting cranky or aggressive I would respond with my own cranky emotions. More often than not I was trying to recover from my own tantrum let alone deal with theirs. Hannah was able to take the time to teach them that their big scary emotions, like hurt and anger aren't dangerous, and showed them nothing but compassion and empathy. The result of Hannah managing them so well was that they had a lot of fun. Hannah had time to make the kids 'belly laugh' with her goofy frolics and rough housing. I was rubbish at this too.

She knew how I felt and was even amazing at dealing with this issue. We would talk about it later and she would remind me that they were not her children. If they were she would also get demented at them as I did, losing patience when they defied me or screeching at them when they didn't tidy up the second I asked. She told me tales of her mum and how she'd called her and her sister 'little witches'. She reassured me that all mums behave like this with their own kids, and *they* are not dealing with cancer. I wanted to believe her, but it's extremely hard to accept and feel like you're not just a wicked hag.

Friends would sing her praises, meaning to encourage and reassure me that we'd made a good choice, but they often failed to connect with the sense of loss and even inferiority that I began to feel in relation to Hannah. They would make comments such as 'the kids love her, Rebekah' or 'you're so lucky to have someone like Hannah, she's amazing' or the worst one I had was 'I wish I had a Hannah' – but they had not faced the most excruciating difficulty that having such a top notch nanny brought and it was this. Eventually the children became so attached to Hannah that they saw her like a mummy. On the rare occasion we were out together and they fell over or hurt themselves they would go to Hannah rather than me, and if they were tetchy and cross they would reach out for Hannah to rescue them from MY arms. It was unbearable. I put on a brave face and Hannah was sensitive enough to always direct them to me, but it was deeply wounding. I lived in the tension between feeling utterly blessed by someone whom my kids felt so close to, but utterly distraught and cursed by the cancer that prevented me from being their mum.

Over time I began to respond to comments such as 'I wish I had a Hannah' with 'do you? I bet you wouldn't want the cancer that has created the need for a Hannah though, would you?' It shocked people and made them feel really uncomfortable but I had to put an end to it to protect myself. Being direct and deliberate in my response seemed the only way to remind people about the reality of how difficult my circumstances actually were. I hadn't even completed chemotherapy and people had already disconnected from the trauma I was living through and seemed more focused on vague jealousy issues over my nanny.

I had and still do have some awesome friends, but the reality of your life being a continual 'soap opera' is that even the closest of people can't fully understand, and the result of this is loneliness. There isn't a mum and baby group for 39 year old women who have cancer, are pregnant with their third child soon to enter family of three other children, no local family support apart from your younger sister whose own life was demanding and stretched too. I found myself in a party of one – most of the time I had to sit around listening to how tired my friends were because they'd been up all night with baby number two or some other tale of a stretched lifestyle and stressed squabbling parents. I would sit there feeling anger and resentment, longing for 'THEIR' difficulties, wondering when they'd realise that problems they shared were nothing compared to mine; often this recognition never came along. The trouble was that even the few people who did try to empathise and genuinely showed an interest couldn't really understand. And I soon understood that if I was to survive this without becoming totally embittered I was going to have to get a grip and woman up.

The Burden of Grief

'The Lord is close to the broken hearted and he rescues those who are crushed in spirit' – those days were dark; I had abandoned Evie AND Josie and felt so abandoned myself. I felt out of options and out of control, so I turned to God and prayed some of the most authentic prayers I ever prayed. I was experiencing grief, sorrow, it was hard to bear and hardly anyone understood. A cloud had slid between me and life as I knew it. I had memories of my pre-cancer life with all my body parts and family life intact, but a large shadow had settled over my future and blocked out any dreams I may have had.

You will never know that God is all you need until it feels like he's all you've got. I felt like that, and began a journey that deepened my faith in a way that I would not change for anything. It says in the Bible that 'We know that God causes everything to work together for the good of those who love him and are called according to his purpose for them'. It doesn't say that 'God causes everything to work out the way I want it to' which was very comforting to me, because clearly things were not working out as I wanted them to.

My hope had to be based not on positive thinking, wishful thinking or natural optimism, but on the truth that God is in control and that he loves me. 'God causes': there's a person behind the things that were happening to me. It wasn't random chance or bad luck, God was still pulling the strings and 'everything' including this disaster and even my death, if it came to that, could be turned into good. This does not mean that everything IS good, but it means God specializes in bringing good out of any situation that his children, that is, those who accept who God is and what he's done for them, face.

Every problem can be an opportunity for building character and the more difficult it is the greater potential for building spiritual muscle and moral fibre. 'Under pressure your faith life is forced into the open and shows its true colours' – our Pastor Alan explained it like this: if you squeeze an orange, orange juice comes out, if life squeezes a Christian, then Jesus should come out. I guess this is what happened to Mark and I, we were being squeezed and what came out of us was how deeply we both believed in a good God.

Corrie ten Boom, who suffered in a Nazi death camp, explained the power of focusing on God. 'If you look to the world, you'll be distressed. If you look within, you'll be depressed. If you look to Christ, you'll be at rest.' My focus would determine my feelings. My focus on God would enable me to deal with all that I faced and all the loneliness I was experiencing from being isolated by a very unique circumstance.

I set my mind that I would not give up, I would patiently persist in this situation. I think I had revelation that to do anything other than grasp this opportunity to mature and embrace the eternal consequences of my character development would only result in the pain of bitterness, depression, dashed dreams and hopelessness. I began to choose less 'comfort' my prayers and more 'conform' my prayers. Charles Darwin said, 'It's not the strongest of the species that survive nor the most intelligent, but the ones most responsive to change.' I had to adapt and change if I was going to survive and be a better person not a bitter person. I was going to have to adapt my views on being a mother, a wife, and a friend; I needed to trust that God was good and set my mind that I would not give in to introspective thinking but would think spiritually rather than naturally. I wanted to run this marathon well and reach the finish line not having given up, but having grown up. I did not go on from this point and continually achieve this position, as you will see, but it was the start of walking in the right direction.

'My God is a good God'

I had to begin there. I had to begin there for the sake of the pain I was feeling over Evie and the pain I was experiencing from loneliness and the pain from the loss of a life that I would never have again. This truth was the key to unlocking the problems that these scenarios caused me, the disappointment and the anger – the Why? Why me? Why now? Why us? I didn't understand but I knew I could trust God's heart towards me was good. His goodness could save me from a slow, nasty, crushing death of becoming a bitter person and take me to a place of being a better person. In his strength I could face my sorrow, I didn't have to deny or dismiss anything that I felt; God leads us through our circumstances not around them.

'Let us run with endurance the race that is set before us, looking unto Jesus, the author and finisher of our faith' (Heb. 12 1-2). I'm a runner, I run to keep fit, I like a bit of competition but that's not the reason I began running. I began running because it was free, it was in the fresh air, and the main reason – I didn't want to get fat. No matter how often I go out for a run my body always complains. It doesn't want to co-operate, my 'bunion' throbs, my 'flat foot' aches and my nose runs almost as fast as my legs due to exercise induced rhinitis (drippy nose).

Things hurt and are uncomfortable. There are of course options. Go home and feel like a quitter all day. Keep running and meditate on how hard and painful it is until I talk myself into walking. Or keep running and focus on the vast expanse of ocean as I make my way along the coastline, ponder the universe and who created it, the changing light and seasons, the ebb and flow of the waves and tides. As I watch the power of God in creation my attitude changes, the pain ceases to matter and before I know it I'm nearly home. Everything improves when I fix my eyes on my sovereign Lord, who made the heavens and the earth by his great power and outstretched arm. Nothing is too difficult for him. (Jer 32: 17)

Loneliness is not the absence of people it's the absence of closeness, a lack of intimacy. When you find yourself in a place that no one else understands and you begin to question if anyone really cares. In a way, loneliness and grief became my route to God because they forced me to turn to him. My rational mind could see that people weren't able to crawl into my body and life and really empathise with my struggle. And this was what I needed. Even Mark couldn't do that; he was better placed than anyone but clearly it's a physical impossibility and nobody can be at your beck and call. When you wake sweating in the night panicking over whether you're going to die, or weeping with anxiety over what effect this is having on your children, or raging over someone who'd let me down, YOU alone have to deal with it. No matter how many times someone says 'ring me if you need ANYTHING – even if you just want to cry', believe me, you rarely do it. I was continually going to find myself let down by people, feel hurt or angry and I didn't want to live this way. Loneliness was a tool that God used to get my attention onto him.

I had nowhere else to go: the loss of Evie, loss of a breast, loss of life meant that all I had left was God. And he was able to show me that even though he was Lord of heaven and ruled the universe, he was within ME and near to ME. As the apostle Paul said: 'He is not far from each one of us.' David in the Bible discovered 'You are with me you will not leave me'. I may have been facing sickness and poor health, but the Lord was with me. I was not alone. When you realise how much God loves you and is with you, your desperation fades into the background, you can forgive people for their thoughtlessness, you can hand the caring of your children back to God, trusting that he is working it out for good, you can stop searching for answers to your problems in the wrong places because you discover God's 'perfect love' and it casts out all your fears. Loneliness becomes the gift from God that allows you to 'turn your eyes upon him and look full in his wonderful face, then the things on Earth become strangely dim in the light of his Glory and grace'.

The Knitted Titty

People are unique. We all have different skills and personalities; no one is like you. It's awesome. It blows my mind when I think about how different we all are. I wrote this poem for my children one day whilst pondering the mind blowing concept of individuality. The poem itself doesn't do the subject justice – I must write a better one.

How people can believe in Big Bang theories and whatever other ideas they have about creation I have no idea. I'm gazing out of the widow as I write this at my beautiful garden; not one single thing in it is repeated. I run by the sea and it is never ever the same experience. I look at my children and am mystified by how utterly different they are to each other. All creation sings of a master artist. A genius mind planned every detail of our world; all of creation points to a person who was intentional and specific about any living, breathing life form. The mountains, the rolling thunder, forest glades – don't those things make you want to thank somebody?

Unique

YOU are unique
From your roar to your squeak
From your head to your toe
From your fast to your slow
From your ears to your tears
From your DNA to the words you say
From your heart to each body part
From your blink to your wink

From your fingerprint to the way your eye glints
From the start of your life to the end of your days
You are unique in a trillion ways
YOU are unique
To the God that you seek.

Rebekah Simpson

Ruthy (my big sister) has an incredibly unique set of creative skills which she used to help me during the six months of chemotherapy. She sent me an album full of empty A5 clear plastic pockets. Weekly she posted me a note or a photo which I could slip into the pockets and use in the present and the future as a source of encouragement.

What fun these letters brought. Quirky, random, hilarious and original, they brought sunshine to my life. The most memorable was her discovery that some people actually knit tits for women who need prosthetics. Some talented breast cancer survivors created knitted 'breasts', very soft and cosy; they knit them in many colours, and even knit the nipples.

They are all original and one of Ruth's letters had printed out stories and photos from the 'knitted tit makers' website. They had me laughing until I wept. One was a photo of a variety of different sized and shaped breasts with information about how to knit the nipples. Photographed amongst the tits there was a Barbie Doll and a rubber duck which was holding one of the tits in the indentation on its back. Ruth's commentary on the photo was 'what's she [Barbie] doing in this picture? Showing off her chest to the rubber duck?' It was so random.

Another post on the website was from a woman who liked to knit herself extremely original tits. One of which was a tit depicting toboggans that she could wear while sipping Hot chocolate after a hard day in the snow. She was so proud of it that she got it out in public all the time saying 'see my titty? See? See?' A cop approached her during one of these sharing times and told her that what she was actually doing was 'flashing', which is against the law.

The result of Ruth's discovery that some people knit their own tits was to knit me a pair. I don't believe this craft adventure was without its traumas. The most significant being a trip to the charity shop to purchase knitting needles. I wouldn't have even thought about going to a charity shop – I would have headed straight to John Lewis' craft department and bought them brand new. This is a significant difference between me and my two sisters – they love rummaging through charity shops. They are thrifty, I am not; I don't chuck money around but I'd sooner spend 20 minutes getting knitting needles in a place where I can just say what I want and a lovely shop worker will find what I need and I just pay for it and walk out.

Ruth went to the charity shop where a whole bag of jumbled needles was presented to her. She had to rummage through them. All different sizes, some bent, some metal, some plastic, not in pairs so even if you found one you might not find its match. I just could not be bothered with all this faff, but hats off to Ruth and others who do. Eventually the charity shop lady asked what exactly she was looking for; what was she wanting to make: a sock, a jumper, a cardigan? Ruth replied, 'I'm knitting a boob for my sister.'

It took her a few weeks to knit these resplendent knockers; they arrived in the post majestic and enormous a few days later. I can't say I ever used them as prosthetics, but they took pride of place on my mantelpiece between two aromatherapy candles and a handpainted watercolour of Grasmere in the Lake District. They were a talking piece for anyone who visited, and I loved telling the story of how they'd come about and the brilliance of the artist behind them.

At some point when Archie was big enough he asked to play with them. It's interesting to me that the girls have never paid much attention to them; Archie on the other hand loves them. I have a range of photos of him through the years cuddling the boobs. To this day they remain one of his favourite bedfellows of choice. It's a funny sight to creep into his room when he's asleep and see his face pressed up against a large soft pale pink bosom with a rose-coloured nipple poking out above his duvet.

I will finish my tribute to Ruth's uplifting powers with a poem she wrote for me.

38 going on 39

(Based around 'you are 16 going on 17 – Sound of Music)

You are 38, going on 39
With an unusual social life
Biopsies, CT scans, pregnancy not planned
You've even been under the knife
You are 38 going on 39
This has taken you by storm
Now you've had your first breast op
No more 'gone south drop'
Firm tittie you've yet to form!
Totally without choices now
Awaiting the next phase
Rid of the tumour
Maintained your humour
And a Nanny to help you laze!

You are 38 going on 39
Certainly not naïve
When the chemo goes in
Just pretend that it's gin
Willingly you'll believe
You are 38 going on 39
Wondering what's in store
Hoping it's handsome male staff
Who are up for a laugh
And willingly up for more!
Totally well-equipped are you
To face this time of strife
And one day, just maybe you'll tell the baby
About its miraculous start to life.

Ruth Smithson

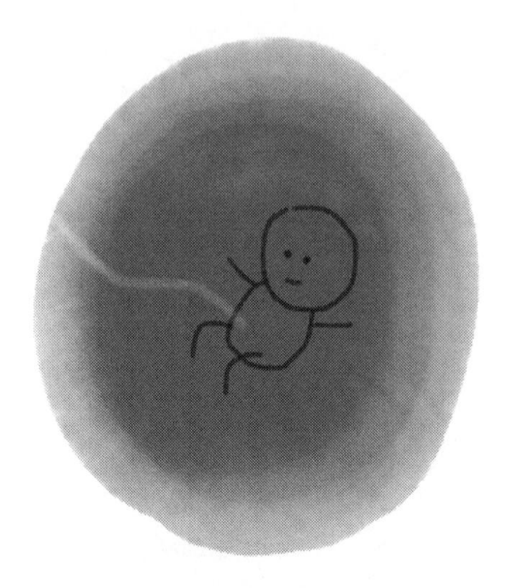

New Life

On the 12th July 2009 I arrived at the RVI to be induced with our fourth child. Our first son. We knew it was to be a boy because I had growth scans every month throughout the pregnancy to ensure the baby was growing properly during my chemotherapy. The sonographer wouldn't tell me for sure until the baby was 20 weeks; all the scans were 3D which meant we were able to pick out details about the baby in very early stages. The first 3D scan I had at 12 weeks post-mastectomy surgery, had been my greatest joy and delight. I pored over it for hours; I KNEW it was a boy – believe me the lump between his legs only had one destiny. Even so, when he confirmed what I already knew, Mark and I both cried.

We had not been remotely bothered whether this baby was male or female. Its unplanned life had God's hand on it from its very start and its journey throughout my treatment had been protected by God's perfect timing. We knew it would be healthy, its gender mattered not. Having said that the news that it was a boy was pretty awesome and our responses showed that. For Mark particularly it was such a blessing. He finally had the opportunity to encourage one of his offspring in sharing beer and peanuts, celebrating or commiserating over the highs and lows of one of the biggest loves of his life, Tottenham Hotspur. Goal won. As for me, I had the opportunity to find out for myself whether boys really were harder than girls – a mummy conversation that I had not been able to participate in; but was extremely weary and bored of hearing. The verdict, now that I have girls and boys: it is personality that defines a difficult child NOT gender. But, if you pushed me to choose I'd say girls are harder.

Induction began around 4 pm. Archie Isaac arrived at 6.15. Mark had learnt his role in the presence of labour: take a hospital chair safely into the far corner and read 'What Car?', only become involved in the final stages when I shout 'Mark, I don't want to have this baby anymore'. He'd not repeated fussing over me after the birth of Evie. What with the constant loop of birthing music that he'd spent hours putting together, endless enquiries as to what I needed, and a monotonous mantra of 'you're doing SOOOOOOO well' which after six hours of all this white noise I was forced me to ask him – with no expletives of course – if he'd like to walk the corridor for a while. I am always mesmerised by the TV show One Born Every Minute when I see couples literally on the hospital bed clinging onto one another, even kissing, moments before baby pops out. I just need to be left alone to get on with it – 'What Car?' and the corner, we had found to be the answer.

This was the most straightforward birth of them all, a bit of gas and air, a few pushes and there he was. Weighing in at just under 6lb with enormously long legs, my third baby, the fourth child in the Simpson clan to be born without red hair. Phew, goal. Archie Isaac Simpson, Archie because it kept the theme of our children's names ending in 'ie' and, of course, we liked it – we wouldn't have called him Leslie, Ronnie or Brodie, for example; sorry if that's your name.

We chose Isaac because it means 'laughter' and I really believed this baby was going to bring some much needed joy into our current situation but also because of the story in the Bible about Abraham and his son Isaac. God gave Abraham a command to take his only son 'Isaac' and offer him as a sacrifice to God. There's a lot of Bible history tied up in sacrifices and the symbolic nature of sacrifice – go look it up, it has nothing to do with God having some macabre interest in asking parents to slay their children and then creating a cliff hanger by changing his mind at the last minute (I'll tell you the ending now – Isaac does not get sacrificed)... thought I better just say that.

Of course, this request filled Abraham's heart with pain; not as much, however, as it would a father in our day, but offerings were common in those times. The point of the story was to do with how much Abraham was willing to trust God and willing to be obedient to him, SO obedient that he was willing to sacrifice his only son. He knew that God had promised that Isaac's offspring were to become a great nation. Maybe he thought Isaac would be raised from the dead, who knows, but the story illustrates that Abraham knew that Isaac belonged to God. Even though he couldn't understand why God was asking him to walk such a traumatic path in God's strength he was willing to obey.

Can you imagine the journey that Abraham took with his son Isaac? They walked for two days, sleeping under trees at night in open country. Two days is a long time to be with your only son knowing what you're going to do to him when you reach your destination. They reached the mountain and began to ascend. Isaac was carrying the wood that was gathered to consume his own body. It's unimaginable; it could be the scene from a current psycho horror film. He was told they were going to worship God so he legitimately asked, 'Where is the lamb for the offering?' Abraham told him that God would provide the lamb. Good answer, Abraham, I don't think I could have come out with such genius, moments away from slaying my child with a knife and then burning him.

When they reached the top Abraham built the altar and on it he placed all the wood. Then he tied the hands and feet of Isaac and laid him on the altar and raised his knife to kill him. Crikey, I don't know if I can continue; what must Isaac have been thinking? The Bible doesn't explain the human emotions that must have been going on at this moment in time; and as I write this I can understand why. My own imagination of this scene of savagery and terror makes it too terrible to try and describe. Somehow we have to enter into the great faith of Abraham as he stood with the knife above his head believing this was not going to happen because he clung to the promise of God that Isaac was to father many nations.

At exactly the right moment an angel called to him, "Do not lay your hand upon your son. Do no harm to him. Now I know that you love God more than you love your only son, and that you are obedient to God, since you are ready to give up your son, your only son, to God."

What a relief and a joy these words from heaven must have brought to the heart of Abraham! How glad he was to know that it was not

God's will for him to kill his son! Then Abraham looked around, and there in the thicket was a ram caught by his horns. And Abraham took the ram and offered him up for a burnt-offering in place of his son. So Abraham's words came true when he said that God would provide for himself a lamb. I do wonder how Isaac recovered from this experience with his father! However, I don't think this is the place to get tangled up in such a debate.

Mark and I felt that we had begun to understand more deeply what it meant to be willing to trust God in any situation. Not to spend our time questioning and debating with him, but to walk in obedience, trusting him for the final outcome. The diagnosis of cancer, the precarious pregnancy with Archie and the nanny issues surrounding Evie had left us no choice but to learn to hand over our most precious commodities to God. I wouldn't be so arrogant as to compare my sacrifices with the sacrifice that Abraham was asked to make. We had been challenged by our situation, and wrapped up in that challenge was whether or not we believed completely that God is love and is true to his word. Whether we could entrust everything to him in our lives and sacrifice the lives of our children to his care; when you're faced with your mortality and you have young children you are plagued with anxiety as to who will care for them when you're gone. We had to sacrifice this control, lay it on the altar and trust that He would not disappoint us. The name Isaac is a constant reminder to us of this story and is a reminder to us that we must live sacrificial lives.

Death v life

Archie was four days old when I started radiotherapy on my chest to kill any rogue cells that may have spread into the bone. I had to attend the Freeman Hospital for 15 sessions Monday to Friday for three weeks. It was a strange experience. Most people in the radiology department of a specialist cancer centre are over the age of 60 and there are no women with newborn babies. You can almost touch the quiet hush of deadly disease, a predecessor of death. There's not much laughing and smiling in those waiting rooms. Tension, tiredness and trauma hang in the atmosphere wrapping ghostly tendrils around victims of cancer.

There was no Maggie Centre in those days to escape to and be loved and cared for by the angels who volunteer there. The concept of a network of drop-in centres across the United Kingdom aiming to help anyone diagnosed with cancer, attached to hospitals specialising in cancer, had not been fully formed. Havens of heaven more like your own home where you could relax in a non-clinical environment and be attended to by people not wearing white uniforms, and forget your cares for a while. In 2010 with my newborn baby I had to sit in the stillness and people-watch, wondering how many of us would survive. Feeling envious that most of these people had reached an age I may never see. I looked at Archie and felt deep sadness.

I recently wrote a poem about the Maggie Centre and how valuable it has become to me since it opened in 2015 and the huge impact that Karen Verrill (the angel) who runs the centre has had on my life from the start of my diagnosis.

The Angel of Maggies

There is a place
A beautiful place
I love to go there
Waves and swathes of
Warmth and hope wrap their tender
Wings around my bruised heart
My broken mind.

The courtyard wild garden
Swaying with meadow flowers
Banks of bright tulips and daisies
Moving in spring breezes
My secret healing retreat
Hidden from clinical corridors
A haven from deathly wards and gloomy faces

I hide amongst the blossoms and blooms
The muted calm colours and secret little rooms
Concerns covered by summer scents
Gentle faces and voices meant
To offer hopeful choices
In quiet caring soft voices

Protected, connected, united
With others on the same winding road
All of us candles in the wind
Not knowing where to turn to
When the rain sets in
Trying to hold the shadows at bay
Cancer has caused us to lose our way

But here in this heavenly place
I come face to face
With a champion fighting my cause
I am a hero within HER heavenly walls

Her compassion drives away my negative perspective
She directs me to a positive objective
She roars like a lioness protecting me
Scaring away the power of illness, setting me free

No-one human could achieve this role
Constantly demonstrating such a selfless soul
So if she's not human; what is she? Shall I tell you
What I think?... she's an angel...truly! I believe this is true.

She's disguised, of course, in heels and smart dresses
Perfect hair and shiny lip glosses
She leaves her white robe in the darkness of the closet
But I'VE seen the tips of her wings
Trailing out from the hems of those dresses
Her angel feathers giving my broken heart gentle caresses
Lightening my burden from Cancer's stresses
Her white brightness lifts my downhearted face
Bringing supernatural hope to my hopeless case

Her giggling stories make me laugh
Transforming my darkness into brightness
Carrying my pain on her wings of lightness
Cutting into my dark deepness
Her angelic strength soaking up all my weakness
She's my forerunner my banner carrier
Waving the flag of victory over my Cancer
She's my counsellor, confidante and friend
Living life with me until my end.

She's my guardian angel
Constant, reliable, unchangeable
Always honest never mincing her words
But like a sweet songbird
Giving me reason to hope
And the skills to balance on cancer's tight-rope

How do I thank this angel of mine?
A few bottles of prosecco, a crate of wine?
I imagine this WOULD cause her eyes to shine
But I think what will cause her wings to flutter in delight
And her golden halo to glow proudly bright
Will be knowing that the strength in HER wings
Are what gave MY wings the chance of new flight

Rebekah Simpson

We found a rhythm over the three weeks: Mark would generally take over feeding and walking Archie around the corridors of the hospital and I would sit and wait for treatment; distracting myself with magazine trash. It was during one of these deathly trips to hospital that I had an awesome encounter with God and heard his audible voice in a way I had never heard it before. It was a sunny morning; sunshine was streaming through the floor to ceiling glass windows that line the open waiting rooms and corridors of the radiology department. A reasonably successful architectural design aimed to flood what would otherwise be a dingy and depressing lower ground floor. I sat warmed by the filtered heat looking out to a paved courtyard garden containing a few sculptures, some raised beds with greenery in and some floating vibrantly coloured silk flags tied to the saplings planted there. They flapped and fluttered all the colours of the rainbow, dancing in the wind, inviting thoughts of freedom to my prison inside. Mark was on a trip to the toilet, I was rocking Archie as he snoozed feeling unnaturally peaceful given the circumstances.

As I looked down at Archie I began praying, I can't fully recall my prayer, but I remember beginning to feel overwhelmed by how tiny and vulnerable he was. I felt I'd let him down, that he had been protected for nine months from the perils surrounding his mummy's illness, but now he was here, what kind of a life was he going to experience? No doubt thoughts of not seeing him grow up would have crept into the edges of my imagination – such contemplations were never far from me at that time. The grip of grief over a future that I may never have watching him grow and become a man began to cause shadows blocking out the streaming sunshine.

Then I heard a voice. At first I thought one of the other patients was speaking to me. I looked up but the waiting area only contained three old men. One was asleep, one was reading a magazine and the other looked too wizened and decrepit in his wheelchair, tubes stuck up his nose pumping oxygen from the canister on the floor to keep him alive, to have spoken to me; poor old fella. There was also a Daft as a Brush volunteer – a charity that offers custom made vehicles to transport outpatients, free of charge, to and from hospital when they're undergoing treatment – sat behind a desk, head on one side pondering something on the computer; and that was it.

I stood up cradling Archie and looked behind me; I wandered slightly out of the area and peered around the corner to see if any gentle spoken male doctor was perhaps having a conversation that I'd overheard. There was no one, just an empty corridor.

I sat down and then I heard the voice again. It was audible, I could hear it with my ears but at the same time it came from deep within. It wasn't MY voice talking to myself as I often do, it was male, it was rich, it was gentle but at the same time, assertive, demanding my full attention.

'Rebekah, all around you is death, but this child in your arms, this miracle you are holding, is my promise of life to you.' That was it. I sat in stillness and soaked these words into the depths of my being. I knew the voice was God his Holy Spirit, he had spoken life into my deathly situation and I felt calm, peaceful and assured of God's intimate involvement in my life. I also felt excited: I'd heard God's voice, how awesome, how utterly and completely loved it made me feel. Maybe a different character would have jumped up and announced to the waiting room that God had just spoken to them; my response was to hold this secret revelation, drink it in, allow it settle into my anxious mind and heart. Saturate and repeat the words until they were fully embedded in my mind as a truth that I was going to live in from this day forward.

I did not interpret this promise of life to mean that I was promised a miracle of healing. I had no sense of that at all. I mention that because when I did go on to share this encounter I was somewhat frustrated by how people chose to take its meaning. Many Christians adapted this experience into a promise that I was going to have a long life, which allowed them to be even more certain that God was promising to give me a miraculous healing.

I took it as a promise that within my situation God was promising me that I would find life, I would find character; I would find the strength to live the life I had day by day and to live it full of life. That he would breathe supernatural life into my dying body and enable me to soar above my circumstances, full of spiritual life. I would not be living under a shadow of darkness buried like spring bulbs that are unseen during autumn and winter months. I was going to push through the dirt and bleakness and reveal an abundant beautiful life that blossomed and was fruitful.

Miracles Again

(I do go on a bit, don't I? Shut the book if you don't like it)

From the very start of this journey, as mentioned before, I have wrestled with other people's views on healing and certainty for miracles. So, here's my chance for a little rant: it's my book, I'm the one who's sick, so I can say what I feel and not be too scared of your argument against me. The view I hate the most is from those who doggedly believe and translate any tiny little bit of progress or any word given as a sign to support their view that I can be certain of and am promised, in God's word, my full healing or a future miracle. Some verses from the Bible have been translated to support this view that I am promised a miracle in my present day experience. Jesus obviously performed many miracles, never turning anyone away in his pre-death ministry. I think this is awesome; I understand that because we are made in the image of him and have his spirit dwelling within we too could perform miracles. The glaringly obvious problem is that most of us don't.

As yet, God has made no such promise of a miracle to me, either through his spirit, or word. I understand the verses and view of Jesus' power quoted regularly but I am still struggling to personally translate those as a guarantee that I (or anyone for that matter) is entitled to miraculous healing in this life in any situation. Maybe one day I will have a different view. I regularly listen and tolerate the view of 'promised miracles to all', I am not closed off to being persuaded, but until my experience and personal testimony and relationship with Jesus shows me enough evidence to dramatically alter my opinion, then I choose to file this under 'open to interpretation' or at least 'open to revelation'.

Such words as 'patience' or 'timing' are frequently pushed in front of me by way of explaining why I have not received my 'Jesus/ Bible' promised miracle. To be honest, I frequently tell myself this half-truth. I do believe there is truth within this statement. It makes a lot of sense; I understand that God is my Father and like any good parent he doesn't give us whatever we want the moment we bleat at him. Asking my child to wait while I finish a conversation, or choosing to delay the consumption of an Easter egg until after lunch are legitimate and important life lessons. You are giving the child an opportunity to learn patience, endurance, trust and many other character traits that are essential for fighting much bigger battles that are still to come.

Of course, the flaw in the examples I have given is that the thing they are asking for is guaranteed to happen in a timeframe they can understand and cope with. I would have to be a very cutting edge parent to say 'you can have the Easter egg but I'm not going to tell you when'. The when then turns out to be 12 years later when they've completed their GCSEs. I think they'd give up on me if I parented like this.

By the stage they are able to understand delay and gratification they also know from experience that you will do what you say. They know they'll get the egg because you've delayed other things; their experience tells them you're reliable and trustworthy, and also that they'll get it in a manageable timeframe. They then make a choice to let it go for a short period of time because they know you love them and that you do what you say.

Some of the difficulty of fully accepting 'patience' and 'timing' concepts when it comes to a terminal illness such as cancer, is that a sensible person, such as myself, who has all their faculties intact (ha ha), understands that timing and patience are important character traits. Unfortunately, I have also experienced that very few people who've played the waiting game in this area, do in fact receive the so-called promised miracle in this lifetime. And this is a gigantic argument against the whole 'you're guaranteed 'complete healing' in God's timing waffle'.

'Mum, I want one of my Easter Eggs.'

'Not now, dear.'

This is followed by lots of moaning and whining from the child and accusations about what a rubbish mum you are; closely pursued with ignorant comparisons to other mums who give their children chocolate all day.

'When can I have it then?'

'Just trust me, my child; I have this eggsasperating situation in hand. My timing is perfect, I know what you need; I have eggcellent plans for your life. They may not include an egg because I have other perfect plans for you. Others may get eggs; some will get them before lunch. Never worry about what others receive because I know eggsactly what YOU need. I'm not going to tell you right now but you must trust me; it may be decades before I give you what you ask, but I command you NOT to worry.'

I guarantee most children would have a prolonged hissy fit if that was the answer you gave them, or perhaps even worse is silence. Your child asks for the egg and you simply don't reply; then a sibling wanders in curious as to what all the screaming is about and tells the child that Mummy is silent because the answer to 'egg before lunch' scenario is already laid out in her parenting manual. This Holy manual can be located in the bookshelf on the second floor – go and find it for the answer, chapter 3 paragraph 2, line 4. Then just believe that one day you'll get what you want.

I haven't even touched on the debate around 'God's will'; that's equally contentious. If it's allegedly said that we have no sickness and that it is not his 'will' for my life, then why do I have it? God didn't give you it, the devil did. Why did God allow that? Does that mean it must be his will in 'some way' or doesn't it? Or did he just make a slip up or go to sleep whilst the devil stormed into my life to wreak havoc? He stood back whilst the devil decimated Job's life, he didn't take Paul's thorn from his flesh; he simply said 'NO! My power is made perfect in your weakness'. I can't even go there over all these questions. There never seems to be a satisfactory conclusive answer; just humans trying to work out the unworkable and make it fit for their situation.

My experience of all these, to me, somewhat inconclusive arguments about healing is that they can drag you down and drown you. The statement that God continues to remind me of is this: seek the healer not the healing. The more you pursue what you **want** from God, the more you're in danger of falling into a pit of fear and confusion. We should pursue God simply for who he is not for what he might do for us. This for me is the solid rock. All other ideas are my sinking sand.

In the Bible Peter learned this lesson the hard way. He is out on the Galilean sea in a fishing boat; 'in the middle of the sea, tossed by waves, for the wind was contrary' (Matt. 14:24). The Galilean Sea was known for its vulnerability to howling winds and churning waves. Peter knew he was in trouble – what should have been a short trip had turned into a night long battle. Winds whipped the sails and tossed the boat with the disciples in it from side to side. I often felt in the middle of a storm, raging around the complex and painful confusion surrounding healing and miracles. Like the disciples, I fought and wrestled it all; as a result of the ambiguity and much evidence proving that miracles were not a guaranteed daily worldwide experience, I felt unable to go blindly along with aforementioned views.

I have been challenged to go to conferences, local, national and abroad to be prayed over by 'anointed healers'. Which left me questioning why my allegedly promised miracle isn't possible when I pray myself? Do I really need to travel half way around the world in the vain attempt to be in a particular place or in front of a particular person? And if these people are getting 100% success rate, which I assume they're NOT because if they were wouldn't it have hit the world headlines like a third world war would? The odds of a miracle are just too poor for me to place my trust in such a truth. I'm even vaguely feeling irritated with myself that I'm spending any time on this at all.

The disciples spotted someone coming on the water and there was Jesus. They didn't expect Jesus to come to them in this way. But in my experience it is when I am in the storms that he is able to do his finest work, for it is then that he has my keenest attention. Jesus' reply to the disciples' fear and confusion was 'Don't be afraid, I am here'. Peter took Jesus at his word: 'Lord, if it be you, command me to come to you on the water.' He walked on the water to Jesus. The story goes on to explain how Peter shifted his attention from Jesus toward the squall and when he did he sank like a brick.

God has asked me to keep my focus on him, and him alone. He doesn't ask me to be naïve or ignorant, oblivious to the overwhelming challenges I face. I've to continue to take long looks at who God is; trying to pay close attention to his word of truth and keep my gaze fixed in him. I feel that overly seeking miracles and healing can be a sign of fear and when we focus on fear our faith starves. I chose to shift my gaze to the steadfast love of the Lord, which never ceases and to seek his mercy day by day knowing that his faithfulness to me was great. The storm ceases because of my focus.

If there were a person whose reputation for miracles was out of this world and unexplainable I'd be on the first peasant waggon out of Newcastle Central. Someone who was not just wafting headaches away by the end of the service or waving hands over sore backs – 'Can you bend to your knees now?'. Full on, phenomenal, unexplainable, beyond anything natural, bona fide, physical miracles done before a public crowd who don't necessarily believe in miracles. Disabled people climbing out of wheelchairs, walking and leaping around, hideous diseases that have alienated people from integrating in their community because their sickness is so repugnant to others, amputated limbs growing back, the dead being brought in their coffins and on one word they rise up to live again and these phenomena happened wherever they went and were 100% reliable for all cases. Then wow. Forgive me, Lord, for the sceptical view I had in 2018.

There was a miracle man who did these things; his name was Jesus. I'm not aware of his return yet; and until that day my understanding is that although awesome unexplainable miracles do happen sometimes via particular people, there remains a huge shortfall of people who receive no miracles whatsoever. Somehow I have to accept this reality and face it as David faced his giant Goliath.

I do believe in miracles: I parent four miracles; I look out of my window to my beautiful garden and marvel at the miracle of creation; I see God's miraculous hand in every function of my body. Do I see many miraculous healings from cancer? Nope, nada, nowt, not one. I'm really going to put myself out there now, even the odd few that I've heard of through someone else I find questionable. I'm going to isolate this view, to keep it simple, to people who have heard about someone being miraculously healed from cancer. I am NOT saying it hasn't happened, but I am very sceptical about many of these cases and doubt they are miracles at all.

My experience of cancer – and believe me I have more information and knowledge of this than most of you reading – is this. That cancer is a hugely personal problem. Everyone's tumour is different and every body responds differently. Some tumours grow slow, some grow fast, some respond to treatment, some don't, some can be operated on, some can't, some are found early, some are found too late. What works in one type of cancer for one person won't mean it will work for others. Some generally have a mostly positive prognosis, some have a very poor prognosis. The variables are vast and the human response even more vast, and medicine is fighting hard to keep ahead of the game. Many people can't fully face the truth of their diagnosis and so choose not to ask questions about the future and therefore can't give accurate balanced information to others.

I am no medical expert, but I want to get the point across that when people talk about being healed, cured, or receiving a miracle in cancer the story may not quite be what it seems. I am going to give a literal example of this from my own experience. When I completed all my treatment for primary breast cancer I was told I could be 95% certain that I was 'cured' – is that the same as a miracle? I don't think it is. Importantly the fact that the only bit I heard was 'cured', I didn't even question the other 5%, that's what I shared with people; everyone celebrating and calling it a miracle, us all ignorant in the absolute truth, even me. Why? Because we all want a miracle when we're facing possible premature death! Beware, people misinterpret consultation information; even I am guilty of that crime.

Medicine has progressed; many people are living with illness that 20 years ago they would not have survived. Praise God for giving people brains and the miraculous talent to use them for the good of humankind's advancement. But it's still not the same to be kept alive by medicine and in the case of cancer treatment, medicine potentially kills the cancer but causes permanent damage to healthy parts of your body, many of which never recover! Work that one out in the light of a discussion on miracles. Many people are cured of cancer or live with it for a long time, but this is not a miracle in the sense that Jesus performed miracles, or that people report and claim as a miracle. I'm not trying to be negative, but it can be so difficult to see people using these tales as proof of miracles and then bantering them around for people like myself to take heart from. There is so much misunderstanding and mis-represented stories of miraculous healings from cancer that I find it difficult to take them as simply as others do. Many people don't even understand that if cancer has spread to your blood or lymphatic system then it is almost 100% certain to eventually mutate into a secondary tumour.

I have had real conversations with people who believe their cancer has gone away, cured, healed, miraculously gone; but on closer inspection their cancer had in fact been found in their lymph nodes – in my mind that means that it's likely to turn up again.

Of course, Jesus can take my sickness away but he didn't and hasn't. In the story of the storm he wanted to teach his followers a lesson: he could have calmed the storm; he could have calmed my storm by removing the tumour or even better not allowed it to happen. I choose to learn to take the apostle Paul's approach in 2 Corinthians 12:7-9. 'To keep me from thinking of myself as important, a thorn in the flesh was given to me, a messenger of Satan, to torment and harass me.'

I don't know what Paul's 'thorn' was, a physical illness or a mental illness, it doesn't really matter. The fact was that God permitted it. He didn't give it to Paul but he did not take it away. He does this because ultimately he is interested in our holiness, not our happiness. If every time we had a problem and God supernaturally delivered us of course we'd think 'yeah', but how would we ever grow as people? How would we develop patience, tenacity and humility? We would constantly give up at the first sign of trouble and become demanding spoilt brats.

God's wisdom allows us to live with the 'thorns'; we are only interested in temporal immediate comfort. He is more interested in the eternal value that is planned for us. Paul wanted to get rid of his limitation but God said no. 'I pleaded with the Lord three times that it might leave me.' I can tell you right now that I've had people plead for me many more times than three. God replied, 'My grace is sufficient for you, my loving kindness and my mercy are more than enough (regardless of your situation); for my power is being perfected (and is completed and shows itself most effectively) in your weakness.'

In other words, bear your troubles 'manfully', pull yourself together and quit whining. Stand up like a man or woman of God and say, 'I will not expect my life to be perfect. I will stand in the power of God's spirit which will enable me to do whatever I need to do and do it with a smile and stop going on and on about what I think I need.'

'My strength and power are being perfected (and is completed and shows itself most effective) in your weakness.' If we have no weakness and whenever we pray all our struggles are taken away, then pretty quickly we would have no need for Jesus at all. We'd use him like a vending machine. 'Therefore I will gladly boast in my weaknesses, so that the power of Christ may completely enfold me and dwell in me.' Oh goody, I have cancer, it's an opportunity to give God the glory for when I am weak, he is strong.

Paul understood and is testifying that God does not take all our problems away; it is in our problems that he teaches us about his grace. Grace that transforms character so that you can bear your sickness and weaknesses manfully and be glad of the opportunity they bring to draw you closer to God. Should we focus on receiving healings and miracles, or should we pray more diligently that we, like Paul, stop going on about them and be glad that our 'thorns' allow the power of Christ to manifest in us?

I haven't given up entirely on expecting my chocolate egg, but I trust that he has allowed this storm because he could use it to teach me some important lessons. Could those lessons be something like this: 'the storms of life are not a choice that you can simply pray away; but fear of the storm and how you deal with it, is always a choice'.

Life, God spoke life into me that day in the hospital. He promised me life. I didn't ask for the details, I didn't need to. I simply took it as it was spoken and felt hopeful for a good life with my newborn son. I am looking forward to heaven and meeting Jesus. Living is hard, it is not for me that I fear dying young; my concern is for my children.

I'm confident that Mark will be fine and go on to find someone else to make his dinner; who doesn't ask for foot massages every night and is a rampant sex goddess. The kids are a different concern. I was left motherless at 35 and believe me it has been a tough journey. She died five months before I was married. She didn't meet any of my children and she's not been there to help me out practically with childcare or for advice on how to handle parenting. I wouldn't have necessarily taken any of her advice, but I would still like to know what she would have said and have her at the end of the phone if I needed her.

I know what it's been like to be motherless and I do not want this for my children. They will always need me. No matter what stage of life they reach, if I am not around, they will feel my absence. I know this from painful experience. It's for them I hope for a miracle; for me heaven is a welcome concept. They have asked me if I miss my mummy, and I've told them I do. When I feel sad I simply focus on meeting her again at the glorious party for eternity in heaven where we are all perfected, no sickness or pain. This life is only temporary and if you know Jesus as your saviour and Lord then one day you will be with him and all other believers in paradise.

We all have to die; it's life's one certainty. When, where and how, we have no control over and why should we fight it? I believe God has that all in hand: we are born when planned and we die when planned; the stuff in between is just the stuff in between. I choose for that stuff to draw me into a closer relationship with God, not so that I can get what I want, but so that I can learn more about his love; and in that love fulfil his number one purpose that I love others as he loves me. If I have 50 years or 80 years pursuing this goal, what does it matter? I don't want to leave my children young and still dependent on me, but the answer is not to doggedly pursue a miracle so that I can be here longer. The answer is to pursue Jesus so that however long I am here I can love them better and point them to him; so that when I'm gone we can all be sure of meeting again in heaven and dancing forever.

Fun with Fundraising

I was to turn 40 in January 2011. I've never been a big one for birthdays – from being a small child the day has been a disappointment. I have forgiven my mother for many traumatic memories and experiences, and have worked hard to understand who she was and why she behaved so unkindly towards me. But the one event that to this day I struggle to understand was her attitude to birthdays.

I can't remember much about my younger birthdays, under the age of 10. I remember other people's but absolutely no recollection of my own. I wonder perhaps if I have blocked them out completely. She had this strange penchant for being different. There was no logic to it and even if there was she did not explain her reasons. If she did they didn't really make sense, and she was so completely unbending in her opinion that it was pointless trying to state your case.

For example, as I got older she would not allow me to listen to popular music, wear any make up, do my hair nicely, wear clothes of my choosing. I suppose she would carte blanche many of these things as being wrong, sexualised or vain. I remember arguing over all these areas, challenging her about music, such as folk, which was just good music, there was nothing wrong in it. No lewd words or girls gyrating around in next to nothing, but she wouldn't have it.

The result of many of these conflicts of interest: I went undercover. Lied basically; I hid make up, I went out looking like she wanted me to look but I changed at a friend's house. When skin tight jeans were in fashion, which of course she was never going to allow me to wear, I just put them on underneath her choice then stripped them off in the back lane, stuffed them in a carrier bag and hid them in a hedge. I saved up to buy my own radio and Sony Walkman and listened to music hidden in the dark, dusty, spider ridden eaves in the attic.

Consequently, I had to lie to a lot of my friends at school, faking knowledge about the latest chart hit, adapting clothes that she bought me in my bed at night to make them more current. It was awful, I felt like a misfit; I disguised it as best I could but nothing could fully take away the fear of being caught by her or the anxiety surrounding her peculiar and extreme rules that segregated me from my peers.

I am not going to describe in detail what she did to me whenever she discovered my sins. It doesn't feel right. It's suffice to say that one of my frequent memories from those teenage years is my sister Sarah standing in doorways crying, shouting at her to stop and threatening her with social services. I doubt they'd have done much in the 70s.

I imagine that birthdays in the early years were peculiar. She was the sort of woman who despite understanding how the average nine year old's party should be, she wouldn't want to do it like that. There'd be activities like colouring in a picture of Christ feeding the 5000 instead of the tray memory game; or she'd play Christian hymns on the piano for pass the parcel, or pin Jesus to the cross rather than a tail on a donkey. If there were party bags, which I expect there wasn't, it would have been Bible verses and an invitation to the Baptist Church Sunday School.

Maybe I begged there to be no party and that's why I can't remember any. It didn't get any better when I entered the teenage years. Often she didn't even remember it was my birthday. In reality this may have only happened once, but even if that's true it created an anxiety in me every year as the day approached that lasted well into my late 20s. Would she or would she not remember?

A few times she got me a card, but no gift. This was equally as disappointing; and forced further lies to friends about what I had received. At this point in my life people were getting TVs, funky Ghetto Blasters and cool Adidas shell toe trainers with matching shell suits. On MY 14th birthday I got a travel iron; it wasn't even one she'd picked out thoughtfully, if indeed one can pick a travel iron out thoughtfully for a 14 year old girl who only ever went on camping holidays with no electrical hook up points.

I think it was the first birthday she forgot. No card, nothing. I waited all day, I can still see myself wandering around aimlessly not wanting to say anything in case I spoilt the surprise that surely must be on its way.

The hours ticked by, I sat outside my bedroom door on the third floor, alone, wondering how best to tackle this issue. Around tea time I went to find her and said, 'It's my birthday today.' She was in the kitchen at the sink peeling potatoes; she turned round and said, 'Is it? Oh.' And that was it.

The winter sun streamed through the kitchen window; she continued to peel the spuds. 'Have you got me anything?' I am cringing as I write this, how excruciating, even in the face of her answer I couldn't give up hope that she hadn't really forgotten. 'Well, you could go and look in the drawer under my bed.'

My heart lifted and I bounded up three storeys in anticipation of what was under the bed. I pulled out the drawer and scanned the array of random assorted products searching for a glimpse of flowery wrapping paper with my name on it. I soon realised that this drawer contained Sale items. Still in boxes, some a bit dusty looking, but as far as I could see there was no birthday gift for me.

I shouted down the stairs 'Mummy' (another obscure preference of hers, she had to be mummy, no one could call her mum – 'would you like it if I called you Becky?' was her argument. I wouldn't have minded; I never understood her point) 'I can't see a birthday present in the drawer.' 'There's nothing particular,' she shouted back, 'just choose something.'

It says it all about the range of items when I tell you that the best thing I could see was a travel iron.

And the above is my explanation for dread that has preceded every birthday I have ever had. Cancer helped me to begin celebrating my birthday from an entirely different angle. I could use it as opportunity to fundraise. That is what I did for most of the birthdays that followed between 2011 onwards.

The format has been different but the function the same. The yearning I had for my birthday to be noted and celebrated found satisfaction in organising fundraisers for Ladies in Pink Scarves. The scars run deep from my mother's attitude to birthdays. I find it excruciatingly difficult to simply ask people to celebrate the day and find it awkward receiving gifts and cards. I don't think this will ever leave me – I have experienced joy in making sure my children's birthdays are special; there will never be a drawer with sale items in my home.

A fundraiser could mark the occasion but also be an excuse to say no to gifts and cards, which I find uncomfortable receiving, and instead asking people to donate to charity. I am able to use my creativity and organisational skills which in turn distracts me from the pain within and elevates my self-esteem.

The first one was a ceilidh, and introduced the creation of the infamous Booby cakes which took centre stage. I asked my sister Ruth to make me a 40th birthday cake; she's extremely creative, talented and inventive. Her final product was 'Beks Pecks 40DDD', two massive iced pink breasts on a silver platter surrounded by 70-100 small booby cupcakes all representing boobs of different shapes, sizes, colours and nipple types with their own title 'The breast of British'. They were the main attraction and raised lots of money. In actual fact they became a trademark product for my future fundraisers.

Fundraising became a big part of my life; either through an event, such as Cream tea and choir or Pamper evenings, running and modelling in Karen Verrill's charity fashion shows. It offered me a positive focus in the negative face of cancer; becoming a voluntary job through which I raised thousands. It led to being nominated and winning two awards: Woman of the Community and then Woman of the Year.

Not sure I deserved Woman of the Year – as briefly mentioned in the first chapter my behaviour later that day certainly didn't warrant such a title. It was a lunchtime event where Prosecco was freely flowing. I don't go out very much especially to posh events all dressed up in a nice frock and heels. I have to confess that I don't drink very often and am not very good at gauging when too much is too much.

I couldn't believe I was even there and shortlisted out of hundreds of applicants. When they announced my name as the winner I was astounded. I almost hadn't gone to the award ceremony at all. The tickets for guests were £50. I couldn't bring myself to ask people to spend that much money when I felt it was unlikely I would win. I emailed them and explained why I would not be there.

Gemma, a dear friend and mummy from the school my children go to, was the person who had nominated me. She's a tinker, loving and selfless, always on the 'look out' for how to encourage and support others. Often to be seen pied piper-like with a band of other people's children following her on the school run. She has generously taken my three to her home on Mark's late night, Wednesday, even when she's felt pretty rough herself.

She has two children of her own and suffers with a terrible illness called POTS, a life altering and sometimes debilitating chronic health problem which manifests itself in many different ways. She rarely allows this to prevent her from offering support and practical help to others. I don't know how she does it, she's always smiling. It's her who deserves Woman of the Year.

The Sunshine Awards rang Gemma as my nominee after I'd declined coming to the event and explained my email. They hinted that it would be hugely gratifying for me and Gemma if we could make the event. Gemma didn't tell me this, she just approached me in the school yard and said she'd like to come with me. In the end, encouraged by Gemma, I filled a table of 10.

I could not believe it when I won; there were some prestigious women at those awards who as far as I could see served a much higher purpose and had raised triple the total of any money I had raised. I guess everyone likes a 'girl next door' story so I found myself on the stage in front of hundreds with my trophy and my head raised high. I lost it after that, and downed far too many free glasses of bubbly.

Which is not where it stayed later; I taxied home to pick up the children from Sarah's who had left earlier to be back for the school run. Embarrassingly the taxi driver just happened to pick Mark up for an event in the same hotel two weeks later. As soon as Mark got in the cab, the driver made the connection that he'd been at this address recently bringing a crazy woman home waving a large bouquet of flowers, brandishing a glass award, screeching with delight claiming that cancer could not stop her doing anything she wanted.

I wish the tale ended there but in true Rebekah fashion, when I lose it, I really lose it. I staggered down Marine Avenue at 3.40 pm in heels and my nicest dress, and actually fell over in the street. I reached Sarah's as high as a kite, got the post-alcohol nibbles and decided to go into Whitley Bay to buy crisps. Sarah was inebriated too and actually allowed me to take her daughter with me – please don't judge us, it's a once in a lifetime experience winning Woman of the Year.

When we got back Kotie started telling Sarah about how 'odd Aunty Rebekah seemed'. Apparently whilst waiting for the cashier to ring the crisps through the till I had leaned on the moving belt with both elbows. My elbows had travelled down the belt but my feet had stayed in the same position which Aunty Rebekah thought was hilarious and crying with laughter she did it three more times. I ate about two large bags of crisps and then crashed out face down on Sarah's kitchen table.

I do not know how I managed to walk my children home that night. I do remember Evie being in charge leading Archie, Josie and I through the streets. Me loudly slurring how much I loved them all, Evie telling me to 'shut up – you're embarrassing us'. But the real pinnacle of this story was arriving home stumbling up to our front door; after wrestling with the key and failing I slid to the floor with the three children surrounding me. Thankfully they found all this entertaining not disturbing, but legitimately wanted to know why I was behaving in such a funny way. My reply, I am ashamed to say 'sometimes mummy's medicine makes her feel a bit odd'. Not my finest moment.

Run, Rebekah, Run

June 2011 a friend invited me to do the Race For Life for cancer research in Saltwell Park Gateshead. I'd never run in my life apart from to the metro station. I have a distant memory of being forced by a battle axe PE woman to run the 200 metres on the school athletics day which traumatised me. I was never destined to do well in it, I was entered simply to fill the lanes and was running against people who liked to run and did it all the time. What a cruel way to humiliate a teenage girl! I came last by a country mile. It was mortifying. I was so far behind that they'd lined up all the runners for the 500 metres before I even crossed the finish line.

But this was different, it was non-competitive and its sole purpose was to raise money for cancer research. I was up for that. I set up a JustGiving site, which was a challenge in itself given how totally useless I am with technology, but by the end of the second day I'd exceeded my £100 target and was soaring towards £2000. The competitor hidden away inside me punched the air with delight – as I've told you before, there's nothing I like better than exceeding my targets. I'm so sad, that when I write a list of things to do and when I'd like to complete them by, something inside me kicks in. I simply like to beat myself; not with whips and sticks, just competitively. There is nothing that satisfies me more than exceeding my own expectations. There is probably something wrong with me; who cares if the laundry is done in 20 minutes rather than 22? ME, I care. I pat myself on the back and move to the next competition: beds, can I strip five beds in less than 15 minutes? Off I go running around the house leaping across beds like a ninja, wrenching flat sheets up from side to side; tearing at duvets, sweating like a dyslexic bloke in Countdown, fastest time, 18 minutes. Still working towards the 15.

It was so exciting seeing that target smashed to pieces by all the amazing friends and family I have. I was astounded and moved that people wanted to support me financially. By the time the date arrived I was nearly at £3000.

My competitive nature is sensible enough to accept limitations, at the time of this race I was not a runner; I didn't deliberately exercise at all. I was happy to walk it if I had to. After all it was less than a year since I'd had a baby not to mention the chemotherapy and radiotherapy. I'd raised a lot of money for a cause close to my heart; I was satisfied with that as the prize for my efforts.

The day came sunny and bright and I boarded the metro along with hordes of other women all dressed in the symbolic pink battle gear. I didn't bother taking the children or Mark; I had no idea what these events were like and I could only see it being utterly boring for our young children stood at the finish line for hours waiting for their decrepit mother to crawl over the 5k finish line. I didn't even understand what 5k was, 3.2 miles apparently, perhaps if I'd known that I would have at least done a bit of training.

I met my faithful friend Beth Brown, who has since run every Race for Life with me and some hilarious 10k muddy races; crawling on our bellies in dirty trenches and swimming through ponds of slurry. We arrived at Saltwell Park and I couldn't believe my eyes; it was swarming with shades of pink. Funky upbeat music pumping out from loud speakers either side of a stage; stalls selling pulled pork, ice cream; and Cancer research wares adorned the paths and field of the park. Families picnicking with babies in prams, children and toddlers smothered in pink facepaints and fake tattoos declaring victory over cancer. Tutus and pink leggings, hair sprayed neon pink everywhere I looked. I was definitely underdressed.

The atmosphere was electric. I instantly regretted the absence of my tribe. This was not just a fundraiser, this was a declaration of war. An intimidating power displayed by 100s of people who were prepared to show solidarity in the face of an intimidating enemy – cancer. I LOVED it. When you sign up for a Race For Life you receive your running number through the post and a paper tabard to pin to your back that you can write who you are running for. When I saw all these squares of paper on the runners' backs with the names of people dear to them written in bold black pen, I cried. I am crying now. It is such a moving scene. A sea of white moving around; bearing the suffering of others on their shoulders, prepared to run for life, not stand still and die.

Race for Life, that's what we were all there for, to race for life, to stay ahead of cancer's grip by raising money for research and provision of drugs that will one day cure cancer and banish its fear forever. It's too late for some of those names, but those who don't have cancer, or those who are well enough to run, do so to fight for the lives who are still here, or generations ahead who will benefit from our current efforts.

I felt a surge of power flood my body. I was going to run this race the best I could for the people written on my back. I had no idea what that meant, but I was determined to take it from my planned fast walking pace to at least include a bit of jogging. We funnelled into the starting area, Beth and I rightly placed in the back of the group called joggers. Even that seemed a little ambitious but many of these ladies looked slightly more rotund than I so I figured if they were in the joggers section I could be too.

Big countdown, lots of whistling and cheering and off we went. Nice and slow as we all piled over the start line, lots of waving to the crowd and shouts of support. We ran downhill on the park path marked out with pink barriers to keep you on the right track; it was as we went down that hill and began to circumnavigate a lake that I realised I was passing people at quite a rapid speed. I glanced behind and could see Beth not far away but not unlike that scene in Forrest Gump when he is running away from the boys who are bullying him, his calipers fly off his legs and he realises he has this ability to really run. And to run pretty fast, and so he does, turning off the road and flying away from them over fields to safety.

That's what it was like for me! I was overtaking crowds of women – some were in wheelchairs so I can't take pride in that; but many of the 'joggers' were running at half my pace. I couldn't believe it, I kept going and soon the runners were far more spread out. I still had no idea how many were ahead of me, but my competitive spirit kicked in and I mentally switched to full power. I turned onto a footpath that ran outside the park along the road and gasped when I saw it stretching ahead uphill for as far as my eyes could see. In the distance I spotted a huddle of runners, maybe 7-10 in the group. They were nearly at the top of this Mount Everest but being so inexperienced with any running technique or judgment of pace I decided I would chase them. After all, the 'running' bit of this event was becoming quite boring; chasing someone, that struck me as fun.

I do not know whether it was my daily experience of chasing my children up three flights of stairs in my house to get dressed and get teeth brushed; or perhaps my 20-30 something years spent climbing and running up fells and mountains in the Lake District that enabled my legs to take the burn of that hill, but take it they did. And before long I was metres behind the group of runners that I had spotted at the top of the hill. I assessed their attire and realised that I had probably reached the running group. But by this time my lack of experience was causing some problems and I was struggling.

I still had no sense of the end, but I was not prepared to give in. They stayed slightly ahead of me, I couldn't see past them so I had no sense of what was ahead of them – the sprinters group maybe? I just knew I had to save face and tail them. A few of them had glanced nervously behind as this gasping, almost vomiting woman who came out of nowhere with a t-shirt that was not a specialised running t-shirt soaked in sweat grunted hot on their behinds. No rotund bottoms in this group that was for sure, fit, athletic and serious were these women. I sensed their anxiety that I might overtake, I knew there was no chance of that, I'd die if I tried, but there was no way I was going to drop further back after my 'Chariots of Fire like' achievement on that wretched hill and give them any opportunity for smugness.

We rounded a corner and I could see the finish, but it was still far too far for my liking, the hill leading up to the finish almost made me howl out loud. But if these hardcore ladies, still a few metres ahead, showed no sign of fear or slowing pace then neither would I.

I couldn't catch them, not the core group. I had a moment of glory as I ran into the final stretch and the crowds were cheering on a straggler from the front group who had drifted back a little. I saw the group of six-seven women cross the line and this lone soul was running for her life before me. My ruthless single-minded nature pushed my pace harder, I felt the crowds distracting strength empower my aching legs; I sailed past the woman across the line seconds before her.

My time was around 24 minutes – I roughly looked at my watch as I crawled to a space on the grass nearby; it meant nothing to me really. I knew I wasn't far behind the core group and realised that they had actually been the front runners out of the hundreds who ran the race that day. They were huddled together sharing congratulatory hugs – I counted seven. So that made me number eight. I wondered how many of them actually had cancer themselves and less than a year ago had undergone chemotherapy and had a baby. Probably no one, I surmised. I felt very proud of myself if not somewhat astounded.

In the papers that day it was recorded that the winner ran it in 21 minutes ish. I felt quite pleased with myself particularly as she was part of a running club; which was news to me because I didn't realise such things existed. I looked at Mark and said, '21 minutes – that's only three minutes faster than me and I didn't train or run at all. I'm going to beat her next year.' Mark said, 'I don't think you understand how much faster that time is compared to yours – you'd have to train really hard.' I had no idea what training was but I was inspired. 'I'm going to do it,' I said. Mark laughed in a kind but rather cocksure of himself way and that only fuelled my determination to succeed at my goal.

After the success of this run I was hooked. I took to running like a duck to water; I began to run five times a week. Hannah would arrive and off I would go. At first I could only run the 5k that I had done in the Race for Life and sometimes I was slower than 24 minutes, which maddened me. As I began to enter this world of running I discovered the Park Run, a five kilometre running event that takes place every Saturday along the sea front in Whitley Bay. They are carried out across the whole country; in actual fact the whole world; you register yourself, receive a barcode, turn up at 9 am and run as fast as you can. The beauty of it is that as you cross the line you hand in your personal tab which has a bar code on it. It logs your time and later that day you receive notification of your time and even better your place in the whole race and even better than that your place alongside other females in your age category.

I loved it, but I hated it too. That's the problem with me: I am wired to rise to competition but the perfectionist in me doesn't cope too well with not being the best and the insecurity in me makes it hard for me to be happy with simply my best efforts. It's a conundrum and a torturous one at that. I became obsessed with reducing my time. My morning runs along the coast perusing the sea in all weathers; marvelling at God's creation; coming back refreshed and ready for the day with my children began to be overtaken. I morphed into a mental case who pondered continuously on how to improve my technique and pace.

I would google exercises and bought a Garmin watch, a sports watch that you can set to bleep when your pace drops. It will record exactly how many miles you cover at what pace for each mile and therefore enable you to begin to hone your run and achieve a better time. It was my new best friend and also a minion of Satan sat on my wrist accusing me with its beeps and buzzing whenever I dared to let my pace drop. I saw my timings improve and my body become lithe and leggy, toned and tapered. I approved of the way my body was changing, I felt in control and strong.

I discovered new friends who were equally wrapped up in running. They directed me to a local running club which I diligently attended twice a week and saw even more improvement and willingly allowed myself to be drawn into extra runs at other times of the week. It wasn't long before I worked out that the 21 minutes that the winner of the Race for Life had achieved was actually an extremely good time and that maybe Mark had been right.

My solution to this was to join the gym. I had tried the gym on short occasions in the past; doesn't everyone? I had never found it to be remotely enjoyable only lasting a few months at best, wasting lots of money on annual memberships. The gym was utterly boring; but I had real motivation now. I surmised that if I strengthened my muscles then I could endure a faster pace.

Of course I was correct but the cost was high. At my peak in 2012 I was training six days a week up to three hours a day. My personal 40-minute gym session which started at 8 am would be followed by a body pump class twice a week (an hour of weights). On other days I would follow it with a combat class; a high energy martial arts inspired workout. I began to include a twice a week a circuit class over a lunchtime. I would do the gym sessions followed by an hour's class, go home, rest, and then cycle to the circuit class at a gym about 10 miles from home. Running club was on twice a week in the evenings so even if I'd gone to the gym AND a class I would still go to the running club.

I grew and grew into an exercise beast and realised I could improve even further if I chose to incorporate running or cycling absolutely everywhere. This included running to every hospital appointment I had, which is about 8 miles, and back again. If I was short on time I would cycle it instead.

I entered local 5k and 10k runs, achieving fast times for my age and a lot of attention. The compliments and adoration would swamp me wherever I went. My story seemed to be worthy of note, particularly when I harnessed it to raise money for cancer charities. In total, through sponsorship, over roughly a year I raised around £6000 through my running alone. I was in the newspaper quite a few times handing over cheques. People were blasted away by this woman running and raising money for cancer when she'd only recently been diagnosed with the disease herself. Throw in the story of Archie and the age of my other three children and it was a tale that wrenched many heartstrings and purse strings.

I fell into running innocently and without expectation; I initially found in running a sense of control over my circumstances; I became addicted to running. All the additional exercise fed the monster within, fuelled my obsession with my running times, but gave me results. As my times continued to improve I would set a faster target and train even harder. I was having regular heart scans due to a hormone drug I was on which can cause heart failure. After one such scan my consultant was feeding back to me 'Rebekah, your recent scan result shows that you have the heart function of a professional athlete; I don't get to say that to many people in my line of work'. I punched the air in delight.

The increasing difficulty with this standard was not maintaining it but continuing to see progress. I badgered Mark continually for new tips; scouring google running sites with my torturous question 'how do you move from 22 mins 5k to under 21 mins?'. Mark frequently had to counsel my disappointment when I plateaued in the Park Run times.

I badgered him for a rowing machine in the house so that I could do random 10 minutes here and there. He didn't really know how much I was doing already; he was already concerned about my compulsion and passion for running, so he may have refused if I'd told him. The cancer card had to come out and be useful in getting around Mark, every cloud has a silver lining; I got my rowing machine. My research had thrown up that with each stroke you take pretty much everybody part is used – core strength is a big benefit, as it is in running too. Brucey Bonus, a piece of equipment in my house that could project me further towards my 21-minute target.

It wasn't long before my alarm was set for 'ridiculous o'clock'. I could row for 20-30 minutes on the highest level before the children were awake and Hannah arrived. Then I would do a timed 5k finishing up at the gym.

You might be asking the question 'what about spending time with the children?'. I didn't, not during the week when I had Hannah. Whatever it was that running had triggered inside me, escapism, denial, competition, control, obsession, fear, it had me in its strangling grip. Any holiday we went on I continued as closely as I could with my routine. Bank holidays, weekends, before any family time could commence, I had to have exercised or I was like a machine gun firing off bullets to anyone who crossed my path.

My success with running brought me so much attention too. People admired me, asking all the time how I managed to be so focused. I took this accolade, priding my discipline and determined personality; but it was really another strangulating twist in the rope that was slowly to hang me.

Having gone through the painful year of pregnancy, chemo and separating from Evie, you'd think my obsession would be to make up for lost time with her, not morph into an extreme endorphin addict. Unfortunately, between 2010 and 2012 that's what happened. Running took priority over my husband, my children, my friends, my God; it had become my idol.

I knew deep down that every day I got to choose whether I spent my time with Hannah and the children or whether I ran away, literally. I'd describe it rather like this: I had a certain number of coins hidden within myself, and each day I would be issued with a new coin. I knew that it could be the last coin I would get. I took each precious coin and decided how to exchange it: exercise or family. Once I'd chosen and spent it I could never get the coins back to spend differently. I found this choice tormenting; the lines between good and bad had definitely become blurred.

I wanted to put my family first, but they were used to Hannah and when I was there it caused tension, so it was easy to persuade myself that I shouldn't even try. Especially as I'd found something else to replace them with that was making me feel so good and so in control and successful; sort of. Spending time with the family caused me a lot of distress; navigating Hannah, all three children's needs and my tiredness. It was so much simpler to just take off and flee; the more I fled, the easier it became. Before long I'd shut down to the little voice inside and the decision to escape became easier and easier.

I got caught up in this new routine and became used to life without stinking nappies, crying, squalling, squealing demands, binding routines, grasping grabbing sweaty dirty hands. In my heart I felt the distant cries of Mark and my children to come back to them, but I was running too fast with the wind whistling for my ears to hear them. I blocked out my thoughts and conscience and began living for my own agenda. Running was never going to deliver the satisfaction that spending time with my children was going to bring me, but I'd drifted too far towards putting my own needs first and I couldn't return to the family that easily, I needed help.

You may think this is appalling and it is; but don't we all have idols? What obsessions do you feed that threaten the balance of your life? Thoughts, images or impulses that maybe started off small but now happen over and over again and now they're controlling you. Maybe you don't want to have them and find them disturbing and unwanted, they bring fear, disgust, doubt. They take up time and get in the way of things that you know are more important. All obsessions are rooted in some type of fear, own up to yours and then dig for what scares you. Are you a shopaholic, workaholic, chocoholic, alcoholic, diet obsessed, money obsessed, body obsessed, cleaning obsessed, acrophobic, mysophobic, agoraphobic or claustrophobic? Google obsessions, there's hundreds. I found a list called The Ultimate list of Phobias and Fears. Makes it sound like fun.

The first step towards dealing with obsessions and the fear that drives them is to accept it's a problem and confront it head on. There are medicines, counselling, hypnotherapy, psychotherapy, cognitive behaviour therapies, and many self-help suggestions. Funnily enough when I was researching fears and obsessions for this section I came across a number of non-religious sites who say you should read religious books whether you're a believer or a non-believer. They are allegedly proven to relieve anxiety and fears. They actually advise reading the Bible. Explaining that fear has been in existence since the start of time and fear of what might happen is part and parcel of life. They say the Bible is a helpful tool in understanding fear and accepting its concept.

Alternatively, life might wham you from the side lines with a whopping Godzilla-like slap in the face, kicking the ass off your piddling fears and sending them into the stratosphere; replacing them with something to really make your knees knock. Full on 'Scooby Doo shaking in Shaggy's arms' type fear with spooky music thrown in. I said I needed help to break this habit and I did; eventually it came but not in a format I would have chosen.

Scaffolding will not be necessary

After a mastectomy some women choose to have cosmetic surgery to remake their breast. I had seen amazing results in The Ladies in Pink Scarves drop-in group run by Karen. Once a month, ladies who had already had reconstruction would proudly lift their tops and gloriously reveal their fabulous fake bosoms. We'd all clap and 'oooooooo and aaaaaaaaah' and then discuss which type of reconstruction was best for us.

There are many different reconstruction techniques available. There are two main techniques for reconstructing your breast: Implant reconstruction which is inserting an implant that's filled with salt water (saline), silicone gel, or a combination of the two. Then there is "flap" reconstruction: using tissue transplanted from another part of your body (such as your belly, thigh, or back). Flap reconstruction also may include an implant.

Both approaches have advantages and disadvantages. Implant reconstruction is an easier surgery, easier to recover from, easier to understand. Flaps are more difficult to perform, more time-consuming, a longer recovery in hospital and then at home. It's all a matter of what's right for the woman and her individual situation. The advantage of breast reconstruction with natural tissue is that the remade breast is softer and more natural than breast implants. The size, fullness, and shape of the new breast can be closely matched to your other breast.

If you're sensible you will not only talk to your healthcare team about the options that may be right for you, but you really need to do your own research, too. Like my friend Claire did; Claire was sensible and thorough, and attended sessions at the hospital on breast reconstruction. Claire investigated the procedure she was interested in by discussing closely with women who already had new boobs. She asked what they felt about the final outcome; and she viewed many ladies' boobies and even felt a few before she made her decision and booked her operation. She decided after her research to stick with the simple option; breast reconstruction with an implant was good enough for her.

I chose flap reconstruction, the more complicated process; it promised a much more natural end result and I ALWAYS like to pursue the BEST. Due to the lack of fat anywhere on my buttocks and stomach, my only option was the Latissimus Dorsi muscle flap reconstruction. Latissimus Dorsi muscle, skin, blood vessels and fat from just below your shoulder and behind your armpit are used to reconstruct a breast. They move them under your skin and around to your chest to rebuild a boob. The blood vessels are left attached to the original blood supply in the back. I had also decided to have a risk reducing mastectomy on the other side, so I would have a double Latissimus Dorsi reconstruction in order to keep both breasts looking the same.

Unlike Claire I did no research whatsoever, if Latissimus flap reconstruction promised me fabulous natural breasts then I was not going to settle for anything less. In my defence there were a lack of ladies of which I could examine who had chosen to have latissimus flap reconstruction because most were able to choose the more straightforward flap reconstructions using ample loose skin and fat on their buttocks and stomachs. So I couldn't do the same research as Claire; however, I have to own up that if I had gone with Claire to look at the ladies who had simply had an implant I may have been surprised and chosen the simpler outcome.

The problem was that I always want the best I can have. This is not necessarily manifested in being extremely materialistic; it's more demonstrated in wider choices. If I set out to do something, be it a children's homework or baking a cake I have to make it the best I can. If I am not satisfied with the outcome I will do it again, and again, and again. I once made six batches of 24 meringues over two days until I perfected the art of getting the chewy bit in the middle.

I knew I had one shot at getting the best boob outcome I could. This was my chance to get rid of the drooping flaps of skin left over from breastfeeding and have the best boobs ever. I'd never liked my breasts;

since being a teenager I'd envied women with perky little bosoms who could wear triangular skimpy bikinis. In lingerie departments I had to wander longingly past all the teeny weeny feminine lacy scraps of fabric boasting the total absence of underwire support until I reached the over shoulder boulder holder section. It wasn't that I had massive breasticles – they were a good size so long as they were well supported – but the minute those babies were released they'd drop to my feet bungee style. I had always had droopy boob issues. I can remember lying about the pencil test when I was a teenager. For those of you who are unaware of this extremely scientific test for ascertaining who has firm 'stand up to attention' breasts, I will explain. Your remove your bra and stick a pencil underneath, the number of pencils you can hold underneath your boob is the measure of how saggy your chest is. As I remember, the range amongst my friends was zero to two, maybe three. I'm pretty sure I could hold an entire set of 12 and the pencil case they came in.

I hated them; cancer had inadvertently offered me the opportunity to have fake breasts. Firm, unmoveable made to order boobies. I was excited. I had already warned Mark that my 50th birthday present was going to be a boob job; his opinion on this does not matter because the matter got taken out of my hands. I can remember around this time the excitement I felt at almost having a chance to achieve my perfect concept of a breast. On one occasion I was having lunch with an ex teaching colleague, and she was asking me about my upcoming reconstruction. I told her with enormous glee that I'd give her a before and after show. We went into the pub toilet and I revealed my one leftover sack of floppy skin and weak tissue, then I sort of pulled up the skin from near my shoulder, lifted the saggy mess with one hand, blew on the flat nipple to make it stand out, and somehow showed her what a beautiful breast I would have! Just in case she hadn't managed to get the complete illustration, I ran back to our table and drew it on a napkin. I wonder now as I envisaged my Pamela Anderson perfection if I'd actually got *plastic* surgery totally confused with *cosmetic* surgery. Do you know what? I think I did. And this confusion between cosmetic and plastic surgery – the first being that you have a large degree of control over your aesthetic outcomes, the second, well, it's make do and mend patchwork quilt effect with whatever you have left after the mastectomy takes every last bit of anything natural away. How could I have made such an error in my understanding? My friend never got her 'after' viewing; indeed it was a very long time before I could even look at them, never mind flash them off in some pub toilet.

January 2012, armed with my lack of research but a focused and clear mind of what I wanted, I met with the plastic surgeon who would provide me with my perfect jugs of joy. It was to be done in two stages, or surgeries. In the first stage I would be given the right breast risk reducing mastectomy, and pouches would be made in the skin underneath the breasts. A small tissue expander is placed in the pouch. The expander is balloon-like and made of silicone. A valve is placed below the skin of the breast. The valve is connected by a tube to the expander. (The tube would stay below my skin in my breast area.) My chest still looked flat right after this surgery.

Around two to three weeks after surgery, I would see my surgeon every one or two weeks. During these visits, he injected a small amount of saline (salt water) through the valve into the expander. Over time, the expander slowly enlarged the pouch in my chest to the right size to take an implant. In my case they had to stretch the skin a lot further than the size I actually wanted to be, due to the fact that he expected there to be a lot of scarring from the radiotherapy and this would need to be cut away.

I looked ridiculous. At their full size they were like two footballs; perfectly round and enormous. Imagine Betty Boop the cartoon character, with her baby face, big eyes and a very small body of which the leading characteristic is the most self-confident bust imaginable. You'll be on the right lines. Although they were very exaggerated, and I had to dress carefully so as not draw too much attention, I loved how solid and forward projecting they were. I had high hopes of the next stage.

I had to wait a month before the permanent breast implant could be placed, during the second stage. In this stage the tissue expanders would be removed from my chest and replaced with permanent breast implants. Then the breast would be made soft and formed to be more natural using tissue from my back. The size, fullness, and shape of the new breasts would be more natural with reconstruction that used my own tissue. I was prepared to endure eight hours of complicated surgery and three-four days in hospital to achieve the breasts I'd longed for. Claire was simply going to have the implants and wasn't concerned about them looking soft and natural; after all, no one really sees them – very sensible, Claire.

How I wish I could turn back the clock and be more thorough in my research. My vanity clouded my judgement and I paid a painful price. Perhaps people tried to direct me into the simpler operation, but I was overtaken by my desire to rectify a lifetime of body dissatisfaction and in doing so I made matters 100 times worse. The results of my reconstruction and this whole section of my journey unravelled to be almost more devastating than the cancer itself.

Hours after the arduous surgery had finished, tender and dosed up on morphine I took a tentative look down my gown to see what they looked like. The alarm bells began to ring and my spirit plummeted as I viewed the bandage wrapped around my entire chest area. I could see no definition whatsoever. I was the proud owner of a mono boob. I could not make out two perky perfectly sized breasts at all, just a continuation of dressing, not a cleavage in sight. Mark was sitting in the room and was so relieved to see me awake – I beckoned him nearer so he could hear my drugged mumblings and he was alarmed to see the horror on my face.

The surgeon came in to see how I was doing. I managed to control the rising hysteria and ask him why I couldn't see two nice mound shapes beneath the dressing. He was calmly reassuring and said there would be no definition for a few weeks due to swelling that is inevitable after surgery such as mine. Not to worry, he was pleased with the results and was confident that in time I would be too. I felt calm and content and flopped back into the warm embrace of morphine.

The days that followed were long as I waited for my new body parts to fulfil my expectations. I had six drains, three each side; they fed into the wounds and body tissues that are cut during surgery and take away fluid to prevent infection. As is my usual style I was up and about immediately, lifting my six drains with me like the lame arms of an octopus. Much to the nurses' surprise I manged to successfully shower on my own. I went straight to the top of the ward as perfect patient.

I was still concerned about the mono boob issue, but I refused to allow it to disturb me too much. I came up with a plan to occupy myself. The nurses had told me I could put my drains in two carrier bags and wander down to the hospital shop or Costa coffee bar; change of scene and all that. I plopped my strange shopping into two Sainsbury's bags and took off for the lift.

It was pure freedom. I did what any proud owner of two new boobs would do. I glanced briefly in the direction of the hospital shop in the foyer and then continued walking past reception and into the open air. I felt like a fugitive; I'm fairly certain if I had asked the nurse if I could walk into Newcastle it would have been a resounding no. I like being a bit mischievous; it's such a thrilling feeling knowing that you probably shouldn't be doing whatever you're doing but doing it anyway. I'm not talking about breaking the law, not at this stage of my life anyway. I do confess to a little shoplifting phase I went through as a teenager; thankfully I was not very good at it. As already explained, my mother had a perverse streak of not wanting us to have any item of clothing that was currently fashionable, so I took matters into my own hands to avoid peer group humiliation.

Moccasins were in fashion, a type of slip on shoe made of soft leather. I really wanted a pair; one Saturday whilst wandering around Carlisle with this longing mulling round in my head I passed a shoe shop with baskets of Moccasins sat outside on the street conveniently grouped according to their size. A swift look into the shop and around me on the street reassured me that nobody was paying me the slightest bit of notice and I'd bagged a pair of size fours and walked swiftly away before you could say 'shoplifter'. I must confess it was quite exhilarating; I ran home with my contraband straight up to my bedroom to unload my spoils. On went the right foot, perfect, on went the left foot. Something felt wrong, no matter how I wiggled my foot just didn't feel right. When I stood up and looked down I discovered what the issue was.

I had picked up two right feet. I spent the next half hour wandering around my room feet splayed in opposite directions determined to make them work. Surely I could break it in and force it to fit my left foot. It dawned on me that people who were experienced shoplifters probably knew that shops left baskets of all one footed shoes on the street in the secure knowledge that they were useless to a thieving rogue. So what did I do now? I did what any sensible shoplifter would do: I took them back to the shop and dumped them back in the basket.

There ended my career as a small-time crook; I wasn't very good at it. But so long as you don't break the law or cause harm to self or others, a bit of cheeky non-conforming and pushing boundaries is healthy I think. I escaped the oppression of the hospital and rebelliously walked a mile to Marks and Spencer's. My goal: to buy a range of pretty bikinis and bras that had absolutely no underwire and skinny little straps over my shoulders. I hoisted up the two carrier bags containing three drains in each, half full of my blood and excess fluids, and off I went like an excited schoolgirl on her first lingerie trip.

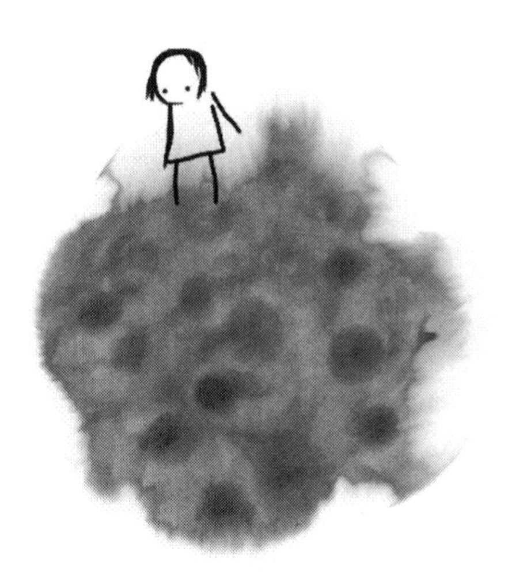

Full Frontal

I should not have been so hasty. Every single one of the items I purchased had to be returned a week later. Very soon after this jaunt the Surgeon came and took off the bandages to reveal my majestic breasts. I looked down at my chest and instead of seeing two perfectly formed and sized pert rounded bosoms I looked with horror at my mono boob. There was no cleavage or space or definition between the two breasts at all. Just a long low hillock of flesh with two sizeable scars running across the top.

He was making admiring sounds at his barbaric creations; I didn't want to burst his bubble – after all, it had taken him seven hours to create this work of art. I managed to squeak out 'why is there no separation?'. He glanced up from his proud examining of my scars and drain entrances and said, 'Oh don't worry, that's just swelling, you will have more definition in time.'

I had anticipated this moment for six months. I can't explain what depths my heart sank to when I saw my chest for the first time. The plastic surgeon left and I sat in silence on the bed trying to come to terms with the result that faced me. The nurse came in to see if I needed anything. 'Are you ok?' I burst into gut wrenching sobs, unable to explain the disappointment I felt with my body. I had built this event up into such an exciting moment I had not considered on any level that I would hate them. I had even promised people private viewings.

She, of course, encouraged me to listen to what he said about the swelling going down. However, I couldn't shake off a feeling of dread that had shattered the boobylicious fantasy that I had created. To this day the experience of reconstruction has remained my most torturous chapter. It is rooted so deeply in many personal misconceptions; my inherent lack of confidence in my body and appearance had pinned so much hope on this operation transforming a despised part of my body into majestic perfection.

As the weeks went on the swelling did go down, definition did indeed improve, but simply revealed a pair of lumps that in my mind were grotesque. Different sizes, different shapes, different heights and rock solid like two small pudding basins. They were the most unnatural, unattractive, unusual looking protrusions I had ever seen. I hated them. Dimpled flesh and odd folds of skin gave each angle a deformed appearance. I was devastated. And small, so very small; I would have given my right leg, left leg and both arms to have my old slightly droopy chest back. I was about to go on a big trip into the dark dangers of my vanity.

You see, unlike Claire, I had wanted the best. She settled for the straightforward skin stretching and implants. That was not good enough for me. My dislike of my body had driven me to take this opportunity to grab the illusion of perfection and forge ahead with no attention or consideration of failure.

Claire had been to a number of groups and viewed the results of different reconstructions. I on the other hand had heard someone banter around that you got a lot better result from having skin transplanted onto the implants and I wanted the 'better' outcome. The gut wrenching reveal of Claire's boobs showed me that her two-three hour operation looked just as effective as my seven-eight hour operation and her recovery much more straightforward.

The nasty sting in this tale is what happened to my back; which of course was the real reason Claire did not want to have the process I had chosen. She didn't want to put herself through any unnecessary procedures when for the most part her boobs were out of sight. So long as they looked ok in clothes then it mattered not how real they looked when covered up. But muggins here was too caught up in some other world and dream of being a lingerie model to think very carefully about such practicalities.

My back was totally trashed; two massive scars running six-seven inches long broke up the smooth expanse of skin that I once owned. It's true, they were neat scars, he was a top plastic surgeon; but in my quest for body perfection I had somehow overlooked that this operation was going to cause the appearance of my back to be far from perfect. As the next few months passed I became more distressed about my back than my boobs. The horror that my perfect breasts had cost me a perfect back and that the perfect breasts were worthy of nothing better than a Victorian freak show sickened me to the core.

Not only did all the lovely lingerie have to be returned but I faced the growing truth that these two deformities were never ever going to be able to fit properly into standard underwear. They were just too odd in shape and too irregular in size and position. Not only that but I could not envisage the elastic of a bra tightened around my damaged back to ever be tolerable.

Worse was yet to come; I will take partial blame for this part of the story, but not total blame. When I met the consultant plastic surgeon I definitely enquired about whether this operation would affect my sporting ability. Namely at that moment 'rowing'; it was my simplest option for exercise at that time. It was in our house which meant minimum time; it is overall the most effective all over body workout you can do which means maximum results. A decent rowing session is hard, very hard in fact, but worth it when demands on your time are high. I relied on it, for body toning and honing and for stress relief.

I absolutely checked out with a number of clinical specialists whether I would be able to row again. It was a unanimous yes. At this point I am going to make all the politically left wing supporters incredibly happy because I am going to criticise private medical care traditionally associated with people who are likely to be hated Conservative party supporters. I am not revealing which way I lean! Mark had private medical care as a perk of his job and until this point it had served us very well. Mainly for speed and the ability to be more involved with working treatment around your convenience. You don't get better treatment, just slightly faster; but let me reassure all the lefties before they go off on one. If YOU needed speedy emergency medical attention you wouldn't be waiting at the back of the line of wealthy private medical people before you got it. You'd jump the queue, that's if a selfish Conservative private medical patient didn't trample on you before you got there.

Compared to the level of attention Claire got under the NHS, under private medicine I was sorely neglected. That'll have all the moralising socialists clapping their hands in glee. Before Claire was able to have her reconstruction, she had to jump through so many hoops. She had pre-operation counselling, she had to attend a certain number of NHS reconstruction groups to make sure she had thoroughly investigated all the options. In these groups there was a clinical nurse specialist and women who'd had many types of reconstruction who all shared experiences, and professionals who listened to what you wanted and then advised the best course of action. She had post-operative physio and advice and had to attend follow up groups for a number of weeks to ensure she was carrying out the exercises conducive to the best healing process.

Maybe this is because the NHS fear being sued if anything goes wrong; I really don't know. But it was worlds away from the service I was offered. Ironically the more blasé I was treated the more I felt superior to Claire. It felt like she was an untrustworthy child in need of constant direction whilst I was a respected adult who called the shots and was in control of my situation. How wrong I was. This lack of thorough guidance overall led to a very tragic outcome and caused a very unfortunate red herring.

My consultation with the consultant plastic surgeon went something like this: 'I have come for risk reducing mastectomy and bilateral latissimus dorsi flap reconstruction; when can you do it?' Bit of ruffling in the diary from consultant; iPhone diary ready to go from me: 'May 15th.' 'Superb, see you in theatre.' And then I flounced out to have my nails done.

No psychological babble, no personality analysis, no checking if I actually understood what I was talking about. For all he knew I could have googled breast reconstruction that very morning and picked out bilateral, bi annual whatever it was 'bilingual-platypusses-doors and eyes flapping-reconstruction' and just thought 'Oooooo I'll have that, thank you very much; my insurance is paying'. And no particular conversation about risk; I will say this again, because the one question I did ask, because it really mattered to me was 'Will I be able to return to sport again; namely rowing?' – 'YES'.

If only. What a sad, lamenting, losers', lost preceding statement that is: 'If only'. Put your hands up how many of you have at least once in your lifetime declared those regretful words over a decision that you alone made. The painful regret of facing that there were other options available, other advice on tap, other choices that you could have made 'if only' you hadn't been too hasty, too stubborn, too selfish. The decision I made in the pursuit of perfect gazongas created the biggest bazooking 'if only' in my entire life.

How many of your 'If onlys' have resulted in the needless conceited irreversible butchery of your own body? I bet the numbers are swiftly reducing. And out of those who are as fluffy headed as me, I wonder how many chose to simply ignore the availability of very clear and informative facts stating the risks involved with carving up your body for the sake of your image? Even fewer of you left I'm guessing. And finally, what if the part of your body that you're unnecessarily agreeing to be chopped up, played an essential part in your ability to successfully perform a task that meant everything to you? I bet I'm standing alone now. I agreed to an operation purely to satiate my desire for perfection. If only I hadn't been such a beeeeeeeeeeeeeeeeeeeeeeeeeeeeeeeeeeeeeeeeeeeeeeeeeeeee eeeeeeeeeep. All I had to do was google a reputable site like the Breast. cancer.org and read the following, and maybe I would have asked more detailed questions.

The brackets are mine:

'While the latissimus dorsi flap may offer good results with few complications, it can have some drawbacks:

You may have partial loss of strength or function that makes it hard to lift things and twist. This can affect your ability to perform certain sports (*alarm bells*), swimming, golf, tennis strokes, **or rowing** (*!!!!!!!!!!!!!!!!!!*). So it's generally not a good choice for bilateral (*both sides*) reconstruction, because you could then have muscle issues (*which will affect these activities*) on both sides.

Most women need an implant along with a latissimus dorsi flap, and some women say the implant feels **firmer** (*not very natural*) than the tissue in front of it.

The fat around the latissimus muscle is stiffer than fat that comes from the belly area, so some women say that their latissimus dorsi reconstructed breast feels **"tighter"** (*think about this one, Rebekah*) than their other breast.

Armed with my two freak shows and a whole lack of 'private medicine' knowledge on recovery time and acceptable sports after a major operation, I tried to accept the disappointing outcome of my own foolishness and resume normal life. I didn't feel ready to go out on a run but around the three-four month mark I felt up for a bit of gentle rowing.

A few weeks on I was suffering from alarmingly excruciating back pain. Being the stalwart salubrious sage I am I battled through the pain in a true 'Mells' fashion. Mummy would have been very proud of me. The fact that this attitude was probably the cause of her 'too late for treatment' diagnosis of Ovarian cancer that killed her was of no matter to me. Fundamentally we 'Mells' pride ourselves on soldiering on no matter what pain we have to endure. 'Pain is for pussies' we would loudly and proudly have stitched on the Mells Coat of Arms should we have one. I doubt we'll have it on our gravestones when we all meet premature death from ignoring nature's alarm bells.

I ignored this alarm bell for long enough to concur irreversible damage from overly exerting my recently operated back. In simple terms I had returned to serious physical exercise before my operation had healed, to a sport that depended on my Lattissimus Dorsi muscle; which effectively no longer existed because it was currently stretched under my armpits and across my two gross dimpled deformities in some failed attempt to give the appearance of natural looking breasts. 'Latissimus Dorsi muscle, you flamboyantly failed; bottom of the class'.

One day I could bear the burning sensation no longer; I hauled myself off the rowing machine and that night I told Mark that I was in terrible pain. He lifted my t-shirt and let out a gasp of horror. He led me to the mirror and showed me the damage I had done. To be honest, I can't really remember looking too closely at my back before this moment. I was too obsessed with the mutations on my front. My back looked like the Himalayan Mountain range. In fact, climbers would have needed ropes and Sherpas on donkeys to help them up the heights of the undulations, peaks and valleys that had volcanically erupted under my skin.

I didn't need a doctor to tell me that the rowing had clearly torn the tissue under my skin from the stretching and pulling action. The lumps were huge and squishy; with a gentle press you could feel the fluid relocating to another area. Like multiple semi-inflated arm bands. Once the Sherpas gave up trying to reach the summits I could hire myself out as a lido and allow small children to jump on my water-filled sacks. My back looked horrendous.

You might be asking yourself why, Rebekah? Why did you do it? Surely it must have been obvious that such an operation would clearly weaken your back and make rowing a very difficult activity to resume. Even if it were to become something you could return to one day; you'd need a lot longer than three months for your back to heal. I know all that now! But I was driven at that time by a lot of fear and it caused me to make some very silly choices.

I had lost control of so much of my life. An alien had invaded my body and eroded parts of it so that they were unrecognisable to me. It had trampled and stamped all over my present life circumstances; made them into a muddy quagmire and taken away any dreams or schemes I may have had for my future. I'd been thrust into a world that I didn't want to be in and forced to inhabit it and learn its language and customs. Heck you have to remember that my children were so young I hadn't even really adapted to the experience of motherhood, let alone accommodate cancer into that world.

I'd gone from being a newish mum, used to be art teacher, probably would return to my artistic roots when the children were all at school sort of person. To a newish mum, used to be art teacher, couldn't make any predictions about what was going to happen to me next week sort of person. One day I'd woken up to find I was having an unexpected child and then one day a few weeks later I'd woken up and been told I had cancer. It was all a rather strange few years so making un-thought through decisions suddenly becomes more understandable.

And there was also the major problem of having nothing to do. I had a superb nanny who had the children totally covered and whenever I attempted to co-parent with her it disintegrated into a mangled battlefield of 'who's in charge'; for the kids, not me and Hannah, which caused me to retreat and search out what to do with myself.

I've already explained the crutch that running and training had become to my damaged psychological state. They had become the drug that numbed the racing thoughts that I couldn't face. They offered me the solution to feeling out of control and gave me a physical outlet and goal that covered up the deeper longings. I hadn't abandoned God and my faith was still deep down in the same position it had always been; but I had silently, slowly and stealthily taken back the driving seat of my life and put God in the passenger seat. Let me show him how it's done for a while. He might need a few lessons on how I needed to resume life post-cancer diagnosis. It was only right and proper that I show him the ropes; prove I can go it alone now. He was welcome to join me, of course, but 'Rocking Racing Rebekah 'was rising up from the grave and radicalising her lost life with her own replacement therapies, again.

How I wish I'd stayed wired into God and prayed through some of the decisions I made around that time. How sad it makes me when I look back and see how much God had held me through the shock and horror of the first 18 months. But how quickly I took back the reigns of my life and resumed my position on the throne. Once I'd had Archie, and had support in place to navigate life's practicalities, I could slowly begin to resume my favourite way of living. 'It's all about me, I know best, I am a rock, I am a strong woman, I've conquered breast cancer, I have raised money, I am respected, I am the centre of attention' yippee. I got bigger, God got smaller.

I return constantly in my walk with God and my wrestle with 'does he heal, or does he not heal, that is my question?'. I frequently remember the testimony of the apostle Paul who asked for the thorn in his flesh to be taken away and God said no. Sadly it was to take me another huge chapter before I fully faced the concept that the thorns in my life are sometimes left there because the pain of them keeps me constantly focused on the power of God. It is this power that I truly need in order to stop me from being a dumb sheep who wanders into all sorts of bother when I stray from the good shepherd. When I start to feel stronger again it's often not long before I spread our wings and want to fly solo. It is flying solo when I have no idea what direction to fly in that eventually leads me to splatting into brick walls and falling to the ground in a heap of bruised flesh and shredded feathers.

The challenge of living a real relationship with God is being able to live it out when you feel like you don't need him anymore. The beauty of trauma and terrible tests is that they hone your spiritual senses, and for me turned my attention to God and what he had to say about things. The tragedy of it was that I didn't continue in that vein when things became easier. I do believe that had I been able to transfer the intimacy and the deep dependence I had on God into my life when it felt that the pressure had somewhat retreated, I don't think I would have made the choice to have all that surgery. I don't think I would have been so driven to achieve bodily perfection. I think I may have been able to not return to rowing so quickly. I would have been more in tune with God's guidance and more led by the spirit to make the wiser choice.

The body issues, the running and training obsessions were all part of the deep pain and insecurity that I had carried all my life. Low self-esteem, inherent lack of confidence and the difficulty to love myself, let alone embrace anyone else's love for me had haunted me for decades. In younger years I had tried various analgesics from drugs to dangerous liaisons; now it was running and the pursuit of two racy rounders. The only person who can free you from the past and any damage you carry is God. Without God I had no chance of healing in those areas, I would simply repeat thought patterns and drive forward my own destructive failed solutions time and time again.

Once my life was out of the danger zone of 'death threats and mass destruction mode' I popped God back in his little corner and I remained the dictator in mine. The issue this ultimately gave me was the irreversible damage I did to my back. It was so bad that it has never really healed. It is so deformed that it has restricted certain items of clothing I can wear. The bulges can be seen underneath anything too close fitting. If I had issues pre reconstruction surgery, then I had out of this world ones post-surgery and post rowing fiasco.

The psychological damage put me in hours of clinical counselling. Specific counselling offered to those who have had surgery that has turned out to be not what you expected. I was so angry with myself. I even pursued the first stages of suing the consultant, but it didn't really go anywhere. There was never a case because as much as he could have given me more direction, I equally could have asked more questions, and overall the time and stress it would cause just wasn't worth it. I needed someone else to share the blame other than just myself. Whichever alley I walked down my honest heart simply found myself standing at the bottom shaking her head in disappointment.

It was not just the look of my boobs and the deformity of my back that was the issue. It was the daily 24/7 pain. Or at least 'pain' is the word generically used to describe any distressing feeling caused by intense or damaging stimuli. It's actually quite a complex subject and defining pain, as I discovered when I was referred to a pain 'clinic', is a challenge. 'Pain is an unpleasant sensory AND emotional experience associated with potential tissue damage.' My pain wasn't so much pain like when you burn your finger and accidently cut yourself with a knife. Mine was more of an itch.

A deep internal itch right into the very heart of the sites where the muscle had been taken away and I had damaged the surrounding tissue from rowing. Worse than that, nerve damage had been caused on the skin and top lying tissue which effectively meant that from the top of my buttocks to underneath my shoulder blades was totally numb. When the consultant in the pain clinic stuck a pin in multiple areas of my back I felt nothing.

A combination of the operation and the post-operative damage left me with a sensation that I was wearing an iron corset which surrounded my entire upper body from front to back. I still have that to this day. I had weeks of physio to try and loosen and soften the muscle which I had torn and ripped apart. The operation had involved pulling back muscle around to my chest; it had to remain attached to its original position so that it had a blood supply and could survive. But of course this had all been damaged too and as it healed it tightened into a vice like grip. I couldn't breathe properly because my lungs were unable to get to their full capacity, because my ribs were unable to expand due to the muscle band that was encircling my chest area. It was horrific.

The difficulty breathing would at times cause me to panic; if I got remotely out of breath I would experience a sensation of suffocating. And then there was the itching. When a wound begins to heal it itches – I guess in simple terms that was what was happening to my internal wounds. They were healing. The difficulty was the numbness on the top layers of tissue. I could feel the mind boggling intensely irritating itch, but I couldn't satisfy it because the area above it was numb.

I would scratch myself with forks, knitting needles, the ends of pens, anything that might have the potential to satisfy this deep itching. It was unbearable. It sent me a bit potty. Mark was given full on scratch duty every night. I discovered if he used his entire body strength to put pressure on the damaged sites then I could feel that inside my back and gave me 'some' reprieve. Eventually I persuaded him to use his feet and to stand on me; one foot on each side of back. I don't know why pressure helped but it did; I couldn't actually breathe during this process but it was SO good on the itch. The average person in good health can hold their breath for around two minutes. I learnt to hold mine for just over four. The world record underwater is a whopping 20:21 mins so it wasn't all that impressive really, but it was worth it to escape from my self-inflicted torture.

What had I done? I berated myself day and night; I cried nightly in Mark's arms. Deep sorrow filled my mind as I considered the results of my own vanity. None of this had been necessary; it was all a choice, my choice. I found it sickeningly ironic that I had had cancer, which in actual fact had caused me no discomfort at all; but the plastic surgery and dependency on exercise, both rooted in fear of being fat and imperfect, had led to a lifetime of discomfort and nagging regret.

Psalm 38 v 17: 'I'm slipping away and on the verge of a breakdown, with nothing but sorrow and sighing. I confess my mistakes to you, my agonising thoughts punish me for my wrongdoing; I feel condemned as I consider what I've done.' It was small comfort to know that I was not the first person who'd made a set of decisions and mistakes that led them to the verge of a breakdown; King David had too. If I had been seeking God's Kingdom first I would not have found myself in a small dark corner. I didn't want to be in my corner running my life, I wanted to be in God's corner fighting the fight.

If we seek anything before God we will find ourselves in dead end alley. Seek first the kingdom of wealth and you'll worry over every penny. Seek first the Kingdom of popularity and you'll relive every unfriendly glance. Seek first the Kingdom of security and you'll be constantly on edge. Seek first the Kingdom of health and you'll be fearful of every sneeze. Or like me seek first the Kingdom of perfection and you'll be constantly disappointed. But seek first God and his Kingdom, and you will find him and in him we can always depend on the best outcome.

I had been feeding my fears and my faith had starved. I felt angry at God; I blamed him for not doing more to stop me – he knew I had cancer; couldn't he just have cut me a bit of slack over the whole reconstruction thing and make it all work out perfectly even though I was ignoring him? The Bible is an amazing self-help book. There are so many characters in there that have 'ballsed' up, or have wrestled on for years experiencing one personal disaster after another.

Jeremiah was the son of a Jewish priest. 'I am the man who has seen affliction under the hand of God; he has driven and brought me into darkness without any light; surely against me he turns his hand again and again the whole day long.' The difficulties he encountered have given him the name the 'weeping prophet'. At the point of writing those verses he was depressed and gloomy. He'd been fighting a good cause for many years, but it was not going well. His world had collapsed like a sandcastle in a typhoon and he eventually blamed God for his terrible distress and physical ailments.

I felt his pain; like Jeremiah my body ached, my heart was sick as a flogged dog's and my faith was puny. I felt enveloped with bitterness and tribulation, trapped in dead end alley. Lamentations 3 v 5: 'God has walled me in so that I cannot escape; he has put heavy chains on me; he has blocked my ways with hewn stones, he has made my paths crooked'. I'm with you, Jeremiah, I feel like he's doing that to me too. I felt as mad as Scrappy Doo when he says 'let me at him, let me at him. I'll splat him! I'll rock him and sock him'. This highly energetic cartoon character is the exact opposite of his Uncle Scooby, who's scared of everything. He is strong, capable of smashing down brick walls; and despite his size can even carry Scooby and Shaggy above his head.

'Ta dadada ta daaaa! Puppy power!!!!!!!' He doesn't let the bad guy get away with anything, he faces the baddies who stand in his way. I wanted to do that to God: 'Ta dadada ta daaaa! Raging Rebekah! Let me at him, let me at him. I'll splat him! I'll rock him and sock him'. Rebekah the raging radgy that was the person I had become; despite it not really being God's fault, the blame had to go somewhere so it might as well be there.

Yann Martel talks about fear in his novel *Life of Pi*. The main character, Pi, finds himself adrift at sea on a twenty-six-foot lifeboat with a 450-pound Bengal tiger as a companion. Pi ended up in this plight when his father, a zookeeper, went broke and loaded the family on a Japanese ship headed to Canada. The ship sank, leaving Pi and the tiger (named Richard Parker) alone on the ocean. While on the lifeboat, Pi begins to analyse his fears, both of the tiger and the sea.

He reaches the conclusion that 'only fear can defeat life'. He describes it almost like a snake, one minute you're perfectly happy and fine, and then something just sneaks into your mind and your happiness just ebbs away, and is replaced with an opposing sensation – anxiety. You begin to tense, breathe faster, fidget, obsess. Your peace has vanished and fear has rested on you.

Pi realizes that fear cannot be reasoned with. Logic can't talk fear away. You have to express fears. You have to understand what's driving you into the same swirling, twirling, twisting tunnels over and over again and fight hard to shine the light of words upon it. Because if you don't, if your fear becomes a wordless darkness that you avoid, perhaps even manage to forget or pretend isn't there, you open yourself up to further decisions motivated out of fear because you never truly fought your opponent in the first place.

We have to pull back the curtains and expose our fears. Like vampires they can't stand the sunlight. Take them out, drag them out if you need to and make them be exposed to cross examination. If you don't you may well find yourself naively choosing to allow someone to needlessly lacerate, scar, deform and destroy your body.

'Non, Je Ne Regrette Rien'

Regret is a sour burden. Edith Piaf, the famous French singer sang 'Non, Je Ne Regrette Rien' (I have no regrets). Well good for her. It is a negative state that involves blaming ourselves for a bad outcome. Feeling a sense of loss and sorrow at what might have been or wishing we could undo a previous choice we made. The less opportunity one has to change the situation you caused, the more likely it is that regret can turn into sadness and cause further insecurities. I couldn't change what I had done and I regret it to this day.

Sometimes choice is a bad thing. The more choices you have the more opportunity to experience regret – there was always another choice you could have made that may have worked out better. The less choice, or no choice, means you may as well accept the situation and make the best of it.

The favourable outcome of regret is that it can have informational value in motivating corrective action. It can help you avoid future negative behaviour; and you can gain insight into aspects of who you are. Self-knowledge is a powerful revelation for maturity and change. Obviously it can have damaging effects too, when it turns into self-blame and this was where I found myself.

I knew there was nothing I could do to reverse the operation and definitely nothing I could do to relieve the self-inflicted discomfort caused from rowing. For I while I just couldn't let it go; the daily constant pain didn't help.

The Bible says in Philippians 3:13 'forget what lies behind and strain forward to what lies ahead'. Nathan Hale elevated the term 'regret' to a high that I will never achieve. In 1776 Hale, a lad of twenty one years old, captain in the colonial army, was arrested by the British as a spy. He was sentenced to hang. His final words were 'I only regret that I have but one life to lose for my country'. I am no Nathan Hale and my surgery has not sentenced me to die; in the grand scheme of things it's insignificant; but frustratingly it still haunts me to this day.

I sometimes feel like Judas, the treacherous disciple who betrayed the Son of God. After his act of betrayal was consummated, Judas was struck by the reality that his wicked intrigue would result in the 'condemnation' of Christ. He repented, regretted his actions but then took the coward's way out and committed suicide. He could have (and should have) been compelled to a higher plateau of spirituality causing a change of heart and life. For whatever reason, he refused that option. It's a sobering and challenging thought that regret can lead to someone taking their life.

The answer is forgiveness; in my head I know that God has forgiven me. The issue is that I find it hard to forgive myself. The apostle Paul had been a determined persecutor of the Christian Way. He was a missionary of mayhem who sought to destroy the church of God. I do feel somewhat comforted when I read that he too touches on lingering regrets, even after he received salvation. In Ephesians 3:8 he confessed he was 'the least of all the saints' – not worthy of the favour bestowed on him, referring to his past and what he once was and did.

When my regret threatens to take me over, I return to Paul and pray that I too will not wither away as he did not, indulging in self-pity and unproductive disappointment. He channelled his memories into fiery zeal and travelled thousands of miles preaching the gospel. I really only have one option and that is to receive God's pardon for 'yet again' taking my life into my own hands. I must resolve that even though the regrets linger, I must not let them control me or disable me. I have to bear the self-inflicted scars and the constant tightness around my chest, the persistent itch that cannot be relieved and not allow my torturous thoughts to cripple my present moments. I have to determine to use my foolishness as a springboard to a higher good that I may not have accomplished otherwise. One thing I can say for certain: my unwise choice has given me unfathomable compassion and eradicated any attitude of judgment on others who make mistakes.

As for forgiving myself and walking in the total freedom of that, all I can say is that I am still wrestling with that. It is better than it was but if I get low and life becomes unmanageable again then it is a demon that creeps up and still haunts me. It has been a huge life lesson about sticking close to God and listening to his voice only; I was still mostly a dumb single-minded sheep searching for pastures on my own, so sadly it was to be a while longer I wandered back into the safety of the fold.

The Red Herring

I have been interested to learn that the term 'red herring' comes from when early settlers hunted. They would leave 'red herring' along their trail because the strong smell would confuse wolves. It means a 'false trail'; today it is something that misleads or distracts from a more important issue and causes people to make false conclusions.

Summer of 2012, having abandoned rowing and still in pursuit of continual exercise, I set my mind not on Christ but on the gym. I went along and investigated what realms of exercise were available to someone with a damaged back like mine. It turned out to my delight, that aside from rowing and a few machines that specifically worked the Latissimus Dorsi muscles, I could pretty much do everything else. This was good news! It did nothing to sort out my deeper insecurities, which of course would have been a better project; but it superficially appeased greatly the need in me to have a focus for my time. The sticking plaster went over my inner wounds and I threw myself wholeheartedly into being a gym bunny. I imagine God at this time up in the heavenlies scratching his head in sheer frustration over my constant avoidance to fully turn to him, surrender control and live a life fully guided by him.

It must be similar to when my kids insist on doing something their own way and I just know they're going to waste a load of time and do it my way in the end. Why? Because 'Mother knows best' – it's a song from the well-known Disney musical 'Tangled'. I sing it all the time to my children. I have spent many wasted minutes trying to persuade them to let me help, or given them advice over this or that, finally taking over in frustration only to make the situation worse. I have learnt that more often than not it is best to allow them to find out for themselves what the result of their choice will be. I scratch my head in frustration, stamp around my bedroom, but I let the reigns go and have to watch them fall over the next pavement stone because they put their wellies on the wrong feet. Then I have to pick them up – 'I told you that would happen' – whilst being blamed for allowing them to do what they wanted.

I think that's what God must have felt about me. 'Rebekah! Stop all this obsessive exercise, it is not the answer to your hurt, I am the answer, I am the way, the truth and the life. Look to me, make me your focus, dwell in my presence daily and will give you peace.' Could I do it? No. Not at that time anyway.

So, I started my new obsession and in the same fashion I went at it like a hammer at a nail. I've already told you how many hours I trained when I was at my peak. This continued for the next few years; four to be precise. Something significant happened around Christmas 2012 that could have been the end of this exercise obsession, but in many ways kept me stuck in the same rut.

During a routine gym session I decided to try out the exercise bike. When I dismounted I felt an acute pain in the base of my spine. I was at the end of my time, assumed it was a pulled muscle or trapped nerve and went home for a hot bath. For a fortnight I wrestled with this pain, pressing hot water bottles against it, rubbing deep heat into it, and daily dosing myself with Ibruprofen. Nothing worked; at the end of two weeks I couldn't even get myself up off the sofa without help. I remember the final Sunday before I caved and went to the GP, sitting, invalid-like, on the red sofas in our kitchen; eating my Sunday roast, stinking of deep heat, my skin burnt from extremely hot hot water bottles. Sarah, my sister, had to pull me up so I could make it to the toilet. Then shouting for Mark to come and help me up the steps from the downstairs loo. It was agonising.

I wasn't worried about it; I honestly thought it was related to the bike at the gym; I wasn't even alarmed when the GP said that given my history he felt he should refer me immediately to the Freeman Hospital for a bone scan. I was perfectly happy for him to do so, might as well be thorough. It didn't even ring any alarm bells when a couple of days later Karen rang me and said she and Mark had noticed my referral come in and they were going to bring forward my bone scan. I just thought they were being nice to one of their favourite patients. Sometimes it's helpful being a bit slow; lack of awareness, at times, can have its advantages.

I was called in for the results of the bone scan a few days later and Mr Verrill showed me a dark spot on my fourth vertebrae. Mark (I'll have you know I'm on first name terms with my oncologist) and Karen knew all about the trauma that I was wrestling with in regards to my damaged back, post reconstructive surgery. He was calm and unconcerned about this spot, he knew I had been suffering a lot of pain, and he knew about how much I trained. The radiographer's report said it was a Schmorl's node; an upward and downward protrusion of the spine's soft tissue into the bony tissues of the adjacent vertebrae. They are quite common and are often a sign of minor degeneration of an aging spine. Not sure I liked that bit, goodness me, they'd be diagnosing arthritis next. I'd already been classified as a geriatric mother, all this under the age of 45; I couldn't imagine what the next 40 years might reveal. His decision was to send me to a spine specialist who had the expertise to advise me on pain management and any other options.

After a number of visits to the Spine Specialist where I passed all the tests for slipped discs and so on and so forth, he scratched his head and said, 'I am wondering if all the information about the damage from rowing too soon after a major operation, and the Schmorl's node, is all in fact a red herring.' I didn't really know what that meant; I knew what a red herring meant, I just didn't know why he was using it in this context. I was still not concerned and he was quite dishy so I was enjoying these appointments, all the bending over and walking in front of him while he analysed my posture from behind. I always loved the 'Carry on' Films when I was younger; 'just 'Carry on, Doctor' view my bottom for as long as you like'; I think I may even have managed to treat him to a Barbara Windsor wiggle.

The outcome from these appointments was that he felt the only way he could know for sure exactly what this shadow was, was to do a biopsy. I still didn't connect with why he felt this was necessary. I was quite happy with my Schmorl's node; it was a cool name for a protrusion and caused a laugh or two when I named it to others.

The night before I was due to go in for the biopsy, Mark and I were lying in bed chatting about nothing in particular. I was drugged up to the eyeballs on painkillers for my back and had probably floated through the last few consultations in a fog of opium.

Mark's mind had wandered to a different level, far away from my haziness of poppy fields and summer meadows. 'If it's not a Schmorl's node,' he said, 'what do you suppose it is?' I answered with my mouth wide open in an unconcerned yawn, 'Just some trauma from exercise I guess.' Silence from Mark, but that was fine because I was drifting off into my drug induced Night Garden. His voice broke into my happy place with another question: 'How do you suppose they do a biopsy on your vertebrae?' 'No idea,' I said, 'go google it. Now shut up; I'm enjoying my hallucinogenic ride on the Ninky Nonk. I can see IgglePiggle.'

Medieval Torture

I never found out if he googled it or not; I was honestly not remotely interested. My friend Beth was meeting me at the RVI, but only because she'd insisted. I was quite happy to go alone, I'd become used to trailing to the hospital and rarely asked for or needed a companion. Mark went to work as normal and I trotted to the Metro blissfully unprepared for the horror of a spinal biopsy.

I met Beth in the foyer and she too asked me similar questions to Mark. I bounced along explaining that I didn't have a clue, I hadn't really thought about it, and I'm sure it would all be over in the shake of a lamb's tail. How wrong I was.

The alarm bells didn't even start to ring when I was taken to a ward, a WARD, as in with beds and curtains, a nurse's station and real life nurses appearing and disappearing behind curtain enclosed beds with real patients in them. I gaily sat on my bed and it wasn't long before a tall, heavily built man with an ample girth, a sallow complexion and dark hooded eyes approached my bed. I have since named him Dr Dark (I can't remember his name, but this suited him).

Just a little aside here; I have frequented for many years now, the oncology outpatients' clinic at the Freeman Hospital. There's a screen that lets you know whether the doctors are on time or how long the delay is. The first time I set eyes on that screen I laughed out loud at the names of two of the Oncology Consultants: Dr Dark and Dr Death. I am not making that up; it is not one of my tales. There are seriously two doctors working in an area of medicine that is indeed very dark and will definitely involve many deaths. How ironic. I wish my doctor was called Dr Death or Dr Dark; I would totally milk the black humour in their names.

The doctor before me looked exactly how I would imagine a caricature of a cartoon doctor called Dr Dark. He wasn't wearing a dark cloak nor did he have jet black hair greased back from his perfect widow's peak; but he did look rather like a sinister Egyptian King and was so tall he'd developed a rounded shoulder stance; his head drooping slightly to his chest. This only enhanced a sort of Hermann Munster impression. He even spoke in a dark voice, expressionless and deeply monotone, but strangely soft, almost hypnotic.

He asked me if I knew why I was there and what I was having done; simple questions that I satisfactorily answered. 'I'm having a biopsy on my fourth vertebrae.' That's what I knew, so that's what I said. Satisfied I was clear on the procedure he imperceptibly nodded his emotionless face and glided darkly and silently out of the ward to 'prepare'. I too prepared by once again donning myself with one of the attractive hospital open backed gowns; then making Beth laugh by opening and closing the back, flapping the surplus fabric like giant birds' wings.

The first whiff of concern that I had was when a hospital porter turned up pulling a bed behind him. I briefly wondered why I needed to be put on a bed, but was distracted by his call of 'Transport for Ann Simpson', and had to remember that Ann was in actual fact me. Brief interlude while I explain the reason he called me a random name you've never yet heard. It's not because I have a penchant for the name Ann, my name is really Rebekah but not officially.

I'll tell the short version: I was named Ann Rebekah Mells when my father registered my birth – my mum felt it sounded better that way round, but she'd always intended to call me Rebekah not Ann. In addition my father spelled Rebekah, Rebecca, which my mum was furious with. Rebekah is a Bible character; this was very important to my mum, as she named all six of us after Bible characters. I cannot imagine the argument that went on between them over this error. My father must have spent months in the garden shed, head down low after this faux pas.

So I grew up calling myself Rebekah and then ran into a few problems when setting up my first bank account. I couldn't register myself under Rebekah Ann because on my birth certificate I'm Ann Rebecca – Rebekah Ann does not exist. You still awake? Good, I'll carry on.

Basically what this has meant in my life is that I have to register on all official documents as Ann Rebecca and then have to endure being called Ann by official people. Before blooming cancer it hardly ever arose as a problem, the number of times I had to sign up for something that required legal detail could be counted on one hand. Passport, marriage certificate, driving licence; but since the plague had hit me it happened every frigging week. I was known as Ann in my second home, the Freeman Hospital, and no matter how many times you tell the nurses that I get called Rebekah, they read on my notes that I'm Ann and that's my label. You don't know how much it bugs me!

I have too many examples of puzzled friends' faces sat in waiting areas with me watching me rise from my seat to respond when Ann's name is shouted for the next appointment. Then the journey home spent explaining this trivial but utterly bizarre choice made by my mother 46 years ago made even more complex by the spelling error of my father. It's going to be the first conversation I have with them when they greet me the other side of the pearly gates.

Ann told the porter, 'I don't need to get on that, I can walk', but he insisted and followed up his insistence with 'you'll need it on the way back'. I couldn't really compute what he'd said before we'd pulled up outside one of the CT scan rooms. I found that short ride quite funny – when I'd had my mastectomy I'd walked to theatre; when I came out I was pushed back to my room in a state of semi consciousness. I'd missed out on all the fun of being wheeled down corridors past all the waiting people.

I felt such a fraud lying down, I was 'sort of' fit and healthy; it felt wrong to lie back, the passers by trying not to look at the sick person on the trolley. Speculating about what was wrong with them; well that's what I do when I see patients being wheeled around. Some avert their eyes but most people have a good gawk. In retrospect what I did was probably worse than simply lying back swooning like an Edwardian woman, hand to cheek, soft groaning, melodramatically faking an illness.

I sat bolt upright on the bed, my hands gripping the bars either side to prevent myself falling off the side when we turned corners. Smiling and waving at people, I majestically glided past many waiting areas. Queen of the trolley, a Royal Trolley Dolly; moving through my domain on my chariot, wafting my hand with a demeanour of breeding; my coachman finally and smoothly delivered me to my destination. I have no idea what possessed me to do this, other than it's the way I tend to react to situations that make me feel awkward. To deal with the embarrassment I make a joke out of it all and the actress in me enters performance mode. This was a classic example.

We arrived and I clambered off, entering into the subdued lighting of the CT room and obediently lay face down on the bed. There were two nurses and Dr Dark who had changed into a blue surgical costume, a surgical mask pulled down under his chin, and a pair of rubber gloves on his hands. In the half light of the CT room he looked even darker; perhaps there was a macabre glint in his sunken eyes. I still wasn't alarmed; how dim can one be? I noticed a trolley to the left of him with syringes and shiny surgical instruments, and I still didn't twig onto what was about to happen.

He explained that they were firstly going to repeat a scan to finally confirm the position of the suspected Schmorl's node. I had no problem with that. The next part was a little more suspect; I would need an epidural. Hang on a minute, an epidural? I'm re-enacting my facial response right now: a puzzled frown, a pause, followed by a slow, dawning realisation that if an epidural was necessary then this was far more invasive than I had remotely understood. Epidurals were what they gave ladies who were having a baby. I'm sure they were used for other things too; but that was the last time I had heard the word bantered around. During the NCT classes and afterwards as various girls in the group either opted to have one during labour; or had to have one because delivery was not straightforward.

I didn't like the sound of it at all; he explained that the procedure he was about to perform required a regional anaesthetic to block the pain in the nerve impulses of my lower spinal segments. Erm, pain? No one had ever mentioned pain; I was beginning to think I should have asked more questions. I wished I'd paid more attention in the NCT classes. The main issue I had been concerned about at that time; was what were the chances of my baby being born with a strawberry birthmark? They couldn't even give me any information on that subject.

He was going to inject my lower back with anaesthetic to numb it and then would perform the biopsy. He did explain what this would entail but to be honest after a longer glance at his trolley of torture instruments which I foolishly thought were probably for the next poor victim, I blocked his drone out and braced myself. I have no idea how long I was in there; the reality, probably an hour. It felt like a lifetime.

The epidural went in, that was fine; the biopsy began. Within seconds of him beginning, both my legs involuntarily flew upwards behind me. It was as if I was attempting the caterpillar break dance move; a ripple went through my lower body creating a wave like a worm crawling. It hurt. They must have added more anaesthesia, he had another go: the same thing happened.

I remember in the 70s dreading going to the dentist, terrified of needing a filling. Dental hygiene was not what it is today; we weren't educated about flossing, regular brushing or the effects of diet on teeth. Or at least there was no education in our home; I can't remember ever being told to brush my teeth. I recall a nurse coming into our Primary School when I was about 10 with these little tablets, we had to chew them; they turned all the plaque on your teeth illuminous pink. I looked like I'd ravaged a paint pot.

Needless to say, I had about six fillings before I was twelve. I can remember every single one; they were agony. The check-up, feeling a stab of pain as he poked around, knowing he'd found a hole but praying desperately I was wrong. Waiting a couple of days, riddled with dread of the impending torment. He would start – there were no injections for fillings back then. It was pure medieval, horrible history style endurance; clenching your hands into sweaty fists, gripping the arms of the chair type of terror.

The only instruction from the dentist was 'raise your hand if you need a break'. How awful, kids these days would never ever be able to tolerate pain in the way we had to. One tried not to raise one's hand because it made the whole agony last longer. But boy, when he hit a nerve in the root of your tooth, you knew about it. Your body would involuntarily jerk and an uncontrolled throaty squawk would release from your wide open mouth. He would stand back, pause his whirring drill; give you 10 seconds, then lean over you and the torture would continue. Those fillings seemed to last forever, and ever, and ever. Independently of my mother and father, I learned to take control of my own mouth care; I am proud to say that in three decades I have needed no further dental treatment.

The sensation of Dr Dark trying to extract tissue from my Schmorl's node was very similar to the pain of a 1970s filling. Like being electrocuted, eventually they found the correct level of anaesthesia and although it remained uncomfortable, the jerking legs stopped. But I was already feeling traumatised.

I have tried to research what happened next, what instrument he was using, how spinal biopsies are performed, but nothing I have found has explained what happened to me. The only procedures I have found are needle biopsies, when a sample of bone is taken directly from a suspected diseased area and extracted. I had a needle biopsy on my breast; it was no problem at all. What he did was nowhere near as simple as a needle biopsy; he did not simply stick a needle into my numb spinal region and suck up the contents of the node.

He was using some type of instrument that required him to screw down into my spine. Due to my lack of research throwing any light onto what piece of equipment he used, I will have to resort to my own imagination, and the sensation that it caused me. Maybe I have fabricated the whole thing, created it out of my fear; I guess it matters not. Whether it was real or not, I think it WAS; what he did and what it felt like are very REAL to me.

After his several failed attempts due to my body twitching like a finger on the trigger of a gun, he was able to move to phase two. This felt like a corkscrew being twisted and turned into my spine. No pain, but I felt the pressure of him rotating his weapon and the force of him bearing down on me. At one point, after two failed attempts to remove enough tissue to be useful for laboratory analysis, he really went for it.

I unfortunately turned my head towards him and saw that his right knee was on the bed near my left buttock presumably to allow him more stability and be able to lever his strength into his arms. One hand, I assumed, was holding the 'corkscrew' in place while the other was rotating; honestly I could see it turning around. He was using his body weight – remember he was a big unit – and was sweating like a sinner in a church, using as much strength as he could muster to screw his way deeply enough into my spine to get the gold he needed.

My eyes were wide with shock; the scene was worthy of a horror film. The nurses kept saying how well I was doing as they gently but firmly held me down on the bed. As I describe this I am also wondering if this really happened. Or did I just drift into some fantasy world and make some of this up? It sounds made up, but as truly as I am here today, I really feel this is a description of what my spinal biopsy was like.

Man, I was so happy to see Trolley Dolly outside the room. I was transferred from the torture table to a wheelchair and lifted onto the bed. I lay back and watched the glaring hospital lights float above my face. I was glad I had not known what was coming to me, I would possibly never have gone through with it. All that to confirm a nondescript shadow that no one was concerned about. I would never have agreed to it.

I have never been so glad to see a friendly face as I was to see Beth that day. I was so relieved she'd insisted on coming with me; whether it was divine provision, Beth's inner sense that I might need someone or her simple kindness, it mattered not. I was moved onto the bed behind my curtain and brought a cup of tea and a biscuit while I regaled her with the nightmare I had just been through. The part where Dr Dark was kneeling on the bed, his trolley of needles pulled up behind him; shady eyes peering over the top of his surgical mask as he corkscrewed, sweating, into my spine, held down by two assistants, had her eyes popping out of her face and her hand clasped over her mouth in shocked terror. I can tell a good story, milking each dramatic moment for maximum effect, I have definitely retold the tale of 'Dr Dark and his Chamber of Horrors' at many dinner parties. I hope there will never be a sequel.

I wasn't supposed to get the Metro home after the epidural, but I did. I didn't want to wait around for a taxi or for someone to come and pick me up. I lied to the nurses and as soon as they gave me the go ahead to leave I was out of that place as fast as my legs could carry me. I ran into our kitchen, straight to the fridge; took out a ¾ bottle of white wine and stood in the kitchen swigging it from the bottle. Mark was stood at the island in the middle of the kid's tea, gawping at me. I paused for breath, allowing my body to relax as the alcohol surged through my veins; then and only then was I able to tell him what I'd just been through.

Death

Two weeks later Karen Verrill rang me up and asked if she could pop in and see me around teatime. She lives on the same street as me; her request didn't strike me as peculiar. She had often popped in to help me out with some concern I had, she'd drained my seromas in the kitchen to save me trailing into the hospital and redressed wounds many times. Although on this occasion I hadn't sought her, I looked forward to seeing her anyway and carried on as normal.

She arrived, I was in the kitchen with all the children who were playing and watching TV, and waiting for food; Mark was still at work. We sat down at the table, my stomach started to churn; there was something in the atmosphere that just told me this was not a coffee date with my friend. 'Rebekah, the results of your biopsy came in today; you have secondary breast cancer in your spine.'

'Am I going to live long enough to see all my children grow up?'

I think you can tell from a person's first response to news such as this what is dominant in their mind. This was the immediate thought that came into my head. I didn't cry, I had floated out of reality and just needed to know the answer to the thing I feared the most.

'No,' she said.

'How long do you think I have?'

'That's a hard question to answer. Currently I'd say the average is 5-6 years. It depends how you respond to the treatments; I've seen some people last 10 years.'

This conversation as I've written it here sounds very black and white and brutal. Karen knew me, she knew I had to know the truth and I didn't need it soft soaped. I had a young family and needed to know the enemy so that I understood exactly what I was wrestling with.

'Many?'

'No.'

'What does that mean?'

'I think Mark has treated one person who survived a decade.'

I understood fully; the likelihood was, medically speaking, that I would be doing exceptionally well if I lived longer than a decade. It was more likely to be around 5-7 years; it could be a lot sooner. No one could really tell me that.

I calculated quickly that Archie would be around nine, Josie 10, Evie 12 and Emma 17. I would be moving into miracle territory if I saw them pass through High School. I couldn't speak. I had avoided mixing with or conversing with anyone who had secondary breast cancer. Secondary breast cancer victims were the primary breast cancer victim's biggest nightmare. They were cursed; an omen of death; the very words 'Secondary' carried a heaviness and a fear that was enough to send you running screaming to the distant hills.

Most primary breast cancer sufferers were able to confidently believe, with the entire backing of proven medical statistics, that after all their treatment ended they were cured. We believed this; we didn't really go around considering that this may not be the case. We rarely talked about it and Karen did an excellent job of lightening anyone's mind and encouraging us not to stray across the line to the dark side. She kept us focused on the present moment; I know now that if she spotted some morbid secondary sufferer sitting next to one of us she would intervene and divert the conversation.

We were largely led to believe that it happened to only a few and it was manageable. More like a chronic illness than a death sentence. Vague reassurances about lots of available treatment and women going on for years reduced the anxiety from a sickening terror of early death to no more of a concern than getting arthritis. Drugs were coming out all the time, the likelihood of there being a total cure for cancer was probably just around the corner.

Our fear was probably more rooted in having to continue the rest of our lives (which we did not believe even secondary cancer was likely to shorten) under the intensity of chemotherapy and the continual shock as a new spread reared its head. At that time, we were all still very much reeling from the news that we had cancer at all; the idea of embracing cancer forever was beyond our emotional capacities. Karen did a champion job of keeping these fears in perspective and subtly persuading people's minds to stay on the present battle.

There was a lovely young lady who unfortunately when she was diagnosed with primary; they discovered it had already spread to secondary disease in her bones. It was so sad; she wasn't the only one, of course, but she was only in her late 20s and had a toddler to care for too. It was hard to ignore someone so young and in some ways a similar situation to myself. She was reassuringly calm about having secondary cancer and I remember her voice clearly – 'as long as Mr Verrill keeps telling me he has medicine for me then I have no worries'. I think we all believed this; that there would always be some way of fighting the silent killer in us all. This young girl died about six months after our conversation; it really bothered me. There was even reassuring reasoning behind this; she had a tumour type that didn't respond well to any treatments. Mine was different; there was much available for me if I had the misfortune that it returned, but it was unlikely to. So, you plod on, navigating these little hiccups and distractions but never ever thinking that one day it might be you.

You see, you didn't really need to know what these poor, minority, unfortunate few women were going through. Karen and Mark plated the cards perfectly and handled primary sufferers with great care. We needed to be pumped full of strength and hope and positivity. Believe in the truth that we would have long lives and one day this would be part of a past; a tough chapter that enriched us and deepened us. A time which, although it was earth shattering when we were in the middle of it, we would go onto be used positively, to help others and make us better people.

Believe me, it was a difficult line not to cross; not to wander over to the enemy camp and if you did, to stay victorious and mentally strong. I remember another older lady who I really liked (she's long passed away now) who also liked me. But talking to **her** always sent icy chills up my spine and a dark sense of the unthinkable would shadow my day following any interaction with her. It was hard to stay off the subject; in the same way that all of us needed to share what we were going through, these ladies needed to talk about where they were at. For me, it was a bit like picking a scab. You know you shouldn't because it's not ready to come off yet, but you just can't resist it; the healed edges are just calling to be fiddled with, you pick away and before you know it you've gone too far. The wound has opened before it was healed and now you have to wait even longer for it to get better. Karen was always at the end of the phone to smooth these fears over or make you laugh so that you could return to the security of the Primary camp.

When Karen became centre manager of Maggie's, she separated the two groups of women; a primary support group and a secondary support group. For the primary group I think this was the right thing to do. It will not have totally removed the fear, or awareness that there are women who have sadly seen their disease recur; but it did at least allow them to deal with the issues that are particular to that chapter. To be honest, that's all you can manage and all you should be managing.

In my stunned state Karen had to tell me to ring Mark and she would stay with me until he could get home. I rang him and said, 'You better come home, Karen is here; it's spread to my spine.' Silence. Then: 'I'm on my way'.

Mark was devastated. I think this may have been the third time I had witnessed him crying. The first was something I'm very ashamed of; it was when we were 'dating' – as you may already have picked up I used to be a bit of a radgy. A situation must have occurred that to me had the ingredients of injustice and unfairness towards me personally. I can't remember what he'd done, I doubt it warranted my poor behaviour; but at that time if I found myself facing those evil twins and the other person didn't take responsibility for their error then eventually I would blast out a pure white rage. I would not calm down until justice prevailed and the person saw the error of their ways. I would literally go mental and it could last for hours; on this occasion it caused Mark to break down. How awful. I don't know why Mark didn't do a runner; I'm hugely grateful that he didn't.

The second occasion was when we found out we were having a boy. He hadn't minded what it was, but when we were told the news, he broke down. It was very moving. The third time was on the news that my cancer had spread. For a few minutes we just held each other and cried. We had not spent any time considering the fact that there could even be a small chance I would be one of the unfortunates. We knew little about secondary breast cancer; but the one thing we both immediately faced and knew was that this was going to be another, much harder journey than what we'd already walked.

And then we started speaking to Karen and got the real picture of secondary breast cancer. Yes, all the information I'd been pacified with was true. There was lots of treatment, it was like managing a chronic illness, many of the treatments were tolerable and those who remained positive like me were often the ones who did very well. But this was only one side of it; we needed the total picture. We had always wanted the complete picture.

She repeated the answers to the questions I'd already asked, more than once. We needed to check a few times if secondary breast cancer really meant that I was unlikely to be alive a decade on; the answer never changed. I love the honesty of Karen; I understand that some people don't want to know this type of detail. I understand that in many ways to many people asking a medic 'how long do I have?' could be a negative bit of information. A millstone round your neck so to speak, the killer of all hope that you **will** live a long life; a timebomb counting down the days and years until the predicted time arrives.

The obvious supporting argument for not knowing is of course that no human can predict the last day of anyone, so what is the point of asking? That just doesn't cut it for me; knowing such weighty information doesn't have a particularly negative effect on me at all, and Karen knew that. She knew I needed such information in order to fight with even more determination. Red rag to a bull was more my response as opposed to a certain death sentence which I would then chew over day and night. Competition loomed, a true test for my character – could I take the baton of death and race fearlessly into the unknown?

We grasped the picture head on; one which is rightly never presented to primary breast cancer patients. That you don't recover from secondary breast cancer; unless you're extremely unfortunate and die in an accident, or find yourself with some other killing disease; then you ARE going to die from cancer. Sadly, that is almost certainly going to be sooner rather than later. I want to say a heartfelt sorry to anyone reading this currently suffering with primary breast cancer and who is now completely freaked out. I want to remind you that this was 2012 – even as I'm writing in 2018 there are new treatments available. Do not panic; even I am still believing that the cure is just round the corner and that I will survive to see my grandchildren. Although I've debated miracles a few times so far, I do in fact still believe in them. You have to, I have to; believing in the unbelievable cultivates hope. It is hope and faith in the impossible that drives you forward to live, and to live well in any circumstance. Once you find your wings you can fly into the face of death and swoop right through it, so don't give up.

Having said that, it is a totally different journey to the one I had been on; and calling it a chronic illness once you find yourself facing it, does not do justice to the full reality. We were looking ahead to a life that was never ever going to be cancer free. This was never ever going to be a chapter that was going to be in our past. Our lives had to embrace cancer, an unwanted guest, an intruder, a thief, bringing with it pain, destruction and devastation and now certain premature death. When I imply that I took it as a challenge and was able to run brandishing my weapons of warfare high above my head, I ought to say that I hid under a rock for quite a while first. Weeping and wailing and feeling like the most tortured human alive.

I wasn't in the greatest place with God at that time, the reconstruction disaster had hit me hard and I had by no means recovered from that, before this bombshell went off. It would have been totally understandable to everyone who knew me if I finally lost the plot altogether. Just gave up on my faith. Stopped believing that God had this all in hand, that he was good and loved me. I'm afraid that isn't part of my story, it just never happened. I had certainly wandered away from a close relationship with him. I had taken back control of my life; but deep down a life-long rooted knowledge that no matter where I wandered, no matter how long I turned my face away from my lord, no matter how far I ran in the opposite direction, I would never ever be able to deny that God is God and it is he who is the way, the truth and life, the answer to who we are and why we're here. Having said this, it was quite a few more years before I came fully back off my highway and surrendered to His way.

Thoughts on a Metro

Recently I wrote a poem about trying to live life when it becomes strangely double sided; until this point I had only really dabbled with concepts of dying. Whilst my disease remained controlled, contained and 'cured' I didn't really have to embrace such reality and it was easier to function alongside others whose lives were less dramatic than mine. I was always moving away from cancer, day by day I stepped towards cancer being a distant memory; a chapter of my life, not my life. I was heading towards regaining the life I had before. Ok, I knew I was different, all be it just because I had the inconvenience of owning cantaloupe melons of differing sizes for breasts. I wouldn't be **exactly** the same as I had been, but my life in general would return to be comparable to that of my peers.

When I stepped over the line into the world of secondary cancer everything became too strange. Unreal and blurred; not dissimilar to a scene from Alice in Wonderland where caterpillars smoke and Cheshire cats leer from trees. For a long time I wandered around in my own head flipping between reality and unreality.

Once, well, maybe more than once, when I was a student I took 'magic mushrooms'. Oh yes I did! My kids may one day read this; they better had because they are the reason I'm putting myself through this daily torture. So, I want you to know, kids, I did it all. There is probably very little that you will do that your dear, boring, fuddy duddy mother didn't do herself. Sex, drugs and rock 'n' roll; I messed about with them all, I was an art student – rebellion is at the heart of art. Challenging people and breaking rules and non-conforming are woven into the depths of most 'artists'; I was no exception.

As a sensible Christian mother I feel a pressure to say that it was all wrong and a waste of time. I regret it and those experiences damaged me and on and on and on and I wish I hadn't and pretend to you that I didn't, but I can't. I can almost hear the gasps of horror from Mother reading this now. Trying to engage their brains to understand any woman who would share openly about her disreputable past knowing her darlings will be lapping it all up. What kind of an example am I?

I can answer that for you. I am an honest, open mother. One who strives to embrace the good, the bad and the ugly in herself; I am a mother who may never get to tell her children about the experiences of her past and how they are all woven into the rich tapestry of who she became. Mine has never been a life that follows a straight line, and it certainly hasn't always been a happy life, nor have I always been a happy person; equally I have had chapters of ecstasy and complete bliss. I am a daughter, a sister, an aunty, a friend, a wife and a mother. I have been happy, excited, invigorated, loved, depressed, lonely, distraught, frightened, fit, strong, whole hearted, vibrant, colourful, loved, hated, rejected, popular, unpopular; all these things and more.

I am a steady person in my heart and head (most of the time!) but my emotions are as wide and deep as the ocean – sometimes they stretch to the heavens and sometimes they reach into the fiery pits of hell. I am passionate, honest and real, always real. What you see is what you get, what it says on my tin is what you can expect to find. I can't be something I'm not, I can't agree with something that I don't, I can't say what you want me to say if I don't believe it's right; I can't fight a cause I don't believe in, I can't leave something alone that I want to fight for. I am not everybody's cup of tea. I have learnt to have a middle ground, but my nature is not to accept rules just because they are there, they are not there to mindlessly and violently break; they are there for all society's greater good but there's nowt wrong with questioning and breaking through rules to find greater freedom.

I dabbled in the ways of the world because I wanted to! I can't deny that aspects of those choices weren't rooted in lack of confidence and a regular sense of insecurity and wanderlust; but within it all I had some amazing times! These times have created some phenomenal memories; some sad ones too, but they have served me well in being an open minded, accepting reasonably non-judgmental person. One who can probably, on some level, relate to a huge variety of people. I can't pretend that it didn't happen and I also can't pretend I regret it all or tell you not to do it.

I am very grateful that I didn't become so enthralled with such a life that my experimenting led to being anything more than that. I have always had an acute sense of right and wrong and I am thankful for this. The challenging, rule breaking side of me just has to defy that from time to time, but by and large good always wins in my battle and I have been able to go off the rails for a while before I reach a place of no return. It's led to a life of ups and downs, that's for sure, but all of the parts are a part of me and part of who I am to this day. This is not a licence for you to go off and be rebels and embrace a life of danger and destruction. Got it?

2012, my life became for a while like my last magic mushroom trip. See, I'd be grasping around for a way to illustrate my experience if I had not had a minor brush with hallucinogenic drugs. I knew it would come in handy one day. God was still in there somewhere, waiting for me to come back to land safely in his arms; but a load of other weird things were whizzing around too, which for a while, removed me from the land of the living.

The particular night I am recalling, I was sitting in pub in Carlisle, home from Bristol University for summer break having taken Magic Mushrooms with a group of friends. One minute laughing uncontrollably, seriously belly aching laughter; the next reaching out in total wide eyed, child-like fascination with the neon coloured jungle of huge Jurassic-like sized leaves that were floating around my head. The pub was no more, I had entered the world of Avatar, I was the hunter in pursuit of the animals making the strangest of sounds, which I discovered later had actually been coming out of my mouth; much to the entertainment of the crowd that I was in the middle of.

Then I was a space man out on the street in the dark feeling the crackling sparks at my feet as I pointed my toes poised to shoot upwards blasted into the starry, starry night. Infinity and beyond, with my silver astronaut suit and protective polycarbonate helmet, floating and soaring high above my life where the stars shoot and there is no horizon to be seen.

Then the paranoia would take over, clinging to the guy next to me, terrified for my life. Something was coming to get me, I couldn't see it or touch it; I could just feel its sinister presence creeping up on me.

Whispering whacky, wicked words of destruction designed to enhance my confused state. It was the paranoia that ultimately was the reason my experimentation with drugs ended. It was horrible and frightening, and I did not want to be responsible for afflicting such terror into my own head. Thank God that my experiences held such horror – it made it easy to stop.

Just read back through those 'states': hysteria, beauty and magic, elevation, transportation, escapism, insecurity, fear and terror. This is the way I would describe the period of time directly following Karen's news: surreal, hallucinogenic, weird, huge and fearful. It is so hard to listen to normal conversation, to be carrying out a normal life in a normal way; all the time wearing a silver space suit, floating amongst starry, muted galaxies looking down onto your life below, never able to fully belong. Trying desperately to explain to people what it's like to live with an acute knowledge that you are dying; in a world surrounded by people whose concepts of death are as far removed as the east is from the west is impossible.

Woman in protective silver suit with polycarbonate helmet floating around the solar system trying her best to tune in via faulty radio system to what is going on in the world of others whose lives are following the regular pattern is exasperating. I became an alien, a non-native, a being from another planet; people didn't understand who I was anymore and although I understood them, I didn't belong to their narrative or life perspectives any longer and never would again. I could feel myself detaching and floating away, an immigrant, an outsider and a stranger on planet Earth. It's probably about the best description I can come up with. In simple terms I live in a different world to most people; it's hard for you to understand. And more often than I tell you it is extremely hard for me to fully participate in the world that you all live in.

Thoughts on the Metro

How would **you** *cope*
In the land of the living
If you lived half your life
In the land of the dying?
Come for a whirl in this
Bizarre sensation
This split life creation
That leaves a strange disconnection
When you permanently abide
In this disjointed dimension
Something constantly preventing
A full connection
To the world of the living
And their thoughtless introspection
It's an interesting concept
If not somewhat provoking
Consider it a window to
A caring revelation
At the very least –
A moment
For deep reflection

Rebekah Simpson

Here We Go Again

I have been hanging my head in total frustration for around half an hour now, trying to find the words or the right place to start this next chapter. I still have no idea; in some respects there is nothing more to say. I'd been told it had come back, I was looking at around 6-7 years life expectancy, I was 41, I was not going to see my children grow up, I wouldn't get to be a granny, I wouldn't reach a time with Mark where the children would leave home and we might have more time to explore other countries, times and spaces. I was facing the rest of my life, which now seemed very short, under treatment for cancer, in and out of hospital, trying to be a mother, never free from disease.

I was going to die, and it wasn't going to be when I was old and decrepit with bits dropping off my body, and nothing working anymore. I wasn't going to be one of those old ladies with a shopping trolley and a permed blue rinse. I'd never get to have brown stockings falling into wrinkles around my bony ankles or have photos taken with grandchildren cradled in my arms, sleeping peacefully on my lap. I'd never reach that point when I might have a stick with a rubber end that I could wave at Mark to fetch me the newspaper. I wouldn't ever have false teeth and a gummy smile or need to wear Tena ladies.

I would never reach my 25th wedding anniversary and recall tales of mine and Mark's life together with cancer only a hazy part of a wonderful journey. No, I was going to die from cancer while Mark and my young family looked on and then I would depart from this life and rotten body and they'd all have to face their lives without me.

I watched my mum die from cancer and it was the stuff of nightmares. She was so normal until the last few months. She was given her diagnosis of Ovarian Cancer and five years life expectancy. She had chemotherapy, surgery, radiotherapy, prayer, prayer and more prayer. It was hard to connect her with death; only a couple of years before she died she still took four or five of my young nieces and nephews on her annual camping trip to Keswick, alone. Her stomach was distended with fluid, like she was six months pregnant, she was exhausted but she was still her. A woman I recognised, strong minded and determined; she'd always taken her grandchildren camping – a bit of cancer wasn't going to get in her way.

It was literally only the months before when she began to look like a person who was dying. Vomiting nearly all day long, unable to eat, strange obsessive desires for food she'd never touch like sweet and sour sauce. Her bed moved downstairs, incontinent; unable to wash her own shrunken, skeletal body. Skin paper thin and yellowing, dark shadows around her sunken eyes, face skull-like.

Propped up in bed like a fragile little bird, virtually disappearing amongst the pillows and bed covers, tweeting all day 'I fancy some broccoli', 'a bit of lentil soup please'. Whatever you gave her she sucked the flavour out but had to spit the mushed up, chewed solid bits into a hanky and cover on the side of a plate. It made me, Ruth and Sarah retch as we tried to meet her needs and care for her in these final stages. You reach a stage when you watch someone suffering like this – incredibly she wasn't in any pain, but she was dying from starvation – and this was slow and horrific to watch. But in the absence of the right to put her out of her misery we had no choice but to attend to her and make her as comfortable as possible until her last breath was drawn.

I have to confess that I handled all this worse than my sisters, I know they had their own struggles with all of this; they aren't mine to tell. I was travelling over from Newcastle and largely living with Sarah mid-week, helping to care for my mum, then home for the weekends. Believe me, there's very little natural 'nurse' in my body. I'm queasy, I'm easily repulsed and I'm not too good with bedside manners; I definitely have the 'get on with it' approach. On one occasion after being sent back to the kitchen three times to redo the broccoli which had not been cooked exactly as she liked it I actually shouted at this poor, sick, dying lady. I can't remember exactly what it was, but I just couldn't bear it any more. I wish with all my heart I had not done this.

Seeing what she had become, this woman who I loved so much, this strong minded woman whom I'd argued and had conflict with for most of my life was awful. Despite all the conflict of the past, deep down I loved her; many times my love for her felt dark and painful but it was still love; and although it wasn't always very clear to me if she liked me at all, I had learnt to see that she did love me. Sure, she'd struggled to express it to me in obvious ways but I knew; I'd learnt to know from the small things. She'd make me cauliflower cheese when I came home from university for the holidays. She'd save up bits of cash from her job in a café and push a wad into my pocket on the platform of Carlisle train station before I boarded the train back to Bristol. She didn't have much but it showed me that she thought about me and tried to meet my financial needs as a student. We'd plan trips out to Mallam Cove, Fountains Abbey, Penrith, Gelt Woods, Grizedale Forest and **many** mountains; in later years she didn't come up them with me anymore, but she loved to drop me at the bottom then time how long it took me to run up and down. 'Where did you get those lovely legs, Rebekah?' – 'From you, Mummy,' I replied. It was the only physical compliment she ever gave me. I have never forgotten it.

All the old haunts from childhood that were so rich in memories that we shared from times gone by. It was the only way I could connect with her, mountains were her love, we loved them together and I am so very grateful that we found a language in which to share a love that we both understood.

So, it was heart-breaking to see her in this state. She had been in the hospice but to put it brutally she hadn't died, so was sent home. Typical Mells genetics, the effect of the respite that the hospice offered gave her a new lease of life; although she'd been predicted days to live she in fact rallied around and went on for another few months. I'm sure Sarah and Ruth would agree that this was not really a welcome turn of events for us; because, with a small amount of help from a Macmillan nurse who washed her, we had to take on the caring until she died.

I am sure there are nicer ways that people pass out of this life from cancer than this, but that is my experience. I will never forget it; it's hard for me to imagine any other outcome for myself. I did not want my children to have to see me in that state. But worse than that, I already know what it is like to live life without your mum. I had first-hand experience of what my children were facing when I died from cancer; that knowledge bore down on me like an oppressive weight and for long intervals I would weep over these imaginings for days.

I was 35 when she died and that was too early. All things I've had to go through and not have my mum. I do not believe it would all have been a bed of roses were she still alive to participate in my wedding, the birth of my children, the raising of them and all the other elements. I am sure there would have been a lot of unwelcomed vocal advice from her, but nevertheless I'd still take that now in exchange for her to still be here. It's amazing how your perspective changes on what matters or doesn't matter when someone dies. Quirks that once pickled your brain become fond little idiosyncrasies. Arguments you had seem such a waste of precious time. Good times dull out the bad in a hazy hue of unreal happiness. Elements of regret swim to the surface and a heart of forgiveness is the only answer.

I miss her; I often ponder the irony of that. It wasn't like I had the mum of story books, or even the mum that many of my friends had. The fact is that my mum was still my mum however she behaved; she was the only one I had and she did her best and I adored her. I loved her and despite how illogical that has felt at times, I just did. In fact, that truth, that I loved her and missed her daily despite any failings or hurt she caused me was the sole reason that I knew that my children would miss me and struggle to cope with life's challenges without me. Knowing the truth that there were times when I hated my mum, hours of counselling, where I had to undo some of the damage she caused, did not and never would alter the fact that I loved her and would always, on some level, need her.

I am not saying that I am a perfect mum to my children. In fact, I'm fully aware that I am definitely not. I do not know what their issues will be with me but I'm sure there will be some. From my own experience, despite the damage I am causing, I know with total certainty that life will be harder for them when I've gone. The younger that happens to them the more painful and difficult that will be for them.

There are so many occasions that will come when I am not there for them; they are multitudinous and immeasurable. For me it is not the big ones, you do adapt generically to Christmas, and family events such as weddings or celebrations. It's the smaller more insignificant, unnoticeable details that were very personal between me and her that I ache for. She was the only person I could call at random times of the day time 10.40 am, 2.35 pm, 11.00 pm, and she would always answer, she was always home. Looking back now I'm not sure how she managed that – she did have a life but my memory tells me that if I rang, she'd pick up. It's such a small thing, I hardly ever talked to her about anything significant, but I miss that little hotline, I miss the knowledge that she was there, just there, whenever I rang, she was just there, always, and then she wasn't. I didn't understand what comfort and security were found in having someone who is always available. How it anchors you, centres you, stops the ground beneath you slipping and sliding like sand between your toes. I still have her number in my phone; I always will. I miss those pointless chats.

I can't say exactly what my children will miss about me. I think it will be the personal quirks and habits, the little things that I do that no one else will ever be able to replace for them. Singing the old Northumbrian Folk tune Coorie Doon (lie down) when I do bedtime whilst gently stroking their backs. They all like their back strokes in different ways, different pressures and different places. Even Mark can't do it the way Mummy does. I have lots of silly pet names for the younger three: Evie Weevie, Evie Weevie Woosie, Josie Mosie, juicy, squidgy widgy, cuddle monster; Archie is Sunny Jim, Mr Bombastic, muscle man, the list is extensive. My cuddles so individual and special for each one, the private whispers of love in their ears reminding them how gorgeous they are, the girls so beautiful and Sunny Jim so handsome. No one else can ever do those things for your children. No other human can love your children like you do, it is irreplaceable and permanent. I said to Evie only the other week 'Whatever you ever do I will always love you. I'm signed up for life, Evie'.

Not long after I received the news of the spread I had two different experiences discussing the death of a parent. They have stuck with me. I don't know how I managed to keep my hands in my pockets and not wrestle them to the floor. 'It doesn't make any difference how old you are when you lose your parents; it doesn't get easier because you're older' or 'I think it's worse to lose a parent when you're older because they've been around longer'.

It's so hard to process comments such as these; firstly, how on earth do they know? Given it only happens once in your life how can you confidently say on behalf of everyone else in any circumstance and of any age that losing a parent later in life is harder?

Secondly, I disagree. How can this possibly be true? If I die in the predicted timeframe that has been muted to me then I will not see my three children reach an age where they leave home. I'm unlikely to see them achieve their GCSEs. I'll be doing well if I see them all make high school. You can't possibly believe that to lose your mum is not harder when you're totally dependent on them than someone who at the very least is settled in a job, with a partner maybe, able to feed, shop, clothe themselves, get themselves from A to B, and probably around the world if they so desired. Are you mad; or just totally thoughtless and selfishly introspective?

What was so hard to face was the sense of desertion. Obviously I couldn't help that I had cancer and that it was likely to kill me off, but that didn't pacify the sense of abandonment that I felt, the fear that I was going to bail on them when they still needed me. I know the tears I have shed every time I realised I couldn't pick up the phone to my mum; I was inflicting **so much more** on my children. I know the emptiness I felt when my mum was missing from my wedding, she never met my children; they never met Granny. I know the pain I still feel when I hear and see grandparents proudly indulge their children's children. There is no one else who is invested in your children when there are no grandparents around or involved. You're alone. There's no one to ask advice or check what's normal; sure, friends do some of that, but your own mother is the only one who fully knows you and is as interested in the development of your kids as much as you are. When you don't have one and you look at all those who do, it breaks your heart.

With my kids I was looking ahead to not only deserting them in the childbearing years but way before that. School achievements, career choices, job acceptances, love choices, house owning, money needs, heartbreak, celebrations, every birthday and I could go on and on. I lost my father when I was 23 and that was hard and painful; but losing my mum was different. Not only was it the end of anyone parenting me, but it was the end of my mummy/daughter relationship before I was ready. It was horrendous, and in some ways still is. I need her now more than I ever did. I'm poorly, sick, sometimes I just need my mum, and that's even though the relationship was often broken and riddled with disappointment. Nevertheless, sometimes a little girl just needs her mum. You seek but you can't find; they're not there and you feel lost and scared. Yes, I have God, I have Mark, I have sisters and brothers, but they are not my mum.

Trouble ahead

Our troubles achieve for us an eternal glory that ultimately far outweighs the torment we have in the here and now. 'It's the fire of suffering that brings forth the gold of godliness' *Madame Guyon*. I had no other choice but to continue to believe that there was purpose behind all these problems that kept besetting me. I was not in a good place in my faith; this continued for the next three-four years as I fought and battled with almost continuous spreading of cancer. I held on, I didn't desert my saviour, I don't think I even had enough energy to muster up an angry prayer. I just held on, I didn't receive any mind-blowing revelations, I didn't spend hours in prayer, I didn't dig deeply into my Bible, I just held on. Like a rock climber free bouldering, I clung to the rock face, sometimes literally by my fingernails, but that's what I did. I clung to the truth that 'God gives and God takes away' and I continued to bless his holy name. Most days it was just 'God, help me to bear this challenge' and that's how I rolled.

Following the spinal tumour in 2012, which was treated with radiotherapy, it next spread to various places in my pelvis. I was eligible to take part in a trial drug, a type of chemotherapy which had been having good results for many women. It was not so good for me.

It was bad enough being told I'd lose my hair if I didn't wear the torturous cold caps again; and of course I couldn't resist the challenge, so I put myself through brain freeze again. The worst terror turned out to be the nurse who was assigned to me. Unlike other wards where you are the patient of whichever nurse is on shift; on a trial unit you have the same nurse every time you go in. A trial drug is a drug that has not been made fully available and all side effects and symptoms have to be detailed and recorded so that a complete assessment of how the drug is tolerated can be made.

My nurse was definitely the love child of Dr Dark and Maleficent, the antagonist in Walt Disney's film Sleeping Beauty. Characterized as the 'Mistress of all Evil', I named her Skeletor. She was tall, thin and willowy with pale skin and extremely defined cheekbones which caused her eyes to appear huge and cavernous like they do in a skull. She could at times seem so mean. Mark said he thought she was fearful and that's why she approached everything with negativity and caution; he's probably right. To me and all my visitors who sat with me during that awful period, she was just unhelpful, doom and gloom; she always looked at the problems.

First problem, the cold caps. She actually said to me on my first meeting with her, 'Why do you wanna use those? Hair grows back, you know.' What a thing to say to a youngish lady who just doesn't want to be bald. I insisted and then she went on to say that the trials unit didn't have their own cold caps. What this would mean to her was that she would have to 'trail' (she actually said that with emphasis, I guess to indicate what a hassle it would be) all the way along to a different ward just to get the machine to plug the caps into. You'd think I'd asked her to trek to China for it rather than along the corridor.

Before I could even respond she had followed this up with how unsuccessful they often were. Then she continued to explain how much colder the hospital ones were compared to the cold caps I had used at home. These cold cap machines ran off the mains; the ones I used at home were kept in my freezer and therefore became less cold over the hour you wore it. Then the nurse who was treating me just ran downstairs to replace them and so it went until the end. It seemed the ones I had used were pathetic, child's toys, anyone could put up with those. The ones the hospital had, well, NO ONE had ever been able to cope with the constant minus 40 degree temperature that these babies put you through. Women crying, begging them to be removed, wrenching them off with half their hair stuck to ice on the inside of the cap.

She went on and on about how awful they were; her finale was truly crowd stopping. They came in pairs; two cold caps attached to the same freezer contraption so that two patients could be either side being frozen to death at the same time. They could turn blue together, awh what an experience to share. 'It would be very selfish of you to claim one of these machines for yourself when two ladies could use it upstairs.' Mark took over and said Mr Verrill had said I could use a cold cap and that was what I wanted, so get on with it, basically. It was not a good start.

Every time I had visitors she moaned and complained and passed comments about noise and accidents and how it was dangerous to have so many people visiting one patient. As far I was aware there were no rules, it was an open day ward, and most of the time there was only about three or four patients in there. She'd tut and be awkward, trying to get around people, hovering behind them like the angel of death, raising her sinister wings before annihilating them in one fatal swoop.

It stressed Skeletor when Josie and Archie came in, but they never stayed long. Hannah would bring them for 10-15 minutes just so they could understand where I was, then they'd be whisked away to the comfort and love of the Maggie Centre to be spoilt by Karen and all the volunteers. Josie actually had her first day at school whilst I was having one of these sessions. I wasn't going to be there to see her all dressed up in her uniform, I wasn't going to be able to do that proud mother thing where you watch them fly your nest for the first time through the school gate. Hannah brought them in and I have her first day at school photo taken on the hospital ward. She'd have a steely look on her face, her thin lips sealed together in abject disapproval.

On one occasion she coldly asked every person I had around my bed to go and sit somewhere else while she 'did her job'. Justifying her iciness and rude manner with some made up explanation about how dangerous it would be if she spilt the chemotherapy on the floor. How she was going to manage that from a laboratory sealed bag I have no idea. She muttered something about there being needles around; and tripping over all the handbags, falling on a needle and piercing the bag. It was ridiculous.

Mark was right; I think she actually suffered from stress. I somehow accidentally uncovered that she had never administered a cold cap for anybody; no surprise in that, she'd have scared the living daylights out of anyone interested. She was anxious about it. Rather than just admit her fear, she had to try and put people off; until me, she'd been successful. I learnt how to manage her. So did all my friends – we didn't really take any notice of her 'intimidating' manner. We just carried on regardless, being kind to her, pacifying her extreme nit picking, obliging her when it was over a matter that wasn't hugely important to us; and largely tolerating but not obeying her negative requests.

She did, however, make a huge mistake which turned into one of the most troublesome and unbearable side effects that I have had to endure as a result of ANY of the treatments I have had.

I was having a trial drug under clinical trial conditions. Clinical trials and the researchers involved in them, use patients to find new ways to improve treatments and therefore, hopefully, improve the quality of their lives. The main difference between being part of a trial and having treatment which is no longer under trial is the amount of detail that is recorded every time you attend.

Researchers want to know regularly how your treatment is working and are on constant look out for side effects related to the drug. You are asked lots of detailed questions regarding ANY new physical, mental or environmental changes, however 'unlikely' they may seem to be linked to the drug.

All these results are used to decide whether the drug should be funded by the NHS. Such decisions are mainly based on how effective and tolerable the drug is; alongside assessing if the results were positive enough to represent value for money. The particular drug I am currently having was under debate for many years due to its cost – £5000 each time it is administered! To date I have had 34 treatments, so if I've done my maths right (which is unlikely), I, alone, just on THIS drug, have cost the NHS £170,000. That is why the trials need to be so thorough and that is where this nurse sorely failed.

Every time I came in I sat and went through the pages of questions. It was only my second visit that I complained of some very peculiar itchy patches on my body. One was on the inside of my right thumb and one was on my shoulder. She seemed completely unperturbed and didn't record the symptoms. She asked me if I suffered from eczema or allergies, which I was able to confidently say 'never in my life'; and then she began to ramble about whether I'd recently changed my washing powder or some other household product. I reassured her I had not and she just looked at me like I was making it up. I can remember her screwing up her bony face, contorting into a puzzled expression, tapping a pen on her clipboard. Her lips pursed while she assessed my mental health. Then she pursued the allergy conversation explaining how she had developed allergies in her later years so perhaps I was too! Cheeky mare, I was a good decade younger than her and certainly wouldn't have been described as in my later years!

The result of this conversation was a non-recorded symptom due to her confident diagnosis that I MUST have developed a reaction to something that had come in contact with my skin. I wish I had pushed back more insistently but you must understand that in my situation you carry a tiny smidge of fear whenever your body manifests something out of the ordinary. A headache is a 'brain tumour', a UTI is 'bladder cancer', a pain in your back is 'kidney cancer', so a new itch on the skin is almost certainly 'skin cancer'. Any new pain (or itch), anywhere, even in your big toe or your armpit can start the mind racing down the dimly lit lane that ends with a sombre doctor telling you the dreaded disease has spread. I will never return to a place where a headache means I'm tired or I have a hangover; and dry eyes only require a quick trip to the chemist for eye drops. They will always begin with the fear that the cancer has come back.

The result of this in the instant I have described was that I immediately accepted her 'professional' opinion; I wanted to accept it. I wanted to be reassured by her that it was as simple as 'washing powder' because it allowed me to feel normal. 'Normal' is what I miss desperately and constantly, I did then and I do now, and I imagine I will for as long as I live. 'Normal' as in, life before cancer; the way I lived at the time she was diagnosing my new allergy and the way I live in the present day is not 'normal'. It is indescribable even in this book. I cannot explain what it is like to try and live 'normally' with cancer; at the same time as 'abnormally' dying from cancer. When your new symptoms are attached to something relating to 'normal' you are ripe and ready to ignore the little nagging voice inside, breathe a sigh of relief and walk forward in the reassurance that your ultimate fear, on this occasion, has not been confirmed.

I wouldn't be bothering to record this if it had in fact been washing powder. The itching continued and her conclusion remained constant, despite the fact that it worsened and spread. But this problem became irrelevant and inconsequential as the chemo continued. It was far worse than my first round of chemo; it took all my energy and gritty determination to face each one, my attention was certainly not on a wee bit of itchy skin.

Sickness, constant diarrhoea, and the most awful mouth ulcers which responded to no medicine at all plagued me for months. The dose had to be reduced to allow my body strength to recover between sessions and tolerate the next one. It became too difficult to discern what damage might be caused by the trial component of my druggy cocktail, and what was connected to the chemo element. I simply felt frigging awful all the time. Then there was the blooming cold caps that I'd chosen to use. The first time I used them began to feel like a walk in the park. What had I complained about? The chemo had made me feel constipated and tired, big deal, but on reflection I'd proudly sailed on through my cold cap induced 'ice cream headaches'. Rather like a figurehead carved on the prow of a 16th century boat; cutting majestically and victoriously through what at the time felt like very turbulent waters but were in fact, compared to this, the lapping of gentle waves.

The cold cap torture became my nemesis, my arch opponent, my enemy. I could do nothing about the effects of the drugs, but I was not going to lose total control by allowing the cold caps to beat me; and they didn't. However, I told everyone that I would never ever wear them again. At whatever time this course of treatment failed and I was hopefully moved onto something else in which the offer of further cold caps was an option, they were allowed to tell me 'NO'. I endured those caps in a spirit of victory, I was a conquering officer having won and defeated my opposition.

Fortunately, or unfortunately depending on how one chooses to view this, I was saved from the jaws of potential defeat in the continuing battle of my 'War of the Cold Caps' by the progression of more disease. It turned up in other areas of my bones which meant the current treatment needed to be aborted. I was to have some radiotherapy on the new sites which would be a lot more tolerable. Mr Verrill was disappointed – he had hoped I would last longer on this treatment. I, on the other hand, felt far more pragmatic; of course, it's always frustrating when I'm told there is more disease, but I'd reached the point of wondering if the whole blend of Skeletor and the Cold Caps were in fact killing me off, not the cancer and chemo at all.

I went home celebrating the day I left that ward for good. Skeletor was there to see me off; I gave her a huge over-the-top bear hug and a magnificent box of chocolates. She of course assumed it was because of the great patient/nurse bond we had developed. I smiled placidly and allowed her to believe so whilst harbouring the inner knowledge that the chocs and affection were more a symbolic representation of the inner party that was dancing in my soul at that very moment. She asked if I'd mind her asking a personal question. My palms began to sweat, my heart to race, my mouth felt like a badger's bottom, I pleaded with God that she wasn't going to ask if we could stay in touch. I nodded (what else could I do?).

'What's your secret?' she said. 'What makes you so happy and upbeat all the time?'

I felt terrible – if she knew what I'd been saying about her, what all my visitors said about her, heck, I'd even asked around as to what the complaints procedure would be if you felt a nurse was miserable and unprofessional. The only reason I didn't do it was because I could not have returned to that ward for the rest of the trial with her there. She might have put arsenic in my medicine.

'Do I?' I lamely answered, somewhat ashamed of myself for putting on such a good pretence to her.

'Yes,' she said. 'There's something about you, you have a sort of inner strength, a peace, that sort of glows from you. In the face of such adversity you remain so positive.'

Ah I thought, it's that 'thing'. It's a 'thing' that most Christians carry; it especially shines through at times when any ordinary human would collapse under the extreme pressure of their circumstances. It's called God. She'd seen something supernatural in me, a dimension that struck her as unusual and had intrigued her.

'Ah,' I sagely replied. 'I'm a Christian – it'll be my faith in God that you can see.'

She nodded excitedly and smiled the first genuine smile I'd seen amongst her usual sourness, stress and sinister responses. I began to have a few mushy feelings towards her; she was simply one of God's lost lambs. I'd been placed on this ward so that this very nurse could experience the love of God and believe! I'd never converted anyone to Christianity – this was my moment. Perhaps I was an evangelist after all? Perhaps the whole hospital would be converted when they heard the good news about the sour faced misery of a nurse whom they all avoided on the trial unit, who'd been seen dancing down the corridors singing 'Jesus loves me this I know'. I racked my brains trying to recall what prayer had been prayed over me when I became a Christian when I heard her say:

'I thought so,' she smugly responded. 'I just knew it. I'm a Christian too.'

I forced a smile and accepted her team spirited embrace. Trying to muster up a sense of 'family' with this woman; trying NOT to judge her on the months of poor responses I and my friends had received from her non-compassionate mercy. Judgment is a 'No No' amongst the Christian community; it's the polar opposite of loving your neighbour. I plunged head long into a slimy deep pit of judgement. How on earth could Skeletor be a Christian?

Not so Peripheral Problems

The weeks that followed should have been spent recovering from the recent treatment, but it became increasingly obvious that something else was lurking, preventing that from occurring. The itchy patches on my palms, shoulders and fingers were spreading at an alarming rate. After a few weeks both arms, both hands and sections of my back were prickling with itchy tingles. The worst thing about it was that there was nothing on the surface to see. Many times a day, as the problem became more intense, I asked Mark to look and see if he could see any lumps or hives that would prove this problem was not in my head.

It felt like 1000s of mosquitos had swarmed my body, bitten me, fed on my blood, attacking me with their proboscis, intruding my skin, searching for my blood vessels and filling my body with their nasty saliva. Irritating thousands of my nerve endings and causing me to itch and scratch until my skin bled. Day and night this went on, a burning and stinging developed as I scratched my skin raw; but frustratingly still no evidence of why.

Of course, I complained about it, but it was generally agreed that it was probably connected to the trial drug and would likely settle in the coming months. It showed no sign of retreating. Night after night my foot massages were replaced by Mark firmly rubbing with the palms of his hands the infected areas. It gave me some reprieve from attacking my skin with pen nibs, fork prongs or hair clips, which offered a sharper scratch than my nails could offer, but in turn shredded the surface of my skin. He did it for hours and hours until one evening I could not bear it any more. In pure rage and frustration I began slapping myself as hard as I could, discovering that if I caused myself severe physical pain it at least distracted me from the incessant prickling. I grabbed a glossy magazine and rolled it up whacking myself with the weapon I'd created, over and over again. Mark tried to stop me, but I'd gone mental with the torment that plagued me daily. Then I crumbled in despair, realising that it was not a solution, panicking that I may have to live in this state for the rest of my days. I hoped that those would not be many.

Whether it was that particular night or later I can't remember, but somehow we discovered that if I wrapped ice cubes in thin tea towels and numbed my burning skin then the sensation would go away. This of course had its issues, ice melting, constant replenishing, and more arms than an Octopus to cover every area. I wrapped both arms in wine cooler covers and Mark would press more on my back. It was blissful but unbearably cold. I'd have to wrap myself in blankets, adorn myself in woolly hats, thick socks, try and get the ice packs underneath my down jacket. Mark discovered a frozen gel pack contraption mainly used to cover the arms and shoulders of an American Baseball player if he'd become injured from muscle strain when throwing or hitting. It covered the entire shoulder to wrist area, velcroed firmly in place it offered better numbing than any homemade device.

This was clearly not a sustainable situation. When Mark was at work I struggled to freeze myself and took to stripping naked and taking regular cold showers or baths. I took long walks on the beach with hardly any clothes on; allowing bitter, chilling North winds and icy rain to lash in from the sea and whip my skin, trying to seek some reprieve. At night trussed up like an Arctic explorer, stalactites forming on my nostrils whilst I froze myself to the bone and poor Mark running around after me because I couldn't move. I wish I could create some humour out of the situation, but there's none to be found. It nearly caused me to lose my mind.

There's a down side to being a stalwart survivor: we don't complain enough. We just 'get on with it'. Nobody knows what suffering you bear because you don't tell them. You say enough so that people know why you may appear 'not yourself' as in not as buoyant as normal, but not enough as to muster too much attention. It's not a characteristic that is bad; indeed I believe it's largely something to be commended – people who seem unable to tolerate the smallest of difficulties are rarely admired and more often than not create a feeling of weariness in others. These days many people lack the ability to 'endure' anything. It's unthinkable that one might go to work feeling a little under the weather or that you may have to wait for the latest iPhone; not just slap it on the credit card which you only pay the interest off.

But the down side of being this way is that things have to get humanely impossible before you're able to complain at all. The danger in this is that it can cause you to suffer unnecessarily and may even be life threatening. What you see as strength is actually a weakness. My mum battled on with some alarming symptoms before she finally took herself to the doctor. By that stage the Ovarian Cancer was too advanced to allow for the option of potential cure. It was declared 'terminal' pretty quickly, a prediction of 'how long left' announced and it pretty much played out to the month. I see this in myself but am learning to differentiate between 'stalwart' and 'stupid'.

I took myself to Maggie's and broke down in a spectacular mess of snot and tears. Karen knew it must be bad and could tell by my clawed skin that all was not well on the inside. Pretty quickly I returned to Mark Verrill for a second consultation regarding this problem. He scratched his head a bit but the light bulb moment came.

'I think this is peripheral neuropathy, not caused by the trial drug, but caused by the chemotherapy in which the trial drug was mixed.'

The delay in diagnosing it had occurred because it wasn't a typical manifestation. Peripheral neuropathy is a result of damage to peripheral nerves but more usually causes weakness, numbness and pain in the hands and feet. It would be more common for the damage to be described as stabbing, burning or tingling, not as itching. It had been this that had thrown us off the scent assuming it was part of the trial drug and not associated with the chemo.

Here comes the killer. On further discussion it turned out that had it been mentioned and recorded as unusual when I was part of the trial then there was a strong possibility that the connection would have been made then. A simple solution to prevent it reaching the level it had reached would have been to reduce the dose of chemo I'd had. A tiny reduction at no risk to the potential success of the treatment would almost certainly have significantly limited the damage.

I explained that the tiny patches that I first complained about had been pushed aside by Skeletor, not even recorded because she believed my washing powder was the culprit. I was enraged. It was too awful to even face the suffering I'd endured due to her lack of attention to the strangeness I complained of. I complained and reported the patches on more than one occasion; her response always the same, a puzzled look – 'it's very odd' she'd say, but not once did that resonate with her as a cause for concern.

I considered again making a formal complaint about her, but I just couldn't be bothered. It was too much to take on in the circumstances. I never wanted to see her again and I hoped for her sake I did not bump into her in a dark hospital corridor. I could be reprieved on mental health grounds for what I might do to her.

I'd never be cured of peripheral nerve damage. I was given a drug that acted on the internal damage; it would take a few weeks for it to have effect. It may recede over time, it may not. As with most of these medicines different people react differently; there's no predicting how your body will manage. It would likely come and go for the rest of my life, another chronic problem to add into my already chronic challenges. Lucky me.

You left me breathless

The radiotherapy was successful on the areas of bone which the disease had spread to. I had a season of relative calm, if you don't include my mental children, my non-existent desire for any form of intimacy with Mark, and my obsessive drive to reach insane targets in my running. Yes, I'd say not a bad dysfunctional chapter if you compared it to some of the previous dramas. Most of my friends seemed to live with a not dissimilar daily experience, so all in all I felt more 'normal', which was very comforting. The gabapentin for the nerve damage eventually worked and I imagine this alone allowed me to get my head above the water for a while.

In 2015 I was seriously training for some races, a few 5ks and a couple of 10ks, one of which was the 10k Race for Life. I was extremely fit and in many respects the best I'd ever been, smashing the 5k park run most weeks with 22 minute times. Although the Race for Life is not an official 'race', its very title summarises a personal journey for all participants. People chase after their life or represent someone they love. They run, jog, walk, or are pushed and even carried, but symbolically they are showing people that despite what suffering they have endured they will not give up mentally, believing in life, living life and loving life. For me having hooked into this 'vibe' it had become a personal goal to cross that line first. Not to beat others or receive admiration but because I knew exactly how much effort it cost me daily, in my circumstances to run at all; so to win that particular race would be my personal reward and signify to myself that in the face of genuine adversity I was a conqueror.

As the Race for Life approached I began to feel increasingly sluggish, fatigued, and struggled to match the pace I knew I could achieve. Over a few weeks it became difficult to run 5k in 24 minutes let alone 22. On one particular Park Run I could see regulars passing me whom I usually didn't see for dust, I knew my pace was slower than normal, but I couldn't accept that it was anything other than a lack of effort. I knew it wasn't fitness because nothing had changed in my routine. I laboured up one of the hills rasping to catch my breath; I was on the homeward stretch and heard a runner coming up behind me. Normally that would spur me on to literally have a race on the last 200 metres of straight, flat promenade but on this occasion I had nothing left in me and watched dismally as I was passed instead.

The runner did not race past me. It was a guy, he pulled up beside me and slipped into pace with me rather than view me as competition. I sensed that it was an intentioned move on his part and I managed to turn my puce face towards him to ascertain what his tactic might be and couldn't avoid noticing that he was gorgeous! He was clearly in good shape and for a moment my legs lost the lead-like feel and developed little wings on which I momentarily flew on instead of lurching forward like a zombie, my knees buckling beneath me. I tried to wipe the crusty, dried saliva from the corner of my mouth and smeared the back of my hand under my nostrils to brush off the embarrassing 'old woman' nose drip that had been swinging there mixed with snot for two or three minutes. I thought 'wehey' I really must stop putting myself down, clearly, even in this state, I have 'Magnetism'.

Then he spoke, as in 'spoke', as in a non-struggling, exercise-induced gasping voice. 'Don't worry, I'm not coming on to you, I saw you really struggling and I'm going to run you home.' I wasn't sure how to respond to this and at the time with my body about to combust and my stomach doing back flips I just grunted something and tried to half lift a hand in thankful acknowledgement of his camaraderie. Run me home he did, like a pro. He took on my pace but ran just a stride in front so that I kept with him. A few encouraging words whenever I exhumed an involuntary pained snorkelling sound. Boy was I trying to hold those in and concentrate on lifting my knees from Zombie drag to fawn like elegance. We crossed the line, I stayed upright and had my barcode scanned with 'Demi God' ahead of me.

After I'd managed to stop retching, bent double with a perfect view of his Nike trainers, he said, 'I'm Gabriel, but I prefer Gabe.' What, I thought!? Gabriel! I knew people who claim to have seen angels, one of my friends sees one regularly and he even has a name 'Hector'. Could it be that an Angel stepped in to help me? Called Gabriel! As in THE Angel Gabriel? It wasn't beyond the realms of belief, particularly when you already believe in the supernatural. I gawped at him, to be honest I still felt like I was going to vomit so couldn't do much other than open and close my mouth like a dying fish. 'You sounded like you might collapse! Hope you didn't mind me helping?' I looked at him and began to see his supernatural Holy glow. He must have strapped his wings pretty tightly into his fitted Nike running T shirt because I could see no evidence of stray feathers.

I tried to mumble out that I didn't mind at all before he continued to explain that he usually ran the Park Run with his girlfriend (the angel concept began to crumble) in the centre of Newcastle, but he was recovering from a sport injury. His girlfriend wanted to come and try a different Park Run, so he'd just tagged along for a little jog as he was unable to run at his usual pace. He saw me and how much I was struggling, wondered if I was trying to make a PB and thought he might be able to help.

By this point I'd reached Mark who was waiting for me and Gabe's 5ft8, 20-something, long legged, tanned, swinging pony-tailed summer-kissed blonde hair held back from her beautifully proportioned face by a funky sweatband girlfriend had walked a few paces to meet him. She was really friendly and smiling at me so obviously a beautiful person inside as well as out and she listened as 'Gabe' and I explained why he was checking the pulse rate (I have put this in for dramatic effect – it's not true) of a scarlet, 5ft4.5 mid 40s, sweaty woman who no longer boasted a flat stomach and zero cellulite (that IS true). She chatted to me a bit and I explained briefly why I was in that state and she was lovely about all that too, as was he. He asked how she'd done – '21 mins 4 secs, babe – not my PB but still the first woman home today'. So clearly a selfless, modest person too because if I'd achieved that time I would have raced towards my hunky man, slammed him on the back and screamed my success in his face, punched the air for a few seconds and then dissected the whole 5k for him, raising my hand in a stop sign every time he attempted any sort of interruption and ignoring the dumpy sweating midget behind him who seemed to be stalking him. She was talented too then, crikey, some people have all the luck, don't they? We exchanged a few pleasantries and then they were gone, Angel Gabriel and his stunning attachment.

One day I was carrying some washing to the top floor of our three storied house. I had to stop three times on the way up. When I reached the final step rasping and wheezing like a 90 year old I sat down and faced the nagging voice inside that I'd been running from for a few weeks. The struggle to exercise, breathless if I climbed the stairs I'd climbed for years, and a slightly continuous dry cough that I'd began to wonder would ever clear up. A google session was needed. I made a cup of tea and sat in the silence of the house reading the words on the screen in front of me. I'd googled 'what are the symptoms of lung cancer'.

- A cough that doesn't go away
- Chest pain
- Hoarseness
- Infections such as bronchitis that won't go away
- Shortness of breath
- Feeling tired and weak
- Wheezing
- Weight loss

I went through them all and compiled a list and responded to my own symptoms in the light of each piece of information described here.

A cough that doesn't go away: well it was a big strong tick for that one. But that could be because I still have young kids and they're always bringing diseases home.

Chest pain: No. Hang on a minute maybe it had started to hurt a bit, but only when running, so half a tick for that one

Hoarseness: Definitely not, no neighing, whinnying and donkey behaviour going on with me.

Infections: No, unless you could include Thrush.

Shortness of breath: Tick, couldn't really come up with an excuse for that given how fit I was and I didn't smoke.

Feeling tired and weak: Four kids, of course I have to tick this one but it's all a bit grey here, so in the interests of this list on this occasion I think half a tick is my honest response.

Wheezing: I breathed deeply in and out a few times, and alarmingly heard a soft wheeze as I inhaled. I hadn't noticed it before but there was no denying its presence. I pondered this one for a while trying to decide whether I always had a slight wheeze. Breathing in and out a few times, willing it not to happen, but sure enough it was there. Barely audible, but certainly there and I could feel a small crackle on the inside almost as if there was some phlegm rattling around in my right lung.

Weight Loss: I wish. Big red cross for that one and a sad face.

Four ticks out of a possible eight. Typical 50% of symptoms I had but two of them were halves so they were not really complete ticks and could be attached to many minor life problems. I sat for a few moments and couldn't really feel that satisfied with the outcome of my list. I had been honest with myself, but unfortunately it didn't really pacify my unsettledness. You see this was a list of symptoms of someone wondering if they had lung cancer. I didn't have lung cancer, I had secondary breast cancer, and I knew that one of its favourite hiding places was the lungs. I knew plenty of ladies who it had spread to there, and although I wanted to believe it would never spread to my organs, the realist in me knew that it could and that it probably had.

Once I'd mentally made this transition I could not shut the door on it. On some level I'd known – there was in fact no other explanation for someone as fit as I was at that time noticing a distinct reduction in lung capacity which prevented me from running at a pace that I'd run at for a long time. Age, possibly, but surely you didn't notice a decline in fitness due to age over a few weeks? I was certain that it would be more of an insidious, creeping, almost barely perceptible slowing down before one day you catch sight of yourself in a shop window with a stick and wonder how it happened. Wouldn't you see other symptoms too like straining to read the TV guide and constantly berating the youth of today for being a waste of space? I didn't do those things, well not all of them, I had recently taken a pack of needles back three times because the holes seemed to be sealed up and I couldn't get the thread through. The kind lady in the Singer Sewing Shop eventually threaded one for me to prove they weren't sealed and suggested I get my eyes tested. It wasn't until a couple of years later when I could no longer make out the CVC code on my credit card unless I was in bright light that I gave in and discovered that I did have eye sight decline brought on by being a lady of certain years.

Whatever that list said or didn't say, I just knew. I kept it to myself for a week or so, not because I wasn't going to deal with it, but because it gets a bit wearisome always being the centre of attention in such a negative way. Knowing that all the questions are going to start and all the misunderstandings; people trying to be interested but not listening properly so they ask you the same thing every time you meet up. The rollercoaster of what treatment was next, not knowing if it was going to be tolerable or knock the living daylights out of you, again. Dealing with people's panic and drama; the shock, the tears, wrenching them out of the idyllic state they'd been living in that allowed them to forget you even have cancer because you're still smiling and met them for lunch last week and never mentioned it; well that's because you didn't ask, you just told me all about your problems. But now the shock, the horror and the gaping mouths as you declare your new spread and they behave as if they didn't even know it was possible. These days I find it all hilarious and am prepared for what comes and actually don't mind at all. Bless all you non sufferers of a chronic terminal illness; I know you do your very best. You're forgiven.

Mark was the first I told of my suspicions. He was gutted, not because he hasn't fully accepted that at some point this was likely to happen, but it's easier for him to be a bit more removed given that it's not happening in HIS body. It's easier to have days when he's not thinking about it, and easier for him to tap into a clearer view of a potential miracle. For him, every time I am told of a new spread he has further to drop than I do. I went through my list of symptoms for him and he tried to take a pragmatic view too, not unlike I had, but the true test for him is what I think. 'Do you think it's in your lungs?' 'Yes,' I said.

I already had a routine 'results' consultation in place to follow up my most recent routine scan. It was only a few weeks away so I didn't try and bring that forward in case it interrupted The Race for Life which was on the Saturday. The consultation was the Monday after; I'd been on this journey long enough to know that a few weeks made no difference and the likelihood was that the scan wouldn't be officially reported on. I know Mr Verrill would have looked at them early for me if I'd asked him to, but I couldn't see the point.

That attitude is horrifically amazing if I look back on where I started. The initial diagnosis had thrown my whole life upside down; the onset of secondaries brought worse turmoil, but each spread after that I had responded to with immense fortitude. I am still frequently asked how I manage to stay so stable in the continuous process I am in, but I truly believe that you would too. It's become a part of my life, my new 'normal'. I could never have imagined it would, but I've had to accept what I have and try not to see it as any more than an inconvenience. I had reached the stage where panicking about new symptoms was a thing of the past. I had a race to run, I wasn't going to let a bit of breathlessness stop me and I know Mr Verrill would think the same – he knew what I was like!

I'd made Mr Verrill laugh a few times at my somewhat blasé responses to new news; but also the way I self-managed drugs I was given. Take steroids, for example, no matter how small a dose I have, I KNOW that they send me loopy. I'm like a rabbit in headlights all day and all night. Every single doctor says 'No. A small dose like that won't affect you at all.' They do, they really affect me, I hate taking drugs and I will only take them if the pain is unbearable, which sometimes it has been. What makes Mr Verrill laugh, and raise his eyebrows, and shake his head in defeated submission, is when he asks me how I'm getting on with a particular drug. I say, 'Oh, I stopped taking that, erm, about three weeks ago. I felt it was time to see how I was without the drug so I stopped.' He'll look a bit alarmed. 'Don't worry, I did it slowly, I read the information inside and realised that if a doctor's consent was needed then I better take the weaning approach, and I've been fine.' I beam at him and he looks at me and says something like, 'I'm not saying anything because you won't listen anyway, you're like my wife.' He calls me Lady Rebekah now. I wonder why?

The day of the 10k Race came, I didn't feel my best but I was sure going to do my best. It was tough. There was this one lady who I'd talked to just before we started; she'd told me she'd participated in the Gateshead 10k a few weeks ago and achieved 48 mins something-ish. I knew I was better than that but possibly not in this state, but if I kept her in sight then it could be helpful for pacing. She was a few strides in front of me most of the way round, I kept her there to focus my attention away from my difficulty to breathe. I had not been able to run at this pace in any training runs due to the inability to catch my breath, so it was tough on my legs which had not been pushed for a while, as well as the control of my breathing.

We reached the last kilometre and I couldn't see the end due to trees and twisty paths but I could feel it was there. I wished Gabe was there to help me see stars and hazy mists but he didn't show up; it was all down to me. I spotted Mark in the bushes, not hiding or anything, just looking for me to cheer me on. He spotted me and yelled, 'Come on, you can do this in under 47' (my current PB) 'if you push.' I honestly thought I was going to keel over and be carried off in an ambulance, but the competitor in me, my desire to win, drove me home.

I played a game of cat and mouse with the woman whom I'd followed most of the way, her in front, me in front, back to her; not because I was toying with her but because I was slowing and struggling so badly that I couldn't hold my position. I bet she thought I was playing tactically, egg her on a bit so we could have a race on the last 100 metres. I really wasn't. In the Race for Life you finish where you start. I recognised the end was maybe 300 metres away. I could still not see it due to an acute bend before the final straight, but I knew how near it was. I had to give this everything I had so I sprinted the last section; it was so awful. I must have looked like a crazy woman, frothing at the mouth; face like an inflated beetroot, arms and legs almost grasping and flailing to try and gain more momentum.

I did it. Arms pumping, long strides, even passing a few women in the last 30 metres; fake smile, worthy of the finale in Chariots of Fire – Vangelis's theme tune playing in my head as I raced for my life. Sadly I didn't win, which had been my goal, and I didn't beat my PB; I did it just short of 48 minutes around position six or seven; winner did it in 44 or something. Monday morning in my consultation I listened to the news that 'the scan results show there is a tumour in your right lung'. 'How annoying,' I said. 'I would have won that frigging race if I hadn't been carrying that extra weight.' My response is actually in my notes. Mr Verrill laughed, as did his student. It's true though, I was more perturbed that I had been disabled by a tumour which had affected my pace than I was that I had just been told I had cancer in my right lung!

I started chemo for the third time. This time was a forever one, as in it was very tolerable and I'd be on it until it stopped working. As in, the cancer defied it. That could be anything from months to a couple of years, what did it matter? I'd never been someone who'd gone to the far end of a fart asking mountains of questions about potential side effects or percentage results related to the drugs success etc. I was just relieved that there was something available and Mr Verrill was rubbing his hands in glee at how fortunate I was to have developed cancer in my lung at that particular point in time.

I know, weird, who gets excited about chemotherapies? Well, seemingly Oncologists do. He's amazing, he really is, but occasionally his excitement over what drug he's got up his sleeve for you can feel a bit strange to witness. Those cartoon images of whacky scientists rubbing their hands together, crazy hair and white coats surrounded by bubbling coloured potions comes to mind. But it's because they're a breed of person who is driven to save your life. Mr Verrill is delighted when he has something to offer me that he knows is fully researched and proven to be very successful and he wants it to succeed as much as I do. Why? Because he is on my side, he wants to keep me alive for as long as he possibly can, because that is the commitment that his job entails. I asked him once, early on, how I would know if I was nearing the end of the availability of any treatment. 'I'd have my head in my hands,' he said. So when I walk into his room and he's on the computer or sat facing the door to greet me then I know I'm home and dry, for now anyway.

What a headache

By the time the chemo started in early August 2015 I was struggling to walk to the end of the street. I had a cough that went on and on and on, and my voice had begun to crack. It was scary how rapid the deterioration was; in the space of a few months I'd gone from running most days to struggling to walk 100 metres. The chemo began and the cough improved but was replaced by the most excruciating headaches I had ever had. I wasn't a sufferer of headaches so I can't say whether these were migraines or just a severe headache. They made me take myself to my bed and not be able to eat, which sounds like the description I have heard from migraine sufferers.

It was the start of the school summer holidays which was most inconvenient; we'd gone to visit some friends who fortunately were able to take over the children. Mark nursed me in darkened rooms when one of these ghastly evils took me over. I assumed they were connected to the chemo, they lasted for about an hour and they responded to over the counter medications, so I wasn't at all worried about them. They were just horrible and were spoiling my holiday, so I despised them purely on that basis. After the first few weeks of the summer break they seemed to stop. I was so relieved but they left me extremely tired and run down and skinny. I say that like skinny was a bad thing, but I have always relished this side effect of any treatment I've had. Like most women of a certain age weight is a battle for me; a set of daily decisions and choices to shut the lid on the biscuit box and eat radishes instead. If once in a while a bit of chemo or radiotherapy puts me off my food and allows the 'waif look' to return and that brings a small ray of sunshine into my daily suffering then who can take that away from me? Sorry if you think that's a bit of an odd thing to say but I have never professed to be sane, have I?

We went on our annual trip to Portugal and wham – those headaches hit me day and night like a railroad truck. I couldn't sit in the sun, I couldn't drink (alcohol I mean), and my appetite was very particular. So apart from looking shamazing in my bikini from the pounds I shed I felt horrendous; this was compounded by the fact that all I wanted to do was lie in bed and couldn't max out the beach effect as a size 6 – darn it.

Mark and I couldn't sleep in the same bed because I was up all night and painkillers didn't even touch the edges; even the sooper dooper max strength man dose extra human migraine ones. One lonely night I made the decision that I had to ring Karen as soon as it was sociably acceptable and tell her what I was going through. I watched the clock as the hours of night slowly faded, mutating into the soft colours of sunrise. 7.30 I gave in, I had to call. Karen answered as I knew she would. She knew we were on holiday and when she saw my number that early in the morning I knew she'd know something was wrong. The bonus of not being a moaner or a complainer is that when you cry on a long distance telephone call from your family holiday to the wife of your consultant at some ridiculously early time in the morning about your pain, then you get immediate attention.

A prescription of the dreaded steroids would be emailed to us and we could take it to the nearest Portuguese Chemist. The backlash to this prescription was the following: if they worked, I could expect complete relief; however, it would indicate that the disease had spread to my brain and I would need a brain scan as soon as I returned to Newcastle. I was desperate for relief but at the same time the familiar dread of what might follow began to wrap its misty tendrils around my heart.

I began the steroids and what do you know: within hours I was headache-free and flying high on more energy than a high speed train. Over the following days I remained free of headaches but behaved like someone on an overdose of amphetamines. Scrubbing the kitchen floor in a holiday rental villa at 5 am is not normal. Mark and I continued to sleep separately because of my incessant writhing and overwired brain that would come up with all sorts of topics worthy of discussion at 2 am. I was in the pool most mornings before 6 am and followed by a round of circuits, stair running and star jumps; the kids were practically begging me to allow them to sunbathe on the beach for five minutes and not have to dig another hole or set up more beach athletics. That was the one and only summer, out of a decade of Portugal holidays, that I did not open a single book or pretend to be asleep when the kids wanted to play. I jumped in the waves, swam in the sea, made running tracks on every beach we went to, built deep holes that I could have buried the entire family in and created monumental cities from sandcastles. I was on such a high that what awaited me in England was just a distant scene in a romantic watercolour.

Within days of landing I'd been scanned and found myself facing Mr Verrill in his all too familiar consultation room, waiting quietly for the news we were all expecting. When he said that my brain was clear I had to ask him to repeat it and show me the scan images. None of us could believe it: Mr Verrill, Karen, Mark, myself – we'd even asked our Pastor Alan along for extra support when we received the bad news. All my symptoms had led us to believe without doubt that I would be told that activity in my brain had been seen. It was the first time in a consultation, following new symptoms, that I'd been given good news. Mr Verrill shared that he also was astounded and had already decided what treatment I would try next. Instead of commiserations we went for celebratory cake.

Mark was really excited that I'd had a miracle of some sort; I wasn't so sure. He still believes that I did. Maybe I'm a lot more sceptical but I couldn't fully embrace his view. He felt that all the signs were there and yet on the scan there had been nothing. I'd even taken myself off the steroids much to Mr Verrill's exasperated mock disapproval, and still the headaches had not returned. I hadn't really been in close fellowship with God for a while so maybe that was why the concept of it being a miracle did not have as much impact on me as it did with Mark.

Whatever had happened I was really relieved. I didn't manage to have the huge slab of cream cake in the deli because my 'fat' radar told me to have minestrone soup. Clearly imminent death from cancer was now not on the cards. This removed the permission I needed to spend my latter days gorging on all the things I daily resisted. If I was to believe I'd be around for Christmas then I had to stick to minestrone soup, no bread, in order to fit into my party dress.

I'd told Mark years back that if I ever got the news that there was nothing else that could be done for me then I was sure as heck going to have a picnic that consisted of all manner of stodgy puddings smothered in whipped cream and washed down with Baileys on ice. I have such a sweet tooth and the capacity to consume more pudding than anyone else at a dinner party. As for chocolate, would it shock you to know that Mark and I once ate one of those massive round Celebration boxes in one night? Mark had gone up to the Spar to buy some broccoli and came back with one because they were on offer at the till. It wasn't even a special occasion, just a random school night. We ate the broccoli first – it's important to have your five a day – and then devoured the chocolate in front of the TV. I handle this lack of control by generally never ever having sweet treats in the house; one biscuit always turns into the whole packet and then I'm so disgusted with myself that I have to have three more packets for comfort.

Christmas 2016 loomed and I used the busyness of the festive season to make a decision to have a break from writing this book. All the reflecting and documenting on the past had started to depress me, trawling through the first year of perpetual trauma, and a life turned upside down in such a cruel and questionably 'pointless' way. I knew my Faith had grown and rereading parts of what I'd learnt was definitely encouraging and inspiring, but it began to exhaust me trying to remember truly and describe honestly everything that occurred and how I felt. I hadn't abandoned my faith, but I had certainly learnt that I, Rebekah Simpson, had a lot more strength of character and fight in her than I'd ever understood and the newfound me had slowly assumed the driving position in my life, somewhat replacing an obvious need for God's help. I didn't return to writing for quite a while; in fact, as events unfolded I was unable to.

I have a brain

January 2016, over a stretch of a few days I began to develop a desperate need to drink. No, it was not the final collapse of a battered and bruised cancer victim eventually succumbing to sneaking bottles of Gin into the privacy of the bathroom and swigging them back in desperate gulps. The need was for Water – pure, simple, preferably icy cold pints of water, no, make that buckets of water – at one point my greatest fantasy was a swimming pool full of water that I could swim around in all day and take mouthfuls of whenever I needed it. Initially I started getting up four-five times a night to alternatively pour a pint glass of Adams Ale down my neck and then within 45 mins peeing it all out, dozing off, then waking to repeat the cycle.

This very quickly cascaded into daytimes where I nearly mugged someone walking towards me in the street on my way home for their bottle of Volvic. I couldn't last more than half an hour before the obsession with the need to drink sent me running to the nearest source. It reached the point where I couldn't wait for it to run out of the tap – I'd just stick my head underneath and swallow desperately from the sweet nectar running and dribbling all over my face and down my clothes. Ecstasy. To make this all easier I bought litre bottles of water and lined them up – ice was on tap – bags of it in the freezer. I learnt the skill of 'downing' a pint, you lean your head back slightly. Open your throat, take a small breath before drinking then swing the glass quickly so that the water rushes to the back of your throat. You have to swallow just before the water hits your throat and gravity kind of takes over. Essentially, it simply pours down. One day I intend to use this acquired skill at a party and beat all the fellas. Good can come out of anything!

Mark took the kids out one afternoon and I drank and drank and drank – eventually I had to turn the TV off because any show that had people drinking in it drove me beserk. I attempted to lock myself in the bathroom. I sat on the floor with my knees up and my back to the door and I rocked, repeating over and over 'I do not need a drink, I do not need a drink, I do not need a drink'. I set targets. 'It's 3.30 – you can have a drink at 4.30.' I cleaned out the entire garage to try and keep myself distracted. But to no avail, I remained thirsty and after about four or five days of no sleep at all, sheer exhaustion forced me into telling Karen Verrill that I thought something was wrong.

I was in the hospital for chemo later that week when my consultant Mark Verrill, who'd been alerted by Karen, came to see me. He said he'd been scratching his head over my symptoms, he'd never come across them before, but he'd settled on perhaps something amiss with the signals from my pituitary gland. The pituitary gland is about the size of a pea and sits below the base of the brain just behind the nose and close to the optic nerves. It is the most important gland in your body for it produces many hormones that control much of the other functions of other endocrine glands. In my case, he wondered if there was some cancerous activity that was affecting the pituitary gland sending accurate information to my kidneys and telling me when I needed to drink or pee. A malfunction, he prescribed a hormone replacement called Desmopressin, and sent me on my way saying that if the drug worked it was good news because my symptoms would disappear immediately, but this was also bad news because it would indicate that there was something sinister going on and I would need a brain scan.

I have become very accepting of information such as this, I have learnt to stay focused on the present moment and not allow my mind to drift into the unknowns. I simply carry on with my life. I guess it's a sign that I have accepted cancer and this rollercoaster that I'm on and have developed the skill of living in the moment not allowing myself to panic about results not yet told. I wish I could translate this ability into the less important things in my life – strange that I can be calm in the face of a potential brain tumour but I nearly blew a gasket the other night because I'd asked Mark to prepare some roast vegetables for tea while I took Archie to Clarks for new school shoes. On arrival home he was wandering nonchalantly up the hallway casually calling to me that 'things hadn't exactly gone to plan'. By that he meant that he hadn't even started!

I could feel the tension rise in my throat and a surge of panic sweep over me. 'What can I help you with?' he irritatingly enquired. 'Nothing,' I said; 'leave my kitchen, I will do it, it'll be quicker on my own.' Brain tumour results I am calm, cool and collected – vegetable delay I am anxious, afflicted and angry.

If you haven't guessed already the desmopressin worked its miracle marvellously and within hours of taking it I was able to happily watch my children enjoy a drink with their meal without running over, wrenching the plastic cups from their grubby little hands and gulp it down in front of them as they looked on in wonder at this mad woman who had taken over their mother's body. I rang Mr Verrill and the wheels were put in motion for another brain scan.

And that's how I came to find myself **AGAIN** in a consultation room in the Northern Centre for Cancer Care, being told by Mr Verrill that the scan had shown there was indeed a tiny tumour nestling in my pituitary gland; I would be given radiotherapy and it would happen within two weeks. I asked if this was the end, could I plan my enormous creamy picnic, when it goes to your brain – is it game over? He said that was not necessarily true, and in the pragmatic manner of which I have perfected the art I did what I have done when being told of any news of spread in my body; I cracked a joke. 'Well at least I have evidence that I DO in fact have a brain.' Then I ask about the practicalities, and I begin to plan.

Brain Fry

Less than a week later I was summoned by a radiotherapy consultant. Mark didn't come with me, it was teatime on a Tuesday – a very busy night for us with football and pantomime rehearsals for the children. We'd been in this situation so many times now: you've been given the results, then you get told the treatment, length of treatment, side effects, risks. Mark always comes to the results but there's no need for us to go to all the hassle of finding a sitter for the children so that he can come and listen to the 'what's actually going to happen' bit. It doesn't faze me at all – in fact I've got so used to it that many years back I embraced it as some 'alone time' for me. I arm myself with Bella or Take a Break, two extremely trashy magazines covering real life stories around such things as wives going totally mental with their husbands and one night butchering them and discarding the head in a random wheelie bin that is dragged out by some mad dog and half eaten, or really thought provoking and intelligent debates based around such themes as 'would you want your kids in the room while you gave birth?' I settle down on the NHS chairs with a diet coke and escape into a world that puts my problems into some sort of perspective and certainly makes me feel huge gratitude for the peaceful, protected and almost 'party like' that my life often is compared to the desolate, despairing, dare I say it depressed people whose lives end in murder, abuse and tragic loss.

I remember this particular 'waiting' room experience because as I flicked the pages of the quality literature on my lap I began to tune into a conversation between a married couple in their 60s. It was a small window into how other people manage the journey of cancer.

'Make sure you tell them how many times I was awake in the night Alf, won't you?'

Her husband opens the lever arched file on his knee and leafs through the bulging, carefully plastic pocketed record and notes which I guessed had been started when she got diagnosed with whatever cancer she had. She must have been going for some time because by my reckoning this file was only going to hold a few more A4 sheets of information before file No 2 would have to begin – it was HUGE – they almost needed a pull along shopping basket to drag it around. Alf found last night's sheet and began to read off it to her while she corrected and interrupted and he diligently altered and edited whatever he was asked.

'12.05 am – you woke coughing, but soon settled.'

'1.14 am – you became quite sweaty and I changed your night-dress.'

'3.08 am – after 1 hour 58 mins of sleeping you woke and had a very bad coughing fit; you managed to cough up some green phlegm…'

'NO NO NO – that wasn't at 3.08, Alf, that was at 4.17 am.'

After about 20 minutes of this I had diagnosed her with my in depth medical knowledge and based on the serious documenting of all these nightly antics as being in the latter stages of lung cancer which she'd potentially been diagnosed with recently.

At some point in this detailed account of last night and my intense eavesdropping covered by my pretend 'Take a Break' masquerade, the radiographer comes out of the treatment room and they beckon her over. They begin to share their diligent document and as she questions them it becomes obvious that in actual fact she was diagnosed with early stage breast cancer, was successfully able to have a lumpectomy rather than mastectomy and no spread to lymph nodes, therefore extremely unlikely to go on to develop secondary metastasis and this was her third radiotherapy treatment out of a course of six. The radiotherapist reassured her that she was managing the treatment well.

The wife said, 'Alf, you better write that down: 4.55 pm 'radiographer says I'm doing well'.'

God bless them. Mark would have filled a whole library of lever arched files by now if we'd been wired like these two. But in that moment mixed up with my envy over the somewhat simplicity of her situation as compared to mine, a smattering of anger that All she had was early breast cancer and a smattering of amusement at witnessing how this couple chose to manage their 'tragedy', I was reminded again of how much of the detail I am able to leave with my God. I trust him with the details and listening to Alf's nightly note taking neurosis I was greatly relieved I could do so.

The door opened and the consultant radiographer called my name and beckoned me inside. Expecting to be told nothing other than how many sessions I would need and when they would begin, it took a few minutes to get my brain off that track and onto the words that were coming out of her mouth. She was explaining to me that because the scan had showed a tiny tumour in my pituitary gland they wanted to treat me with a very new form of radiotherapy called stereotactic surgery. It is the most minimally damaging form of radiotherapy made up of a three dimensional coordinate system that can locate tiny targets inside the body, in my case the pituitary gland, and then perform radiotherapy on that specific area and in doing so minimise or even eliminate damage to surrounding tissue. This was all very good news – having had radiotherapy four times I, more than anyone, understand the side effects from the damage done to other organs as the radiotherapy zaps through everything to hit the tumour. When I had radiotherapy on my spine the radiation passed through my body from front to back, straight through my stomach to hit the tumour in my 4th vertebrae. All fine – the effect on the tumour was fabulous – cleared it all out and future scans have only ever shown healing bone, death to the spine tumour, yippee. Effect to my digestive system – uh oh.

In a world full of discord and disputes sometimes we have to speak about the things that bind us to one another rather than break us apart. Sometimes these things are random acts of kindness and generosity and sometimes these things are random acts of the digestive tract – and in my case, a damaged digestive tract from exposure to radiation. The result: increased and chronic back draft, botty burps, breaking wind, grundle rumblers, gurglers, grunts, pips, puffs, pop tarts, squeakers, steamers and stinkers. In a word: lots of extreme farting.

Farting is part of the universal human experience and I have never been ashamed of it. Personally I find wind hilarious, particularly when elderly members of my family, not exactly 'open' about personal matters, let them drop by accident in my living room and then carry on reading the newspaper while my kids ask loudly who did it and hold their noses in disgust shouting 'errrrrrh, Archie, that smells like one of yours'. I have to leave the room find a hidden corner and cover my face to muffle my childish giggles.

Maybe you don't find wind funny – in my opinion that is an enormous shame for you. Perhaps before you dismiss fart humour as lowbrow and juvenile you should allow yourself to be caught up in this 'back draft', just allow the 'wind of change' to 'blow' through this section so that as you read you too can stand with some of the greats, Benjamin Franklin (founding father of the United States) or Louis CK (comedian) in saying 'You should fart proudly, you don't have to be smart to laugh at farts, but you have to be stupid not to'. Come on, bottom guffs are part of the universal human experience, they know no borders, every person from every corner of the globe breaks wind; loosen up, it is simply funny. Certainly funnier than cancer, that's for sure, so, I hope you can work a bit of this philosophy into your daily routine and give yourself some rippling good pleasure.

I'll leave this subject with a good place for you to start: next time you feel one brewing, pause, stand still and as you feel it about to erupt, say out loud 'listen to this – too good to miss…' And then blast it. It's a great skill to be able to time the end of 'miss' with the release of gas. Practise when alone so that when you're next at a party you can proudly amuse the crowds with your skills. One sign of how comfortable I am with a friend is when I feel relaxed enough to let rip in front of them and not fear their response. Have I done it to you yet? No? Maybe we're not as good friends as you think.

By the end of an average day I would look like I was six months pregnant, my stomach was so swollen with gas that all I could do most evenings was lie on the sofa and let them go. And boy did they hum. Poor Mark, every night as he massaged my feet he'd be blown away by the gale force power of blanket lifting, blasting, butt cheek flapping wind, poisonous, putrid and perpetual. Marriage – for better for worse, for richer for poorer, in sickness and in health – our marriage has been tested many times to the extreme of human endurance and believe me painful nightly flatulence that drowns out the sound of the Antiques Roadshow is definitely amongst one of our greatest private challenges.

So to hear the consultant start with some information about there being a type of radiotherapy that could potentially cause no damage to surrounding areas of my brain and therefore be a lot more tolerable was really good news. It rapidly went downhill: my 'Itsy bitsy teeny weeny tiny' tumour which was barely identifiable on the scan and was mainly proven to be there because of my peeing/drinking issue was only 4 mm away from my optic nerves. If they didn't get the measurements spot on I would almost certainly lose my sight – the risk was too great to proceed without further information which could be obtained in the form of the results from a deeper scan. If they felt the margins were too small they would NOT be able to perform the stereotactic surgery and I would be given full brain radiotherapy which is a lot more invasive, the biggest side effect being that I would lose all my hair – no cold caps could be used – it would certainly fall out and may only grow back in patches. The final punch was being told that it was illegal for me to drive and I would not be allowed to drive for two years following treatment and only providing I had no further spread in that time.

After she finished speaking there was silence in the room. I just looked at her; she looked at me. She broke the silence.

'It's fucking crap, isn't it?' she said.

For any of you who are totally anti swearing, and generally speaking I am one of those, I want to explain why I have not censored her statement. I have never heard any of the highly professional doctors and consultants swear in all the seven years I have passed through this valley. Not even a blasphemous 'God', a word that is not even deemed a swear word now, no different to saying 'golly' or 'gosh' or 'goodness'. They are well spoken, respectful and in actual fact rarely display an emotional response to the terrible news they've just delivered to you. They are professionally detached whilst exuding a silent care and compassion that helps you to remain calm, centred and trusting that their passion is to save your life. When this reasonably elderly consultant, top of her game, radiologist chose to summarise my consultation in this way I didn't think 'oh how rude and offensive', I agreed. That's exactly what it was. 'It was f*****g crap' – sorry but sometimes there are no other words. In that room another woman, possibly a woman with four children who knew more than anyone what this news was potentially going to do to my coming year, faced a young woman who had already been through seven years of indescribable loss, pain, surgery, and poisons and was facing more loss, pain, and poison and she simply spoke from her heart. It was exactly what I needed to hear alone in that room and if you're judging my acceptance of such language then it implies to me that you have not had to stare into a chasm of darkness such as mine.

This is the one and only time I have actually cried in a consultation. Although she had described the information in a very balanced and thorough way, all I heard was we get this wrong and you'll almost certainly lose your sight – we haven't had a lot of experience using this technology because it's so new – you can't drive – and if we decide this isn't suitable for you, we'll blam your whole brain, you'll lose all your hair and be very sick for months and months. Even for a hardened cancer battler like me this was pretty hard to take.

Over the next two weeks everything was once again thrown up into the air with no sense of how it might land. But unless you have an 'Alf' like interest in the boring details of when the scans happened and the hourly timings of my stressful nightsweats then I'll just move swiftly on. The only vaguely interesting thing worth spending a couple of sentences on was the creation of my 'gimp' mask, as I called it. An impression made of my head and face in a kind of yukky green, cream coloured, flexible silicone mesh that was covered in tiny holes but with a grotesque mouth cut out of it rather like the mouth of a blow-up doll and crude holes for eyes and nostrils. It had bolt holes on the sides that screw your head to the radiotherapy treatment bed so that when the machine blasts you with radiation you can't move, rather like a scene from Frankenstein's laboratory. The mask ensures that the radiation hits the precise places where the disease is, and you get the best blamming possible.

No matter how necessary it was, it was still freaky, but my kids would love it. I asked to take it home at the end of my treatment. The children have a day at school where they have to dress up as an alien – normally I'm scrabbling around the night before trying to create something original out of a cereal box, purple and green coloured clothes, tin foil and old teeny boppers (a type of headband with pompoms attached to bouncing springs that protrude upwards from the band – perfect for alien antennae). My costumes never even feature in the top 10 – it's devastating, the kids don't really care but when they come home and tell me that 'Gertrude won again' I sit sniffling over a mug of tea and curse Gertrude's parents who are so wealthy they probably have a tailor on Savile Row create the infamous winning garments for their little 'darling'; and then I recall all the times as a child when I didn't win or I wasn't picked for games, and the trauma is relived (have you picked up by now how competitive I am?). But next time, little Simpsons, this spooky darling is going to ensure that one of you will bring the prize home to Mamma, utterly unique, not to be made by any Savile Row expert or found in Smiths Toys or Argos, grotesque, green (well almost) and gruesomely alien like, 'come on, this one's in the bag'. I was ready to go, merely awaiting to be beckoned by the radiology department to find out the date I would start.

Blam the Whole thing

A few days later I arrived for my radiotherapy consultation expecting to be seen by a radiologist who would simply describe in more detail how long my treatment was going to last and give me the sheet with the dates and times I would arrive. Instead I was ushered into Mr Verrill's consultation room – my right hand man and stalwart companion in the goal of keeping me alive – and beckoned to sit down. I'm a straight talking girl and he's a straight talking man, but I'd barely perched my bottom on the edge of the seat before he began. 'I have your scan results. The deeper, more detailed scan has revealed multiple sites of disease in many places in your brain. It's pointless carrying on with the idea of a more focused treatment on the pituitary gland – we have to give you full brain radiotherapy.'

What was he talking about? I had tumours in my brain, everywhere. How had this happened? How had I moved from what seemed like a manageable little lump in my left breast to BRAIN tumours. It was surreal and it actually made me laugh – obviously not because it was funny, but because it was so insane and unreal and unimaginable. It's one of those places that you DO NOT want to hear the word cancer mentioned. I immediately thought 'this is it, my final card is about to be played, it's over'.

'Am I going to die?' I asked.

'Rebekah, we'll have to shoot you for **you** to die,' he replied. (Don't be alarmed at this statement – Mr Verrill and I share the same sense of humour.)

The following weeks were an example of how loved my family are and how 'kindness' is a virtue that, given the chance, many people possess and want to exercise it. I have to tell you about some of the people who sacrificed 'time' out of their own busy family lives to put myself and my family first at this yet again difficult time. Throughout this narrative I have mentioned specific people and how much they mean to me and some of those people stepped further up to the mark, but there were new additions. Some of you won't know them but this could be their only opportunity to ever have their names mentioned in print so it would be cruel of me to not give them their moment of fame! So, I'm going to shout them from the rooftops, write their names on the skyline. My heart was once again broken, all my scars had been opened, but the people who stepped forward made the 'impossible possible' (paraphrasing James Arthur, a singer – winner of The X Factor some year or other).

I love The X Factor, incidentally. My sister Sarah bought us tickets to go see the X Factor tour in 2010, the year One Direction came third. I remembered that date, didn't I – that's because I had a massive crush on Harry Styles. I screamed 'Harry, Harry I'm over here, I love you, Harry.' He definitely winked at me. Probably like most people I am fascinated by the truly untalented people who audition and obviously can't sing a note in tune. It taps into a personal fear that my friends and family are never truly honest with me, especially Mark. I am constantly asking him if my bottom looks big now; I used to have quite a pert little behind but as the years have rolled on it has become more 'dimpled' shall we say. Each time I ask he says 'No, dear' – I know that's a lie.

After my consultant's news I had to work out how we were going to manage for the weeks during and following brain blam. I like a plan; just as well really because goodness only knows how we'd have managed to keep our lives running if I didn't. I was preparing for about eight weeks of me being out of the picture, this was a full on preparation for battle – all practical bases had to be covered from the start to the end of the day. Mark had to continue his job with the hours he was doing and I wrote myself out of the picture entirely; easier to tell people I didn't actually need them than to be scrabbling around in a state of emergency last minute to find people who could step in. Being a bit of a control freak it's difficult for me to accept that I can't control everything. I had to accept that I wouldn't be able to control the events that might happen over the next few months but I could certainly take hold of planning who might be able to do it on my behalf. It was to be such a time of feeling the spirit of community and in many ways was one of the richest experiences of love in action that I could ever have imagined possible.

Some may see this as a lack of faith that God would provide for us when the time came, or maybe they would see it as the hand of a woman who had to have everything under her control. I would say it was the example of a person who had learnt from her journey that God takes care of the stuff I actually have no control over and I could trust him to handle the unexpected for me, but that it's my responsibility to take care of what I can.

I could use the parallel of money to illustrate this point: God gives us everything, it is all his, including whatever we earn. He asks us to manage that money responsibly, to give a portion each month back to him through the church, and to save an amount. The rest is for our bills and essential expenses. Whatever is left over is to spend as we wish on whatever you choose; I choose Gin and holidays.

When you live this way not only do you find you always have enough, you often find you have abundantly more than you need. God always rewards obedience and blesses you more than you could ever imagine, the more you give the more you get – it's MORE, MORE, MORE all the way with God. I could give many personal accounts of this happening we gave, but what we got back was ten-fold what we gave away. It may not always be a financial harvest that you get back, but God knows what we need at a specific point in time and he will pour that appropriate blessing out on you to bless your obedience in following the principle of giving the best of what you have first to him.

We had such a positive experience very quickly following this consultation and it somehow enabled us to believe that however bad things were about to get that we were going to be ok. Mark and I went out for a meal one night to a favourite local Turkish restaurant of ours. I had vaguely clocked who was around us where we were seated, you know, checking out if I knew anyone, which women were slimmer than me, what they were wearing, did they look like they worked out, that kind of stuff. I know, I know, so superficial and judgemental. No one caught my eye, so I could relax; despite cancer my outward appearance was doing ok in the world of other female 45 year olds. Who knows how we compared internally but sometimes that just doesn't feel like the most important thing even if in fact it is.

So, that left me staring across the table at my lovely hubby in silence. I've had a journey with the old 'silence' thing. I remember well pre-sickness and children, sitting across the table from Mark on many a night out, footsie, flirting smiles, and flowing conversation that later led to cuddling, kissing, and canoodling in romantic candlelight – what happened? Life happened.

At one time I felt uncomfortable with the silence; I thought it was a sign that we had reached 'that' dreaded place. The place I had observed pre-marriage in the naïve and idealistic vantage point of a 20 something watching married couples sit together in silence. I could only imagine it meant they'd reached a point in togetherness that was constantly tedious; complete boredom was what they now shared. They dragged their dreary relationship and world weariness into the restaurant and could only manage to sit in extreme apathy looking across the table at the one who 'once upon a time' lit up their life; but now all they share is dullness, detachment and the dirty doldrums. It would never happen to me. I would talk about 'anything' rather than be silent, and would even create an argument rather than have nothing to say.

'Why aren't you talking to me? Are you bored? We used to have lots to say, what's happened to us?' and on and on I'd go until a bickering session would fill the space, but at least we were talking. Honestly, I was, I still am, such a crackpot.

But here I was gazing at Mark in complete silence, I felt so grateful that I had my best friend in the world with me. The only person in my life that I am able to be silent with. I've learnt that silence is pure, and peaceful. When I was younger I was so insecure and had to break the silence with anything, but I have come to see that constant chatter is a waste of a dimension that has a quality all of its own. I LOVE being with Mark because I feel so safe that I can shut up and relax in the silence.

We finished our meal and asked for the bill, but she said 'your bill has been fully paid by the couple who were sitting behind you, you owe nothing'. We didn't know them, we didn't speak to them; we could barely remember them. I do not know why that couple paid for our meal, but what I do know is that from the weary walk we were on, this act of kindness from complete strangers lifted us sky high. We have continued to experience such kindness from others despite the demanding journey we seem to be on forever. Giving to others holds such a blessing for oneself. We have raised thousands for cancer charities, and continue to give support financially to people who are in need. We don't do it to 'get', but this experience in the restaurant felt in some way to demonstrate that you do indeed 'reap what you sow'.

God promises that if we concentrate on blessing others, he'll take care of our needs. Luke 18 says that God guarantees this blessing: 'I guarantee this. Anyone who gives up anything for the Kingdom of God will certainly receive many times more in this life and will receive eternal life in the next world to come'. You cannot out-give God, in the giving game God will always win. The monetary aspect of this illustration had a value to us because we don't need someone to pay for our meals, we can comfortably pay for our own. God gave us over and above what we 'needed'. Probably more important was the spiritual aspect – God knew we needed a touch from him to encourage us to lift our faces heavenward and KNOW that HE was still with us. 'Give and it will be given to you. A good measure, pressed down, shaken together and running over into your lap. For the measure you use, it will be measured to you' (Luke 6:38). I really needed a physical sign that despite my recent wanderings God was very much present in our lives. We didn't walk out of that restaurant, we skipped, we were flying high, we had wings, we soared home with renewed strength and joy filled our hearts.

When you live life from a position of knowing that God is in control, obviously one wanders away from this concept from time to time as I myself have admitted to you, but fundamentally you do return to knowing that I owe him everything. Therefore my position will always return to trying to obey him in ALL matters; this looks like physical practical choices in my life to follow God and listen to the Holy Spirit. When I do that, at the right time, I am assured of reaping a rich harvest. The principle works in any area of life. God had given me a family and my responsibility was to serve them and provide for them as best I could in all circumstances.

It was my job to get on and make the family work even if that meant temporarily replacing me with others. It was not an option to avoid that responsibility and foolishly hope it would all work out; weeping and wailing and falling to the ground, gnashing my teeth and pulling my hair out in self-pity, or to sink into a deep dark hopeless depression blaming life, myself, other people and so on and so forth. I HAD to simply walk ahead and make it all happen, trusting and hoping that help would come as and when we needed it.

I started with the main issue, the children. Once Archie had started school, Hannah had moved on to other employment, although she continued to help out on a Saturday. Mark leaves for work at 6.45. I needed people to come in every morning, get the children up, dressed, fed, and out for school. Mark picks them up Monday, Tuesday and Friday, but Wednesday and Thursday are his London days or very late back days, so I needed commitment for a school pick-up and help until they went to bed two days a week. The next issue, food; you can survive off frozen meals and takeaway for a week or so, but one-two months did not feel like an option to me. I needed meals on wheels – people who could daily bring the food we needed and were happy to take the world's fussiest eaters' needs into account. I hate to see waste; a wonderful lasagne made with lots of love could easily have ended up in the bin because someone added chunks of pepper or the onion was cut too big. So, I needed caterers with thick skins and be able to please the taste of four of the world's pickiest Master Chef Judges.

With the exception of my younger sister who lives round the corner with a young family of five, neither Mark nor I have any relations nearby and therefore had no choice but to turn to friends for help. I began approaching people who I knew would be right for the jobs. There were only a tiny few who could cope with the children in the mornings, and not that many more that I felt comfortable enough to be specific about the food. Within two days the perfect people had come forward, tried and trusted friends and my elder sister who was prepared to travel from Carlisle every week to do an early morning. I had all my needs sorted and felt a huge sense of relief. I had done what I could, I'd planned and covered the crucial components, and felt hugely blessed and grateful for how easy that was. But there was to be far more provided for us than basic morning school runs.

As the news of my situation became known locally there was a tsunami of people offering help. I had sorted what I saw as being essential and Mark and I would cover everything else somehow, but it was not to be. I rarely rely on anyone else to do things for me. I come from a position of assumption that I am capable of whatever I set my mind to and that others or life owe me nothing. Up until this point Mark and I had largely managed whatever practical challenges cancer had thrown at us. Of course, we'd had help over the years but largely we were capable and astute enough to stretch our boundaries, be it financially, emotionally, mentally, spiritually or physically to master the challenges that we had faced. We were still expecting and prepared to live this way for the coming few months no matter what it entailed. I believe God put everything in place for us so that every single tiny detail of our home life was covered far more than we asked for or even felt we needed.

The hall of Fame

Jo and Emma

My friends Jo and Emma set up and co-ordinated an online care calendar for us that created a care community of local friends who could sign up to different tasks on particular dates. These covered meals, cleaning, laundry, lifts to and from hospital, or children taken to activities such as swimming, gymnastics, football etc, gardening and more. Beds were going to be changed EVERY week! I did challenge this one and confess that my beds didn't normally get changed every week, more like once a month, but the two yummy school mummies Jo and Emma who volunteered for this job insisted on it. At this stage no one listened to anything I said anyway; the running of my life had been taken over by a host of extremely focused and diligent busy bees and I kept being told to 'let it go, let it go, you can't hold us back anymore'. It seemed that they felt it was essential with me potentially being sick and all that I should have my beds done weekly. I quickly learnt to agree and as my sickness developed I was extremely grateful for their weekly smiling faces, humour and compassion – they were angels. Apparently a number of people had been scratching their heads for a long time over how they could support me or help; this was the first chink in my armour they had seen, so they took advantage of my weakness and muscled in with their helping hands.

I absolutely suffer from 'Independent Woman Syndrome', I'm not easily influenced by others in matters of opinion or conduct; I can think and act for myself, thank you very much. And in many ways, not all areas of my life, but many, I like to be free, not especially subject to another's authority or jurisdiction. The world is an exciting place and I like to question and challenge that. This hasn't particularly been an issue between Mark and I because we largely see eye to eye and we have very different roles that play to our natural abilities and skills. We know what those are and we allow each other to be in charge of what we do best and submit to one another's judgement in those things. I like independent women, I respect them and it's definitely something that would catch my attention and make that woman an attractive proposition as a friend.

But of course it has its difficulties. I applaud myself that I'm not a burden to others in any way at all and that I handle my life correctly on my own. The problem is that the natural default to independence can mean that you make things harder on yourself when you actually do need help and are being offered it. Friends and loving community are there to lighten your load and help you in times of need, but when you've lived an entire life of 'doing things on your own' and making a pretty good job of it, then it's no surprise that I found it very difficult to allow others to step in. Sadly, I also confess to the despicable traits of a teensy weensy bit of arrogance; my aforementioned leaning towards needing to be in control doesn't help either.

Independence, arrogance and control – wow, what a nasty cocktail. I'd like to move quickly over these three admissions with a simple sentence summarising why it was difficult initially to say yes to the helping hands community. 'I CAN DO IT WITHOUT YOU' (independence); 'I CAN DO IT BETTER THAN YOU' (arrogance); 'I CAN DO IT JUST THE WAY I NEED IT' (control). In the words of Frank Sinatra 'Yes, there were times, I'm sure you knew when I bit off more than I could chew. But through it all, when I had doubt I ate it up and spat it out. I've faced it all and I've stood tall and I did it MY WAY'.

'Let go and know that I am God. I rule the nations. I rule the earth and I rule daily life, Rebekah, in your home in Whitley Bay' (Psalm 46:10

– obviously the Bible doesn't specify the bit about my home). All these willing people had been in my life so that at such a time as this if I could let go, become dependent, humble and abandoned to others so that they could be the hands, feet and bodies that covered all my practical needs. I could simply focus on my health and claw back time for the children rather than spending precious time on chores. I simply had to focus on myself during what became the most horrendous experience I had yet had, but of course I wasn't to know that yet.

So, I had to decide, who was going to remain in control and that choice was a battle, but sensibility won and I handed my life over to the volunteer co-ordinator of helping hands aka weekly bed changer and life savers Jo and Emma. We had a key safe fitted so friends could access my property freely to carry out chores, no need to knock, access all areas; just a request that they shout loudly on entry in case I was performing my pole dancing routine for Mark. A matter of days later I was looking at my life mapped out on a computer screen as to who was doing what and when and even emergency back-up people if the first person was sick. It was weird, but I'd made the decision to let go and had to roll with it, trusting that it would turn out to be another part of my life journey that would no doubt bear much fruit in time. I decided I might as well embrace the new 'me' and had a bell placed by my bedside so I could beckon my servants when I needed them. I had no idea what 2016 was going to unravel and how much I actually needed all these helping hands.

The Maggie girls

Jill, Nic, Lyndsey, Gemma *and* ***Ruth***
(you've been named, ladies – fame is just around the corner)

September 2nd 2006 was our wedding day. We'd hoped it would be one of those hot, sunny autumn days, the leaves just beginning to turn on a few trees and only a few blackberries in the hedgerows remaining, having been picked to bare by passing ramblers and hungry children looking for the dark, plump succulent treasures hidden amongst the thorns. I had visions of beautiful photos taken in that low warm light that early autumn brings and is so beautifully described in this quote from a poem by Keats entitled To Autumn – 'Season of mists and mellow fruitfulness, close bosom-friend of the maturing sun'.

Think monsoon and that would be pretty near to the weather in Carlisle on the 2nd September 2006. No romantic mists or mellow fruitfulness and no sunshine at all, let alone a mature one. I'd have settled for a weak sun, cloud covered, showery interval type of day over what we got. It was literally stair rods from early morning until it was dark and all outdoor photo opportunities were long gone. All the wedding photos are of people huddling closely together in a doorway of one description or another. Dresses wet with a dirty tideline seeping a few inches up from the ground and hair flat, damp and sticky from sodden hairspray, dilapidated sad-looking flowers hung their heads under the constant hammering of the relentless downpour. It didn't dampen our spirits, though, we laughed and loved and looked forward to life just as wedding day couples do who are blessed with clear blue skies and bright hot sunshine, damn them all.

If you're a smart Alec you'll have realised that if 2nd September 2006 was our wedding day then 2nd September 2016 would be our 10th anniversary! Which felt like an anniversary worth celebrating especially after the decade we'd just had: we'd survived the death of my mother in 2006 which was sadly only months before the wedding, so she didn't actually make it; three children; cancer; an unexpected 4th child; lots of fundraising interspersed with more and more and more cancer; we still loved each other; we still loved God; and we still laughed. That is worthy of a celebration getting all the people we knew and loved into one place and having a bash.

Previous to the news on my brain I had already put the wheels in motion for this grand party; Karen had very kindly agreed to me using the Maggie's Centre for the event. It was the perfect venue: I'd spent so much time in there over the last three years since it was built, receiving support and giving support at times of need and times not of need but just because I like it and like the people there. It's on the same site as the Northern Centre for Cancer Care (NCCC) and had provided so much free, practical, emotional and social support to me and my family and friends. The Maggie's Centres are the legacy of Margaret Keswick Jencks, a terminally ill woman who believed that the journey of cancer could be greatly improved for people if they could hang out in a more private, light filled space whilst waiting for test results, and be surrounded by loving people and beautiful artefacts and gardens. Each centre is different, but a similar ethos is provided – carefully chosen and comfortable rooms decorated with calm, serene but modern and local artwork, where you can meet a friend, speak to a volunteer or go to sleep are on offer. The central kitchen area is homely and welcoming, a large table for people to sit around and read the paper, meet others or view with pleasure the sheltered courtyard garden as it flowers and changes colour through the seasons. It's amazing and many of the people in my life knew I went there but couldn't possibly have any idea what life saving provision it was. It was the perfect opportunity for them to tap into the facility that had given me so much help.

My intention, had multiple brain tumours not come knocking at my door, had been to use this special day in our lives to pull on people's heart strings yet again and raise lots of money for Maggie's. A raffle, cake sale, a band, food, games for children; I saw it as an afternoon event that would spill over into the evening, people could come and go and the vibe would change but in essence I'd spend a day fleecing people for charity using our anniversary as an excuse. I might be lucky this time and have the hazy, dazy, lazy September sun that didn't turn up for my wedding day, but could do this time and guests could wander in the Maggie's garden amongst the late blooms and the sleepy bumble bees.

With the inconvenient interruption of multiple brain tumours, I wondered how I was going to achieve this idyllic fantasy. In actual fact in the entire year that followed I didn't lift a finger towards any of it. A group of big hearted, committed and loving mums from school who became affectionately known as The Maggie Girls took it over entirely and made the whole thing happen and exceed my expectations. On top of that they took it upon themselves to organise a raffle that blew everyone's mind. They were a force to be reckoned with, a military operation that stopped at no obstacle; they tanked on with a single mindedness that was frightening and raised around £10,000 pounds for the Maggie Centre on behalf of me.

Watching them do this for me was phenomenal; these ladies gave up valuable time from their own families and chose to ride the train of my life for a while. I will never ever be able to thank them enough. And not only were they doing the raffle but a few of these ladies were also helping me out weekly with laundry, after school childcare and cooking. It makes me cry, such love in action, I can never ever repay them.

The Wing Women

***Sarah, Betty, Mrs D** and **Claire** (here's your mention too)*

My emergency last minute.com – masters of everything, refusers of nothing, they always find a way to help me if they can and if they can't they find a way around it. These ladies have known me a long time; very little reserve stands between me and them. Put it this way, I feel comfortable enough to break wind in front of them and then carry on talking. In my mind, that is the ultimate in feeling loved and accepted in a friendship. I'm not sure they would agree but they're still around, aren't they?

One of these women almost daily made herself available to pick up any last minute jobs, she was my Girl Friday, my beck and call girl, my dear sister Sarah. Her previous nursing vocation meant she was willing to do absolutely ANYTHING, even check that the protrusion from my bottom was piles and not an outward growing tumour that in my deluded cancer fearing state sometimes I became anxious about.

Another reorganised her work life so that she could come skivvy in my house every week. The lovely Beth, every week she came and would do absolutely anything I needed, no job is too much, no request too great. She and her husband Richard love my unruly kids and regularly offer overnight stays and holiday entertainment and their son Jo who Archie has a bromance with.

Can you believe that Jackie had her hair cut off for no other reason than to demonstrate her solidarity and understanding for what I was going through? I don't think I would do that for someone. I decided to have my hair cut very short BEFORE I started treatment I didn't want it to fall out in clumps, or strands to be found on the pillow, or become all thin, wispy and witch like. This wing woman came with me and had hers cut very short too. What can I say? What a friend. She too extends to cook, cleaner, jet washer, junk remover, early morning child minder armed with muffins and chocolate chip cookies – for breakfast! The kids loved it. She also introduced eggy bread to them which has become a fixed Wednesday morning treat; only I insist on it being wholemeal, my tribute to healthiness amongst all the fried butter.

And the mass catering that one of these friends has done for me is unbelievable. Claire would make batches of portion sized meals for me, always bespoke and to fit in with my dietary needs. She'd pack them all into take away containers and let herself into my house and put them in the freezer. Always thinking ahead as to how she can help, a lift to hospital for a long session of treatment would include lunch too, homemade soup in two little flasks, with spoons, and even sides of buns or bean salad in little pots.

All these ladies have been so faithful for so long, they spot a problem and they're on it. The list of things they turn their hand to would take thousands of words and I have hundreds of examples of the many ways they demonstrate love and friendship to me. They've been committed from the start and I know they'll be there until the end.

There are many other people who upped the ante at this time to put their loving arms underneath our lives and carry us to a better and brighter place. Other friends and family whose own lives meant they were restricted by their own struggles to help practically with ours, or who lived too far away but who thought outside the box.

My friend Dawn definitely deserves a mention. She is the sweetest, most thoughtful person a girl could ever hope for as a wing woman. I met Dawn when we lived together in a rental property as young postgraduates. We hit it off immediately and would spend hours sharing our souls and pondering if we'd ever get married. We had bedrooms next to each other (I had the small one, Dawn had the massive one with a bay window – just pointing that out, Dawn). When it got too late to continue chattering in the communal living room we'd move to our bedroom and lean out of the windows talking until the sun began to rise.

She lives the other end of the country from me now, but she has been so faithful in being involved in every part of my life. Phone calls that always make me laugh, cards, flowers, letters, and in the midst of my recent trauma paid to have my favourite monthly subscription of a magazine delivered to my home; she always brightened my days with reminders that I was loved.

One Final Laugh: Nicola

April 6th – the only specific date I'll ever be able to share; I only know it because it was the day after Mark's birthday. My 'Lotsa Helping Hands' designated driver Nicola Booth had picked me up and we were sitting in the waiting room of the radiotherapy department in the Freeman Hospital. Nicola is one very special person in my life, a friend from decades ago, first acquired when she joined Hotspur Primary School where I'd been teaching for a few years; I was around 25, so probably about 20 years ago. We clicked straight away, we're both straight talking, expressive, passionate and compassionate people, same sense of humour, and boy could we talk. Sometimes my jaw has to work so fast just to keep up with Nicola that it literally aches after a few hours. We ramble away, dissecting life and people and stuff. We've gone through a lot of personally difficult and traumatic chapters over 20 years and have weathered many painful storms and we're still going strong.

I can't recall at which point in my cancer journey Nicola presented me with a cheque for enough money to pay for Mark and I to fly to Spain. She had organised with a close friend of hers to allow us to stay in a villa she owned there. We even had spending money, and childcare had all been arranged. For months she'd secretly been gathering all her friends, who had never actually met me, but were willing to raise money via Nicola's many mini money-making fundraisers that she organised in order to send Mark and I off for a break in the sun, child-free, cost-free and planning-free because she felt we deserved it. I love her to bits, she's barking mad, can be as crazy as a bag of squirrels but she is one amazing person and friend.

I don't see Nicola that often – she lives over the other side of the city where she still works part time as a teacher and is an amazing single mother to two teenagers. Unsurprisingly because she's so friendly, warm and caring she has lots of friends who are at a similar place in life to her, so can still do things in the evenings like go to pubs or concerts, which only exist as dusty, hazy memories in my life. We've adapted over the last seven years to meeting up during the daytime, our most regular haunt being the hospital where we'd blend friendship catch up time into the hours I often sat around waiting for an appointment of some type.

Here we were sitting together, she hadn't seen me since I'd had the final news about the full brain scans – of course we'd texted but there were a lot of details to fill in.

I have Nicola's permission to share this little story in case as you begin to read you think I'm being irreverent to someone's pain, because I'm not. It was a source of much needed hilarity on a level that I certainly hadn't expected to be having on the first day of my brain blamming. It has forever given me a funny memory of that date and we still laugh about it now as does everyone I share it with. We'd maybe been talking for about 10 mins with Nicola trying to get to grips with what I'd been told and how I was going to be affected when she began to become very emotional. I asked if she was ok. I know Nicola deeply cares about me and worries about me a lot, and she's somewhat out of the eye of the storm because she doesn't have any connection with the more regular people I see in my daily life such as mums from school or church people. She has to wait sometimes months to see me in the flesh and then get all of the details of what is going on. These meetings are often quite soul-stirring because Nicola is a very passionate, responsive and loving friend. I gently flagged up and confronted her distress that she was attempting to swallow down and of course this simply allowed the floodgates to open and she began to cry.

Once it started it wouldn't stop, gasping gulps of tear-filled sorrow came gushing out. I took her arm and began to reassure her that everything was ok, I was going to be ok. We were seated in an open waiting room with about 30-40 people awaiting treatment for cancer too and a busy footfall of others walking down the corridor. Two nurses passed who clocked the situation and very kindly and gently approached me and asked if we'd like to use a private room just up the corridor. I asked Nicola if she'd prefer to go to this private space; her words were not legible through the snot and gasping but she nodded and began to get up. The nurses showed us to a small empty room and said that they'd inform the desk of where we were. 'What name should they give?' 'Ann Simpson, grrrrrrr' – I'll always have a moment of irritation when my 'not name' has to be conveyed.

The nurses took me and Nicola who continued to cry all the way up the corridor, and deposited us in a private room until all the tears ran out. I didn't mind at all, I prefer people to be real and express themselves honestly. I'd rather an outburst of tears from a valued friend than the stiff upper lip, unemotional, hard hearted, 'never mind – it'll all come out in the wash' approach that shockingly I STILL run into. There was a soft knock, the nurse had returned and popped her warm face round the door. She looked at me and said gently, 'Is Ann ready now they've called her name?' Me and Nicola looked at each other and howled with laughter. The nurse looked a bit puzzled – she was obviously dealing with some right loons here, she left one having a breakdown and now she's watching us fall off our chairs screeching with laughter. I managed to explain that I was in fact Ann – this was Nicola, my friend, it was me who was having the treatment, and Nicola had come along to support me! This set off another ream of laughter, the nurse joined in and the three of us stood outside that room with aching sides; the scenario had so much comic value in it, I loved it. Thank you, Nicola, for making such a happy memory for me, it's made me laugh out loud again today and will continue to do so forever.

Hell On Earth Begins

By the 3rd day of full brain radiotherapy I was feeling nauseous constantly, I could only eat lemon sherbets and drink ice cold water. I lost 5lbs over the first weekend (every cloud has a silver lining, eh). The fastest weight loss diet EVER presenting 'The lemon sherbet diet'. Day one, a dose of radiotherapy followed by four lemon sherbets, one for each meal. Continue this process for three weeks and lose anything up to 14lbs. Not a diet that I imagine will have many takers. By the end of the first weekend I was vomiting constantly, or should I say retching because I hadn't eaten for four days; the safest place to lie was the toilet floor where on one tragic occasion Evie discovered me. I hate that my children had to see me like this: pale, hollow eyed and haunted. She stroked my back and held my hair while I puked into the toilet bowl. My 9 year old should not have to tend to her debilitated, declining, diseased mother. It's tragic and it breaks my heart. There's nothing more to say.

We had to ring the emergency telephone number and explain my situation. I do not give in easily or cry wolf or make a fuss over nothing; I dislike making contact with the hospital outside of scheduled appointments because there's inevitably a long process where you are passed between people until SOMEONE is found who is entitled to make a decision about what to do for you. It takes time and believe me the last thing that I want to do is spend ANY extra time in my life on this wretched disease and hospital – between them they've taken more than you could ever imagine. It has to be dire for me to ring and ask for help but the way I felt was unbearable.

Imagine you'd been at a three-day festival living it up 24/7. All day singing and grooving, hands raised to the bands, dancing like you just don't care. Eating an array of street food any time of day or night, moist pulled pork with sweet vinegar slaw, melting halloumi and avocado burgers, soft salmon fish fingers with wasabi mayo, Massaman curries smelling sweet and hot, drinking a little more beer than you know you should.

You've had a blast, but then you come home and the lack of sleep whirling twirling gyrating irregular eating and the overkill on alcohol begins to hit you. Body dragged through an army assault course, aching in places you didn't know you could. Head hurting like a hundred hammers hitting, hard stomach bloated, gut churning, skin grey, eyes heavy, deprived, dissipated and depressed. This is how I felt but with no fun or frolics at a festival to tell of.

Late that Saturday night lying on the bathroom floor, I waited while Mark drove to the hospital to pick up some anti sickness drugs. I felt despair, total and utter despair. I had been told I 'could' be bedridden and unwell, but I had not been prepared for this. The drugs stopped the vomiting but there was no return of appetite and the nausea was persistent and present at all times. Steroids made sleep illusive and sporadic, my body and mind craved rest and recuperation which seemed out of my reach. I dragged my geriatric, sickly, skinny, emaciated body through the hours that seemed to drag on, my skin burnt and blistered, bald as an eagle, exposed, vulnerable, feeling barely alive.

I had to repeat the process Monday to Friday for three weeks, fifteen sessions in total, each one more gruelling than the last. I had to endure the weird conversation of one young assistant radiographer:

'Hi, what have you been up to over the weekend, been out anywhere nice?'

It was hard to answer this question given I could barely get to the toilet. So I answered her in a joking fashion: 'Yeah – I was out on the toon' (Geordie for town) 'on Saturday night, dancing, twerking on the dance floor until the early hours.'

'Oh great! Where do you like to go?' Honestly, was she for real? I mean even without cancer I don't look like an obvious party girl.

It took only six days for my children to stop running up to see me when they came in from school. Occasionally one of them would pop their head round the door but largely they adjusted quickly to life without me. It's not the strongest species who survive but those who are most adaptable, and it would seem that my children are very adaptable. I had a glimpse into what life would be like in my home when I died; guess what, they'd all be fine. The stars would continue to shine and the sun and moon would push time on, the tides would still turn and their lives would continue to grow and change without me.

Should I have been happy witnessing their ability to accept life so simply, the laughter that resounded throughout the house almost mocking my suffering? Maybe a better person would move into such a spiritually elevated place. As for me I had not reached that mature and selfless place and I simply felt blackness. I'd had a ghostly glimpse, pre death into the space I had vacated – it left me falling into the depths of my own mind-created grave.

Of course, one can rationalize now that in my debilitated state I was simply reading their behaviour in a very negative way and of course they were incredibly sad. I'm sure there would be tears and grief and wailing and mourning and maybe even a bit of gnashing of teeth and as their lives developed they would have times when they re-visited the early loss of their mother and so the grief becomes uncovered again and so on and so forth. But despair is a terrible thing and this was my first experience of it. The complete loss and absence of hope is a frighteningly dark and lonely place to be and by far this was the worst I had ever felt.

Many people came in and out of the house making my home function as they had planned and committed to. Of course I was grateful but as I lay in my darkened room and listened to people clattering around living normal lives, lives that I wanted, it fed that creeping deceitful monster in my mind that whispered darkly in my ear 'You're useless, you have no role, no function, what will you do if you never get better, you do nothing for others and you're going to die without seeing your children grow up and they'll hardly remember you because most of their lives you were absent'.

Watching TV, talking to others, visitors, reading, walking, fresh air, sunlight, good food, cuddles, texting, social media, and company. I could not bear any of it, everything drained me of further precious energy that I desperately wanted to reserve for at least a two minute snuggle with my children as they were brought up to bed. People wanted to come, they promised just to 'sit' in my room and read and if I felt like a few minutes' chat then great and if not they didn't mind. People just wanted to do anything they could, I only had to text 'help' on the Facebook page that I set up for close friends and family to stay connected with me and informed during this horrible time. One friend even commented 'heck – you have to be quick off the mark in responding to your needs on that page – I can't get a look in'. Multiple people would come running to do my bidding. It's grossly unfair that I could not milk the situation and behave like royalty for that one period in my life. I just did not feel well enough to see people, text people or relate to anybody on any level whatsoever.

This nightmare went on for weeks, my physically weak state prevented me from using any of my former strategies that previously enabled me to at least stand firm in my faith and believe in God's goodness. I had up until now remained solid in the belief that my suffering developed endurance and in turn that produced a more rounded character and out of that mature position I could always have hope. I had never really doubted that there would be a point that God himself would restore me, but as each day dragged by that hope just slowly seeped away and total sorrow engulfed me.

About five weeks after I'd started the radiotherapy I was due one of my three monthly routine scans to look at the tumours in my lungs and check my liver. I have become used to these scans as I've shared with you before and have had enough of them to realistically accept that more often than I'd like, they do in fact show up a new spread of disease. Even with that reality in mind I am pragmatic and positive and have generally approached them very rationally. I spend little time worrying about the outcome and have a very practical approach to whatever the outcome will be. As time has gone by I have developed a strong mental attitude which prevents my boat being too badly rocked. This was not the case this time.

In my sickly state I was panic ridden by the concept of this scan; sheer terror filled me for days as the date rushed towards me. I hate water slides, particularly ones that are black inside meaning you can't see where the next dip or turn is. Every year when we go on holiday to Portugal I have been dragged onto 'The Black Hole' by my children purely for entertainment value. My heart races, even in the blazing Portuguese sunshine I sweat with anxiety; when it's my turn I have to face the fathomless darkness, wriggle awkwardly into the rubber ring and plunge into the abyss. You have never heard the likes of the screams that come out of me, all the way down, mouth wide open, screeching, squawking and squealing at the top of my voice 'Noooooooooo I don't like it' 'Aaaaarrrrrrggggghhhhhhh help me'. When I reach the bottom and am flushed out into the plunge pool and glaring sunshine, standing around is always a crowd of people including my kids laughing uncontrollably at the noise I've made. The impending scan was having a similar effect; I had tipped over my breaking point and was living in a paroxysm of utter dread, anxiety and apprehension about the outcome of the results. I cried like a baby every night and when Mark came home from work I begged him for reassurance that the results would be ok.

I knew in myself that I couldn't take any more, if it was bad news and the cancer had spread further in my lungs or to another part of my body, I felt I'd totally break down and give in. For about three days beforehand my whole body was in a state of panic, my throat tightened up making it difficult to swallow, my heart pounded and raced, I couldn't breathe, and I was jumpy and twitchy. I had never experienced anything like this in my whole life. I'm aware that some people suffer debilitating panic attacks frequently and I now understand how dreadful they are. I was unable to function, it was like I was being chased by monsters; I wanted to run for my life but instead I found myself frozen to the spot. The only prayer I could manage was 'heal me, help me or take me home'.

As with most 'scary monsters', when we actually do stand in front of them they lose their hairy and scary grip. That's what happened here. I turned up to the scan and was told 'it was all fine' and then I ate lots of cake – LOTS of cake, and for a moment in that crazy, deep, lost place I allowed the comforting ooze of naughty sugar to course through my veins and allow my crazed mind to be comforted – just for half an hour.

Freedom Called

As the next few days rolled on, I was still enduring the radiotherapy treatment, but didn't return to the frenetic feeling I'd experienced in relation to the scan. However, I still had a generally disturbed feeling of not quite being able to get my feet onto solid ground. Maybe I just needed more miracle-working cake?! One day, alone in my room, the oddest thing happened to me. Something took over my body and an enormous howl came out of my mouth, the cry an animal would make if caught in a trap. It was the cry of a woman totally broken from ongoing illness and mental anguish. I howled in distress, I was on my knees in the centre of the bed and I leant forward and beat the bedcovers. I know not how long I maintained this base, carnal, animalistic position but at some point my screams turned into angry, aggressive, aggrieved shouting. The cry that splurged out of my mouth was 'freedom' – 'freedom' – 'freedom' and I screamed and shouted and beat the covers until there was nothing left to express.

I lay on my side quietly crying and then I heard a voice. Here she goes again with the whacky God stuff – I've tried to make God intertwined in this story in a non-challenging way, but honestly there are some chapters that I simply can't avoid telling the story exactly as they were. So here I go; it was a voice I recognised but had heard physically only a few times before, a voice that was clear as a bell; on this occasion I could hear it all around me, and from deep within me. It was so audible that I sat up and looked around the room to see if someone had used the key safe and sneaked into my room. It was God.

For those who are reading this and don't believe in God as a real entity that communicates with us personally and in many varied ways, you will probably be thinking that I imagined it or conjured it up out of my own need to receive comfort. I assure you this was not the case; I have no way of proving it but why would I make it up? I believe I have illustrated many times throughout this story that I am an authentic, honest, practical, logical, rational, fully accredited, sane person with a sense of humour and a normal life. So try and get over your scepticism and have a little faith – maybe it could change your life! (Preachy bit over and done with.)

There are two reasons aside from my ears actually hearing this voice that confirmed it was God and not me. Firstly, the conversation that followed. I would never have had such a conversation with myself; and secondly, the outcome, which more than proves it was a supernatural experience and not a human one. My cry for freedom had been an unusual one in the first place, more likely I would have just cried, or whimpered my 'heal me, help me or take me home' request, and then turned to Mark later for some TLC. But to scream for freedom in such a brutish fashion was just not my style, it was something deeper within me that cried that word, and I believe it was the Holy Spirit speaking on my behalf.

'Freedom from what?' said the voice.

'From cancer, you buffoon.' (I did actually say that, so frustrated was I by God's odd question.)

'Freedom from suffering, from sickness, from life,' I screeched back in total anger.

Wasn't God supposed to know everything; had he not been following the last seven years; or had he been too distracted by more important tasks such as the Earth's rotation or ensuring gravity works effectively and we don't all just start floating off into the universe? I honestly felt like it wasn't me who'd lost track of things, but that God had.

'You don't need freedom from your cancer, Rebekah, I want you to park the cancer and I will show you what you really need freedom from.'

Come on, why would I answer myself with that? I didn't even know at this point what that meant. If I was to have imagined a response to my raw cry it would have been far more along the lines of 'poor you, it must be really awful' as a whole magic treasure chest full of Ben and Jerry's Phish food ice cream and Lindor chocolates descended from the heavens; closely followed by litres of Hendrick's Gin and a magic wand that waved all my sickness away.

This voice was definitely God speaking deep truth into my life, deep into my soul. It stilled me, it got my attention and caused me to raise my head and for the first time in weeks I felt a glimmer of light shine into my blackness. When God speaks to you like this, everything within you becomes enlightened, you have been given the truth and the truth can set you free. You have revelation and it's revelation that changes your mind, heart and outwardly your behaviour. If this had not been a spiritual encounter I would have been able to push this conversation to one side and continue to wallow and wail alone in my bedroom. Someone eventually would have temporarily comforted me telling me it was ok to feel like this, it's understandable and it'll pass, just hang in there. I would have felt a bit better and the strong emotions would subside, but I would have not have developed any strategies to deal with such despair and the next time it happened, I'd be in the same place. But this encounter had no such outcome; it changed the course of my life; my perspective was forever altered.

The Encounter

I had encountered God in such a tangible real way; his voice audible and everything inside me sat up and listened. I felt compelled to listen; it wasn't a choice to listen, there was nothing rational or explainable about this experience at all, it was so powerful. I can't influence your response to this incident – **you** have to decide whether you think I am a lunatic, on the level with a man who says he's a boiled egg, or simply a good storyteller with a fantastic imagination, or a sane woman who had a real encounter with God. I don't really think my description leaves you any other options: I hope you can just believe me.

If you struggled with the last paragraph you will really find this one hard. I am sorry! The last thing I want to do is give you a reason to stop reading, so please stick with me. I fell into a deep and peaceful sleep of which I have not had since the 'Big C' got me in 2009. I had a dream. I dreamt that I was on an operating table; I could see the theatre and various surgeons and nurses. The top surgeon in this theatre, I recognised him as Jesus and he was going to operate on me. He told me he was going to perform an autopsy on me, open the very life of me up and expose what was in there. His focus would not be on my organs; he would not be looking to remove the cancer, he wanted to show me my soul. All the hurt, the rejection, the areas of fear, bitterness and anger, disappointments, disputes and devastation that I dragged around with me but hid from the public eye whilst this pot of nasty stuff continued to slowly affect and destroy my private life. My marriage needed attention, my children needed a better version of me, my bad temper and reliance on self certainly needed looking at. These were the real reasons I did not experience the freedom I cried out for. He wanted to show me the truth about what held me back. It was not the cancer, it was me, what was lurking inside of me and how it affected my attitude to my circumstances.

I saw my life on a map with boundary lines drawn around different zones and titles to define the areas: my children, Mark, church, extended family, friends, hobbies, thought life, beliefs, attitudes and feelings; basically all areas that made my life mine in the past, present and what I'd become in the future if I didn't sort my mess out. I noticed that each zone had a red shaded area of varying size, some were almost entirely red, others less so, and some had little red on at all. The red represented the areas of my life that I had control of and if I was honest I knew they weren't functioning that well. It was these areas that were restricting my life in the here and now and held me back from being able to live my life in total and utter freedom and fullness despite my circumstances. I had this 'moment' where I realised that it might be possible for me to feel utterly peaceful inside, have a genuinely all round happy home life; not a partly happy home life, without **anything** changing on the outside.

Oh golly, I desperately want to present this 'experience' in a way that is not off putting to a massive group of readers. I want to remind you that I am not trying to ram religion down your throat and I really don't want you to feel awkward. I think I've dealt with the fear of what you might think about me, a lady who is of 'seriously unsound mind' because I probably am. Not in a certifiable way, more in a left of centre, whacky, wonderful way. So I ask you once again, at worst to bear with me, at least read it as a factual explanation that is quite radical, and at best read it and be fascinated, inspired and believe that it could be real.

It's so hard to explain without getting into stuff that I don't want this book to be about. Yes, I want it to be a book of truth and so God has to be in here because I believe he's true; but I am no 'spiritual teacher' and I'm definitely NOT a 'life coach'; gosh one day I might write a book on all the escapades I had in my 20s. Think along the lines of 'Diary of a 20 Something Screw Pot' describing the rollercoaster of a decade in a young woman's life where she tried EVERYTHING and I mean EVERYTHING in order to find out what the meaning of life was and then you'd know that I am not a Holy Jo.

Once you decide, as I had done many years ago, that God is real, therefore Jesus is real and the Holy Spirit- defined as the Trinity, it sort of demands a response. As in, 'Ok, I believe all that'. Once you acknowledge that then you ought to find you want to know more about it all. This would likely involve finding a church that can help you; and other people who feel the same as you. Now, the bit that freaks people out, you'll then find that you're a 'dirty wretched sinner' (lol – I'm laughing because I KNOW what you're thinking – and I am not going to comment because this book will lose its focus!). I could say this in a softer way but I wanted to shake you up a bit!

After that you will be dosed in the revelation that God adores you, he chose you to exist before the world was even created and he WANTS you. He forgets that you've been a rascal in your life up to this moment and shows you how to be who and what you're actually designed for – in other words, your purpose for being here.

Now, the journey begins – again, I'm not going to go into all that and what it means. The only bit you need to know to understand the experience I have just given you when I cried out 'freedom' then 'autopsy' etc is this. In simple terms, depending on your character, present life, job, hobbies, and all that, you begin a journey of living with God as a real truth and this will cause you to think differently. The main way you think differently is that you want to put God first not yourself, but this can at times be challenging. I am one of those people who find it hard to depend on someone else. So my journey is riddled with 'who knows best battles'; it has been a lifetime of giving up the need to be in control and I expect it always will be. I know that when I 'let things go' I find 'freedom'; my life is so much more relaxed. Ooooooooooo, what a wonderful feeling that is!

This dream revealed to me that aside from a few small chapters in the last seven years I'd largely been managing off my own reserves; I'm a very determined, strong minded, 'dare I blow my own trumpet' talented lady. Yes, mathematically I'm a dunce (not PC I know, but I was born in 1971 and it was ok to use that word then so that's what my Maths teacher called me, get over it; anyway it's actually true and I can't be bothered to google dunce for an alternative word), but aside from that I have never really failed at anything that I have decided I WANT to do.

I had already harnessed Cancer for the greater good – running and raising so much money for charity (did you know I was once 'Woman of the Year'?). Deep down, when I was alone, I knew those 'worthwhile' activities were preventing me from really facing some of the more important struggles I had. I needed to peel another layer off my independent streak, move my attention from cancer and the public benefits it had brought me, but also the excuse it gave me to not face more important issues.

Wiggle

The way this worked for me was to face and accept that my private life did indeed need a bit of attention. There's a story that I knew from my days in Sunday School; I could have hunted for one that illustrates a similar message but from a 'non-Christian narrative' to keep it 'fair'; but this is the one I actually remembered and I'm NEVER going to get to the end of this wretched book if I have to do some more flipping research.

There is a pool called Bethesda outside Jerusalem. A great number of people who were sick, blind, and lame waited by the pool for the waters to stir. An angel went down to the pool at appointed seasons and stirred up the water (cool – imagine that, an angel turning a pool into a Jacuzzi). The first to go in after the water was stirred was healed of his disease. There was a man there who had been ill for thirty-eight years. When Jesus noticed him lying there (helpless), knowing that he had been in that condition for a long time, he said to him, 'Do you want to get well?' The invalid answered, 'Sir, I have no one to put me in the pool when the water is stirred up, and while I am coming (to get in there myself), someone else steps down ahead of me.' Jesus said to him, 'Get up: pick up your pallet and walk.' Immediately the man was healed and recovered his strength, and picked up his pallet and walked.

For the first time ever I read this passage in a completely different light. I had never liked the story; I think it shows Jesus as a cruel hard man – it was obvious to me that the poor crippled man couldn't get himself to the pool edges to receive the benefit of the stirred up waters. I thought that kind, soft, loving Jesus should have said, 'I know you've been there for a long time, and are not fast enough to get yourself to the pool when the waters stir. I will carry you to the pool and for the patience you have demonstrated over thirty-eight years you will be healed today.'

My version of the story should then have ended with Jesus reprimanding all the other sick people for their selfishness. For not organising themselves into a queue and making sure the cripple, who'd been there the longest, was next. Surely one of the sick people whose illness allowed them still to walk could have lifted him in.

I began to see this story from another angle. His answer, that nobody had helped him to get in, basically illustrated his avoidance of responsibility. He then goes on to blame others 'while I am trying to get in, someone else goes ahead of me'.

Jesus didn't feel sorry for him and step in and help him; instead he was rather stern: 'get up! pick up your mat and walk'. In other words, stop being a whine bag and avoiding your responsibility and get on with it. I began to wonder why the man had not just sidled an inch nearer to the pool every day. He was crippled but we know not how severely; he could have 'wiggled' his way nearer. If he'd wiggled I became convinced he'd have sorted his own problem in potentially a few weeks. I knew for sure that if I had been him I wouldn't have lain there pathetically for thirty eight years knowing that the healing pool was probably only a few feet in front of me. I mean honestly how lame (excuse the pun); if anyone had dared to get in the pool before me after I'd wiggled for three weeks, believe me they'd have got a good beating with my Zimmer frame and a few choice words. He could speak! What was he thinking about all that time? I would have been screaming at people after two days to drag me into that blasted pool – what on earth was wrong with him?

'Victimitus' was his real problem, what was inside him was what was killing him. Being crippled wasn't his biggest difficulty, it was not being able to see he had a poor selfish 'woe is me' attitude. I'd lost all sympathy for the cripple when I saw him in this light. In fact, if I were Jesus I'd have given him a good talking to then left him there for another thirty-eight years to figure it out.

I realised that there were areas in me that I'd allowed myself not to take responsibility for because I had cancer. A bit like this cripple, I had blamed my situation and made excuses not to deal with a few personal areas that needed attention and that were my responsibility to face. It seemed overwhelming at the time, nasal gazing was not my first choice of healing activities on my list of post radiotherapy recovery tactics. But instead I was screaming and crying and moaning to God that I'd had enough and couldn't he just give me the easy selfish option and 'beam me up, Scotty' to heaven?

So in the absence of any better option I decided to try the wiggling approach to my 'victim' mentality just in case I did live for another 38 years, by which time there was a possibility I'd be divorced and none of my children would be speaking to me and Cancer would still have a bigger place in my life than the wretched thing deserved.

Genuine change in life begins with YOU changing. You 'wiggle', you decide on a goal and then take small steps towards that goal. Inadvertently, secretively and unconsciously I'd wanted cancer to change for my life to change, or Mark to change for my marriage to improve, or my children to change so that I could be the model parent. It wasn't external that was going to change my outward situation, it was internal change. The external was just a distraction; In many ways, although I wouldn't have owned up to it, I **had** allowed cancer to limit my potential; I hadn't realised that it was my mind that limited me reaching my potential. You might be thinking 'it didn't look that way to me, you ran, you fundraised, you always seemed so positive and driven – I don't think you limited yourself at all'. That's true, but when I became too poorly to engage in those public strengths I felt totally defeated. Internally, privately, I was left looking at what was left of me and my family. Facing a future where running was unlikely to be possible I knew I needed a new strategy.

The physical effects of cancer did of course mean I couldn't do some things as well as I used to, but my freedom came when I realised that it also gave me opportunities to achieve other things that I would perhaps never have tried had cancer not entered my life. It was my attitude that dictated what I could and couldn't do, not my illness. I wonder what things the crippled man thought about and used as distractions to waste thirty-eight years – the mind boggles. But waste them he did. He could have been healed and living a new life with his working limbs, but he was focused on the wrong problems.

Wiggle It Just a little bit

As mentioned there were many areas I needed to apply the wiggle technique; in actual fact, because wiggling is a slow process I will likely be busy wiggling for the rest of my life. Genuine change, be it physical or behavioural, does not happen in one day. It's easy to say I'm starting that diet tonight when you've just consumed half your body weight on a hearty Sunday roast. It's not real change, though, if the next day you grab a plate of doughnuts that you bought for the kids and ate them when no one was looking.

Or to decide after they left for school today that you'll never be 'mean mummy' again after a morning of screaming at your children because they dared to make a mess in their rooms when they were having great fun. Oh yes, it's easy to promise yourself this whilst alone, calming down at 9.10 am with a gin and tonic. I'm a paragon of virtue for six hours of my day, I get along with everyone, the delivery men, the postwoman, the neighbours, my coffee date, my editor, anyone I need to speak to on the phone, the gardener, the cleaner (Do not judge – I'm not a posh nosh, I am poorly), hospital staff and the list goes on. All those people think I'm amazing, I smile, I chat, I always complain in a very nice tone; biscuits and coffee and some fluttering of the eyelashes to the maintenance men BEFORE I tell them the skirting board they fixed in the hallway is NOT straight.

It's not genuine change though if by the time 4.30 pm comes and the children have had fun in their rooms again and 'Lord alive' dared to make another mess and I've screamed at them, then hidden in the utility with a glass of wine and consumed that entire plate of frigging doughnuts, is it?

It takes a long time, a lot of commitment and much determination to change anything in your life for the better. I feel thankful that cancer drove me into the ground; I do not believe I would have made such dramatic changes in the secret private circuit board that lay within myself that dictated the vibe and atmosphere in our home for the people I loved the most, my family, if cancer had not come knocking at my door. It took six years of doing really well on my own reserves with everything that life was throwing at me before I completely broke and really focused on what was most important to me. The final part of this tale describes what the result of my attitude and choice to completely leave BEHIND my discreet victim mentality and wiggle myself into a wonderful world where what was on the outside was TRULY a reflection of what was on the INSIDE.

The Avocado Incident

Remember I was a sick victim to the evil rogue radiotherapy – I'd languished in bed feeling awful for months, forgotten by the kids and unable to face friends. I'd had my 'freedom' revelation and encounter with God and I had to wiggle towards a better place. It all began with an avocado.

I had this compelling feeling that I had to get out of my sick bed and make myself smashed avocado on toast with a poached egg. I know, it's bizarre, but that's what happened. I knew I didn't have the ingredients to make this meal so I realised I was going to have to walk to the Spar to buy them. I hadn't been out of the bedroom for quite a long time, and certainly not to do anything such as leave the house, go shopping and make MYSELF a meal during the day. I had been sufficiently supplied with meals on wheels from faithful friends for the family. I, on the other hand, was still pathetically existing on my 'Lemon Sherbet' diet.

Smashed Avocado on toast with poached egg was a favourite of mine from Jamie Oliver's Everyday Super Food; just doing a bit of advertising for you, Jamie, you can thank me when I'm a celebrity too and you've read my book. I really didn't fancy anything even close to a meal, so Avocado, that was just an insane suggestion. I argued with myself for a few minutes; I told you it's a slow process this behavioural change lark, and even more so to control freaks like me. Then I reminded myself that I was going to be different in ALL areas, however difficult that was, and this was my first challenge.

I slowly got up and got dressed; this in itself was a huge achievement. It involved lots of resting but one huge excitement as I slipped my jeans on and they nearly fell off me; I liked that bit. In short, I miraculously made it to the shops, made myself lunch and gobbled it all up. I sat back and laughed. I needed a reason to get off my sick bed, I needed the feeling of success by achieving the impossible, I needed the energy and sense of well-being from fresh food, fresh air and exercise, I needed an appetite which was created from exerting myself and I needed the blessing that came from listening to the inner voice that encouraged me 'You can do it – you don't need to wait to be better. I am with you and will give you the strength'. For the first time in my life I had properly heard God speak, give me a challenge which I took, achieved it, and felt total and utter pride, joy and excitement at how much more I could go on to champion in if I lived every day in this fashion. This was not my 'end', it was the beginning, the beginning of a different life.

I think that the Avocado story was a simple start to a process that I needed to engage with. The public 'me' had to take a holiday, while the private me had to clean herself up a bit. The Avocado tale was the beginning of me eating better, which as we all know is a foundational requirement for health. It was the power source that enabled me to begin dealing with my inner self and radicalizing our family home.

The Goggle Box

I'd always been a fan of reality TV, you name it, I watched it: Big Brother, Celebrity Big Brother, Big Brother's bit on the side, I'm a celebrity get me out of here, Geordie Shore, Ex on the beach, Towie, Made in Chelsea and many more. They were recorded on a series link so that I never missed a season or an episode. I was recuperating from the Avocado adventure and relaxing in front of a bit of 'Ex on the Beach', when I began to think a totally radical and alien concept. I started to consider that these trashy programmes were actually quite depressing and pointless! I paused the episode just at the cliffhanger moment when Dade (I've changed the names) who was reclining on the sun lounger with his Penis Colada – oops Pina Colada – ogling the very large knockers in the very teeny bikini of his new bird Taleesha, whom he'd already sucked the face off on this Island retreat.

When horror of horrors his girlfriend comes gliding towards the camera standing figurehead style in the prow of a sailing boat (well actually it was a motor boat, but for the purpose of effect I've called it a sailing boat) like Amphitrite (an ancient sea goddess) straight towards the cosy scene of her boyfriend slobbering over his new bit of stuff. This strange thought continued; 'Rebekah, perleaeeese can you stop wasting your time watching this trash on TV?' Why wouldn't it shut up? I needed to see what was going to happen when Myeesha (the girlfriend) who was looking extremely aggressive reached Kade and Taleesha; but this pesky voice wouldn't stop. It was gobsmacking, I couldn't believe it, I was about to witness a handbags at dawn fight or maybe more a Factor Four suncream bottle attack with the effect of causing their tans to have Dalmatian-like white spots on. This nagging, persistent, inner disturbance made me hit the stop button.

Do you know what happened next? I began to ponder how much time I'd have if I simply stopped watching this baloney. The shows weren't influencing my behaviour and attitudes; I hadn't forgone my moral values to live a lifestyle like they do on Geordie Shore. I hadn't exchanged my sweat tops for sequined boob tubes, or my momma knickers for crotchless lace or a sensible double gin and tonic (only the one, on a Friday night!) to drink shots and then going home to the 'Shag Pad'. But there were possibly other things that if I simply pledged to myself that this rubbish no longer had valuable space in my life I would find something to do that was much more rewarding and may even allow me to give something back to my family and friends who had given so much to me. So, I deleted them from saved shows; it did take a few painful hours to get rid of Geordie Shore, but I did it. I cancelled all the series links and wondered what to do now.

I had the next mind blowing thought – 'I could watch the God Channel instead'. That would be more than a Wiggle, I argued back 'that would be proper bottom shuffling and I am not ready for speed, I'm just a 'baby' wiggler'. I might as well say at this stage that not too far down the line I'd stopped all daytime TV; I **did** watch the God Channel **and** created series links of my favourites; I'd subscribed to some daily audio inspirational Christian teaching from a well-known lady in Christian circles called Joyce Meyers, who I had never heard of because I wasn't into those sort of obsessional daily rituals. Now I think I'm in love with her – no, I haven't changed my sexual preference, but I think I'm definitely feeling some kind of womance towards her (female version of bromance). Fortunately for her, she lives in America so I can't stalk her or camp outside her door.

This lady has changed my life, not as much as God obvs, but her audio and TV show have taught me God's truth on how to be better on the inside which is all that really matters and it showed me the importance of the Bible and me actually reading it every day. I had to retrieve my Bible, which was at that time being used as a doorstop for the living room door. It had a tendency to slowly close without it. The room had a log burning stove and the door needed to be propped open to allow ventilation or you literally cooked – the Bible had been there for nearly a decade. Now I had a use for it so it was replaced by a squat bull wearing a tartan coat with ginger tufts on its head; reminded me a bit of Mark.

I'd always found the Bible really boring, but suddenly it came alive and the wisdom for every area of my life was overpowering. As I persisted in listening to Joyce, reading the Bible and even adding Christian songs to my Spotify playlist – which oddly sat quite well between Robbie Williams and Pink Floyd (seriously) – I began to find a real inner peace that enabled me to actually be nice to Mark and the kids for at least a week rather than three minutes. This whole experience was turning me into a real life 'happy clappy hallelujah wierdo Christian type'. I bet the next thing will be putting a fish sticker in our car and hanging around street corners belting out 'Sing Hosanna' next to a blackboard with 'Jesus loves you on it'. Nooooooooo!

Mummy and Wife

All this new exposure to the Bible illuminated so many more areas that I could wiggle in. I realised that I expended so much energy on running to the hospital and back and being strong and powerful and influential and winning awards and races and doing fundraisers and conquering the world using the cancer to define me and reaping in all the praise and the money and the newspaper attention and even Royal attention – yes, I had tea with Camilla Parker-Bowles who is the patron of the Maggie Centres – and being on the news and being an amazing woman who had gone through this awful journey but didn't let it stop her from doing all this awesome stuff that I had nothing left for my family.

Sad, very sad, even sadder was that I knew it was happening but I didn't want it to stop. It had become easier to live in the light of my public glory than in my reality of the debris I'd left at home. I knew this had to stop.

It was simple: I had to stop ignoring the little voice inside that said 'go home, simply be at home and learn how to love Mark and the children more wonderfully than you already do'. I'd been so neglectful that initially this was very hard. How did it work? One can't just conjure up a new version of oneself and then start being it and expect the kids and Mark to just go along with it.

Ta-da: short tempered, impatient, rude, blunt, sometimes totally beserk, always distracted, sarcastic, critical, grumpy, moody, controlling mummy has gone, disappeared for good and been replaced by an angel of light, a calm, sensitive, gentle, genuinely funny (as in not cruelly sarcastic), kind, affectionate, joyful, peaceful mummy. And from this day forth, my dear husband and mind boggling awesome children, our home will forever be a haven of calm love and laughter. Obviously this wasn't possible – or was it? Would faking it at first eventually lead to it being authentic and real? There was only one way to find out: wiggle it.

The Wiggle Outcome

I had gone through a huge internal encounter which had changed my attitude completely. The only way to prove that to myself and show others was to be that radical – to actually BE different. Even if it felt like a pretence at first; only doing it is doing it, so I did it. I just decided, in the same way I had decided to take up running and to prove to myself I had improved I'd set a goal and trained to achieve that goal. It was exactly the same process to change my inner self. I decided I was going to be different – I wanted to be calm, affectionate, peaceful, loving, stress-free, positive (to name but a few), so I just started being those things!

I wiggled – tiny things at first like putting down the spatula when I heard Mark open the door, returning home after his day and going to greet him, asking him 'how his day had been' instead of screeching from the kitchen 'Maaaaaaaaarrrrrk – I have a hot pan in front of me – Josie is hiding behind the sofa cos Evie is trying to hit her with a sword; Archie is eating mud in the garden and Emma will NOT lay the table. Where have you beeeeeen?'

I started to kiss him before I went to bed – not full on Frenchies, not at the start anyway, just a peck on the cheek at first which then became a peck on the lips which then became a slightly longer peck on the lips and then… you can imagine.

If my 'red alert about to combust button' began to blast in my head when a child said 'NO!' usually caused me to respond by screaming 'how dare you defy me – I'm counting to three and if you haven't cleared those toys away there'll be no more sweets for the rest of your life and no one else will get them either!' Which then disintegrated into everyone crying over no more sweets, no clearing up was done, and all the children would shuffle away to find comfort in Mark and I'd be left alone feeling like a crap failure of a mother who maybe could have helped small child clear up, rather than demand and then scream at them brandishing extreme threats that would never be carried out because I relied heavily on sweets to bribe the little darlings into good behaviour.

I decided going forward I would deep breathe, count to ten and calm down BEFORE I spoke. I would try to keep my voice level and understand what was making them want to be defiant and then think about an alternative way of handling it all.

These are just a few examples of how change began. At first these wiggles felt almost impossible and I failed over and over and over and over again. Some days I wept with disappointment but then I'd blast out some Holy music or pause and consume some encouragement from the vast amount of scriptures I had written down in notebooks that lay all over the house around anger, impatience, love, joy and many more, and I'd wiggle myself back to a place of peace, ready to face another day.

Sorry became my closest friend. I swallowed my pride and my own need to always be right and I'd return to Mark or a little person and ask them to forgive me – I would hold them close to my fake bosomed chest and tell them how much I loved them. Slowly and surely as I wiggled, persisted and determined to keep going to reach my goal for a home truly full of love and calm, it began to come true. This was 2016; it's now 2018 and I still get this wrong but I promise you, my home life, my marriage, my sex life, my inner feeling of tranquillity and the outer sense of calm that is between me and Mark, and me and the children, is unrecognizable.

The truest result of my behavioural change was when one of the children said to me (this was about nine months later): 'Mum, you've changed, you're different, we have so many more cuddles now and we actually spend time with each other'. That is beyond words the biggest reward I have had on my wiggling journey.

I can't tell you all the areas in our home that were transformed because many of them are far too personal, and my husband told me not to! The first draft of my book described EVERYTHING in a LOT of explicit detail; I tried to convince him that it was all for the purpose of helping others who were likely also to be struggling with similar issues (you know, don't you? Sssssshhhhh – **sex issues**). But he just wouldn't have it. So the chapter on 'Wiggling in the bedroom' has been cut.

Just between me and you, I really DID work on some very large meaty intimate wiggling which I can't go into, but let us just say I have slowly moved out of the dry bushlands and entered into the moist vibrant valley. And this, my friends, is a miracle.

Cape Fear

I had to stop allowing fear to hold me back. Fear in me didn't show itself in an obvious way at all; neither did its bedfellow, 'anxiety'. In many ways I'm not fearful at all, in fact I'm fearless. I love physical challenges such as rock climbing, zip wires and skiing; in fact, I'll give most physical challenges a go if the opportunity comes my way.

I travelled to many far flung places as a student and as a single lady, I loved travelling and I loved doing it alone. I've had lots of adventures with my backpack trekking in central Turkey, Canada, Spain, France and more.

I am sociable and friendly and confident in conversation, pretty much able to discuss any topic with any person. Ironically, it's very rarely the 'big stuff'; for example, I don't worry often about any aspect of cancer, but I could carry a tight knot in my stomach over the children and **their** future. Of course, worry is irrational, so spending even one night being anxious imagining that one of my children who had a real hissy fit last night will probably be in jail in ten years for attempting to stab someone who'd looked at them in the wrong way, is totally pointless. Or feeling sick for days and hiding from people because I have slipped into a state of paranoia with the 'people don't like me' syndrome sparked off by a friend not saying hello to me in 'Home Bargains' when in reality they probably hadn't even seen me. Blaming 'me' for everything that goes wrong is a favourite starting point for anxiety, worry and fear and can unsettle me for weeks. I guess we all have a mask that we put on, we carry on smiling and appearing confident and hiding our real insecurities.

I had a very poignant experience during the 'Wiggle Revelation' regarding the management of my discreet but very real disposition to fear and anxiety; which definitely began a radically different approach to the difficulties I have always had in this area. Almost a solid stepping stone from the sinking sand that fear and anxiety privately created in me, to the more solid ground of genuine confidence based in a much deeper sense of genuine security rather than something I mustered up for the public. It was a version of what God had said to me about Cancer – 'Park it, Rebekah – leave it to me'. I had to do the same with anxiety and fear: 'Park them – give them to me'.

How on earth does that work? What does that even mean? It meant having to learn a new mental discipline, create a new pathway in my brain; almost exercise my brain to not simply continue to 'indulge' thoughts that led to a complete meltdown, but to practise the habit of replacing the destructive, pointless negative thoughts with calming, peaceful thoughts. This is where the Bible study I was doing really came into its own. I found hundreds of truths regarding the antidote to fear and anxiety, hundreds. What I had to do was begin to combat the habit of defaulting to destructive thoughts by recognising when it happened and replacing the thoughts with good thoughts.

It was hard work – it still is, but lesser than it used to be. To aid this process a very strange thing happened. I had gone to bed and fallen asleep like usual; my difficulty wasn't falling asleep it was staying asleep. I had this awful nightmare that I was in a small boat at night time. The sky was inky black and stormy, the moon and the stars obliterated by dark clouds, hiding all light that they could offer. The sea was as black as the sky and my little boat was being tossed backwards and forwards on the stormy sea. I was heading alone, straight into the hugest waves, only identifiable as waves in all this blackness by the white crest at the very top. They were enormous, towering metres above the smallness at the prow of my little wooden rowing boat, tsunami in scale. I looked upwards and could see with certainty that the huge wave ahead was moments from crashing down onto me and causing certain death.

I woke sweating and crying, I heard that 'inner voice' whisper 'Rebekah, you are safe in your little boat, you are NOT in it alone, I am in it with you and I will steer you safely through the storm – trust me'. The translation of this dream was obvious to me, the storm represented the worries and anxieties I regularly sank into in the depths of the night; the reassurance that I am not alone with them was the reminder that peace is possible and available to me ALL the time. The person in my boat was Jesus – the boat represented my life and the calming reminder was that he is in my life with me and is there to calm the internal storms so that the external storms are manageable.

Now, listen in, what happened the next morning was to me a very strange occurrence. My alarm went off at 6.50. The first person I wake up is Evie whose bedroom is on the top floor. I have to climb up the long flight of stairs and then turn a right hand corner and up the second much smaller flight. It's a typical Edwardian style layout, a beautiful mahogany banister snakes its way from the bottom of the house over three floors to end its winding journey in the Gods. As you come up the first flight straight ahead of you is three built-in shelves that largely contain books from MY past life. Some of the classics like the Bronte sisters, Jane Austen, Dickens, a few favourites of Shakespeare, some poetry, and lots of C.S. Lewis and a few other Bible related non -fiction books. All from my much younger days where I used to dream romantically and sit wistfully in the garrets of my childhood home reading Wuthering Heights, wondering if I'd ever meet my Heathcliff.

Amongst this dusty library there was a collection of discarded Bibles. My Father had been a Baptist Minister and when he died I received part of his collection of biblical books – extremely valuable to me because of the love that he had for them. Alongside his grand collection, at some point – probably when we moved to this house a decade ago – I'd popped amongst his a Bible that I'd been given as a Sunday School gift, known as the Good News Bible. It had even been covered by my dad in a recycled semi-see-through plastic bag. He was a stickler for covering books; he recycled everything he could, an early believer in the Green Movement. His shed was like a museum, rammed full of potentially 'useful' articles, he spent a lot of time in there and was delighted if a screw or something went missing in the house because he would have one somewhere in there that could replace it.

These 'Good News' Bibles were extremely popular gifts in the 70s as a first Bible for children. They were worded in a way that young children could read and contained black and white illustrations to accompany the text. This Bible had not been moved from the shelf for as long as we'd been in the house. As I rounded the corner from the big stairs to the little stairs, plonked right in the middle of the top stair was my old 'Good News' Bible open wide.

I approached it wondering who had chosen to get that old thing out – it hadn't been there last night when the children had been put to bed, so what was it doing there? I got nearer, I was about to close it and put it away when I noticed the half page illustration that the book was open at. My jaw dropped open – the illustration was of enormous waves, cascading and tumbling around a tiny wooden fishing boat. The title above it was 'Jesus Calms the Storm' – it's told in the gospels of Matthew and Mark. The disciples had gone out fishing at night – Jesus was with them but had fallen asleep – a huge storm had blown up and the disciples were very afraid. They woke Jesus up and his response to them was a bit of a telling off – 'what are you afraid of, have you so little faith in me?'. He then goes on to calm the storm and they're all amazed at his supernatural powers.

It was exactly the dream I had had that night. How on earth had someone got the Bible off the shelf, chosen the only one with illustrations and been reading the exact story on the same night I had my dream? How odd. At breakfast I asked them all, 'Has anyone been looking at the old yellow covered Bible kept on the shelf on the way to the attic?' I might have well asked them if anyone wanted to wear pink knickers on their heads today. A resounding 'No' was the response and the continuation of chomping and slurping Weetabix resumed.

As I pondered the strangeness of this little event I eventually had to settle for the fact that it had got there in some supernatural fashion. I don't believe in ghosts, and certainly not ones that know your dreams; so the only option left to me was God. I'm not that sure that God would have physically moved the book but slowly I came to the conclusion that it must have been an angel. Ok, there I go again with my fantastical imagination. If you have a different opinion, then feel free to have it, but an angel makes the most sense to me. This experience increased my faith dramatically and encouraged me to embrace the key to the path of releasing my fears and anxieties. Every time I felt the tightness in my throat, the first sign of anxiety for me, I would recall my dream and the strange Bible incident and it would block the worrisome thoughts that would begin to swirl in my mind.

The overall principle that was revealed to me was that Jesus is in my troubles and he can calm any situation – get your mind off the darkness, Rebekah and on to the blessed truth that there will never be anything that happens in my life that with Jesus in my boat he can't calm.

Fear: a really big bad wolf with huge teeth and sly eyes, always lurking in the bushes waiting to gobble me up as I wandered life's paths, filling my basket with flowers. This big bad wolf knew how to hide and loved to jump out at me when I was least prepared. But I had a solution now: I could jump in my boat, sail into the eye of the storm and know that peace and calm waters would be found. I didn't even have to wait for some magical time where there were no fears – the revelation was that the fear could be there but it needn't overwhelm me.

Arty Fartsy Pants

As love and peace began to reign in my home, and inner calm became a more regular state, and wasting time on poopy TV and obsessional exercising had begun to vanish, I found I had time to return to my arty roots. I felt compelled to create something that I could give away, my mindset had shifted a bit from me to others; the spiritual encounter had dropped some sort of power surge into me, giving me the energy to consider blessing others. I had a desire inside that I'd never had before to find alternative ways that I could give others joy. I'd had so much support but always felt incapable of returning the favour.

I got my sewing machine out and began to design, create and make dressed small dolls that I would simply give away to anyone who expressed an interest; with the sole purpose of the joy that is found when you 'give rather than get'. They all had names carrying particular meanings related to 'Joy' such as Ada, Bea (Beatrice) or Maeve, and were all unique. I was turning into Mother Teresa.

I could only manage short periods of time but creating and making gave me so much satisfaction and made me feel like the real me. Creativity has always followed me; from an early age I won drawing competitions in Carlisle's Cumberland News and excelled in Art at school and university. Creativity led me to teach art, and eventually to work part-time as a teacher and part-time as an artist.

The running thing, that was so wrapped up in fear and unrest, but the re-flowering of my creativity budded from a love and a seed that is in my DNA. My love of running 'was like the foliage in the woods: time would change it, as winter changes the trees' – but my love of the arts and literature 'resemble the eternal rocks beneath, [*maybe at times hidden*] but necessary, a part of my very being'. (Adapted from Emily Bronte,

Wuthering Heights where Catherine describes the difference in her love for the two very opposite men in her life.) I am a very creative person, and it will always search for an outlet for it **IS ME.** When it is quashed it agitates to find release and somehow along the way a whole lot of life had swallowed it up.

Children had swallowed it up first and then cancer. I'd lost my way and this horrible sickness had ironically become the stepping stone to me re-opening my heart and re-introducing secret parts of the past me to the present me. They embraced each other like long lost friends and flowed into life initially in the form of 12-inch rag dolls.

Wiggle Your Way to a Wonderful Life

I feel I need to write a second book titled 'Wiggle Your Way to a Wonderful Life'. The blurb on the back might read something like this:

Do you ever find yourself stuck in your life
and wonder how you got there?
Do you remember being passionate and driven to pursue your dreams?
Maybe you dreamt of exploring the world, or dedicating your
whole life to serve others who suffer, or creating a work of art.
Where has that life gone, you wonder, is it even possible
to rediscover those long-lost feelings of freedom in a life
that now feels full of responsibility and reliance.
Yes, it is!
To find the freedom you crave you need to learn how to wiggle.
It's a simple process that can make your dreams come alive.

I can't cover all the wiggles I made; I picked some simple, reasonably light ones to illustrate the immediate benefits I found from allowing my perspective to move. I said goodbye to obsessional running and hello to healthy 3x a week running, goodbye to screaming when I felt stressed and hello to kindness that came from my peaceful soul – how was your day? Thank you for earning money for us so that we can have a lovely home and holiday. Goodbye worry and anxiety, hello confidence and inner security. Goodbye jealousy, hello the ability to love myself and see myself as wonderful. Goodbye protective independence, hello the beauty of intimacy and dependence. Goodbye to negative thoughts and attitudes – 'life is always going to be hard'. Hello to hope – 'Good morning beautiful life, what adventures will we have today?'

Goodbye to self-will and hello to God's will. In essence this was the root of it all. I could go on and on and on about the many layers of dead skin I shed and shed them I did and still am. At times it was hard, but the benefits far outweighed the difficulties. But like a butterfly emerges from its chrysalis I began to find my wings and fly.

I used to buy into the concept that it's ok to be your worst at home surrounded by the people who love you unconditionally. I used to think it was ok at home to unleash my inner beast and be the devil incarnate so long as I was Angel Gabriel to the outside world; but I don't believe this anymore. It's a lie and I wasted so much time believing it and being a fraud. I am so grateful that cancer broke me down so badly that I was able to encounter God in the way I did and have my entire perspective changed.

I still scream at home and show my worst to the best people in my life – I'm not frigging Peter perfect – but I do not lie to myself and believe it's ok when actually it is NOT. It's simply a waste of special time with special people who deserve the very best of me.

As all these underlying fears and anxieties began to seep out of my life I could determine in God's strength to not waste a single moment or opportunity living in stress and conflict or an unfulfilled victim lifestyle. I began my marathon wiggle, my new journey; I learnt to say goodbye and farewell to all the nasty stuff inside me and hello to the peace, joy and love that blossomed in my home. What a new life began to open as I shed all the grime.

'So long, farewell
Auf Wiedersehen, goodbye
Goodbye
Goodbye
Goodbye'

Sound of Music

The Writing's on the Wall

It all began when I was still going through the above process, and I was still very poorly from radiotherapy, but significantly, despite the direness of my physical health, the wiggles had begun to free me and I was finding a completely different perspective on my life was emerging. Phil, one of my brothers, rang me out of the blue one day. He rarely calls me. It was an incredibly powerful, unexpected phone call; we discussed very personally my illness, which, since I was diagnosed in 2009, and it was 2016 when this call took place, we had never had. The astounding thing he said to me was 'I think you should write a book'.

My brother Philip – where do I start! Never mind me write a book, I think he could write a book on the story of his life. He is an extremely talented man and despite his seemingly tough outer skin he's actually an incredibly emotional, loving man. He is academically very capable; he won a scholarship to university and achieved a first in Mechanical Engineering and as a result had a very successful career. He moved out of this successful career and bought an old run-down cottage and farmstead on the boundary of the North Yorkshire/ Lake District National Parks. It's in the middle of nowhere and extremely beautiful. With his own hands and skills he renovated the house and two of the large barns to provide a high level of group accommodation right in the heart of the fells; it's amazing.

I can't say anything else about him for fear of his already huge ego quite literally exploding. He is one of those annoying people who is excellent at everything and wins everything – never ever play Monopoly with him.

His words 'I think you should write a book' were the beginning of my release into skills I had never before exercised. This was my very intelligent, talented BIG BRO telling me I could write a book. I don't think I can explain how 'capable' that made me feel. If Mr Smarty Pants was telling me I could do it then maybe I could. I had, in fact, had two attempts to write my story, previous to this conversation, but they just had not flowed. I only wanted to record the detail for the children, but both times I tried I'd become so bored by my own drivel that I knew for certain it would be of little use to them. I tentatively set about the process of writing and sent the first few chapters to him. When I got his feedback I was elated – 'It's amazing,' he said. And that was all the encouragement I needed to continue. His advice to me was to 'make sure you don't preach at people!' I hope I haven't.

This writing lark has been a slow process for me; I had no idea how to write a book and I had no ambitions regarding the outcome. It was meant as a memoir for the children, I may not be here to tell them my story, and there will undoubtedly be spaces in their memories that I'd like to fill with the actual facts of what happened rather than figments of their imagination. My biggest fear is that they will suffer from the absence of a mother even when I was alive, that they will only see and feel the outcome of how cancer took me away from them. And it has – it's the biggest sadness I carry, that I have, through no choice of my own, been extracted from their lives, physically and emotionally and they will have felt the biggest impact of that.

So, this book is the only way I can try and explain to them what was happening as a background to them growing up. I truly hope that it helps them to forgive me; I have neglected them at times, I have been absent, I have not been able to cope with them, but it has never ever been because I don't love them. I tell them every day how much love I have for them, I pray with them that they will know how loved they are, I cuddle them as much as I can, I speak positively to them at every opportunity I have, I do my best out of the place I'm in. But still I feel it isn't enough, still I fear that they will see mainly the space I didn't fill, the dreams I didn't help them achieve.

I pray that I will defy the statistics and live until I'm a crooked old lady – but it's so unlikely; I don't think I'll be with them during all the developments of their lives, school results, maybe university, careers, relationships found and lost, maybe marriage and children. Then there's all the small details, telephone calls to distant places that I can't imagine, emails, advice needed and rejected, watching them stumble, watching them prosper, being their mum always there, always fighting for them, willing them to push through. The only female in their lives that has been there from day one, I have tales and experiences of them that only I have had, that only I can tell.

The love of a mother is a one-off love, nobody else can claim it, nobody else can replace it, nobody else will ever be who I am and love them like I do. No other woman will ever feel as strongly and passionately, would give their own life for them, die for them, have sleepless nights over them, cry tears of pride and joy over them. Only me, and at the moment it looks like they'll be robbed of that immense love long before they should be. This book is an effort towards leaving a bit of me with them; I am so grateful I was inspired to do it and that I have had the tenacity to achieve it. I thank God that he has helped me when I've felt like giving up. All the wiggling I did and the layers of heaviness I carried were shed and created room to explore other skills; illness and family have slowed it down but I have done it. You, my lovely children, may not actually read it, but that's ok because I pray that just owning it will fill you with comfort, a treasure chest of truthful revelation on who I was, strengths and weaknesses, highs and lows. Of course it's just a flavour, a glimpse, I know I haven't been everything to you that you wish I was, but know this: I tried the best I could, I really did, and above all else, even at the times when it will have looked like I didn't, I want you to know that I loved you all differently but equally with a love that was overwhelming and mighty in its power.

I'm a poet and I didn't know it

December of the same year – 2016 – I was asked if I would say a little Christmas reading as a representative of a cancer patient who had received care and support from the Maggie's Centre at their annual Christmas carol service in St. Nicholas' Cathedral. I was more than willing to oblige, it was five days until the event, so it was a relief that all I needed to do was to turn up and be given an appropriate piece of text. I was also told that if I wanted to find something more personal to read then that was fine too, I just had to let them know the day before.

It was a Friday, the Carol Service was the following Wednesday; it was the weekend, life was crazy, Christmas was less than two weeks away, preparations were in full swing, the kids were high as kites, parties lined up, multiple school nativities to attend, present buying – you know what it's like. I went to bed on the Friday eve, exhausted, only to be woken at around 5 am. I sensed an inner voice saying 'we're going to write a poem for the carol service'! As I have already explained to you I'd gone through a significant encounter with God and many areas of my life had been challenged and radically transformed, so I'd become accustomed to this sensation of hearing a voice that directed a decision I was about to make or gently guide me each day. I knew this voice, it was the Holy Spirit, I know it sounds off the wall but what happened and how it happened are real, which only confirmed that I was not dreaming and it had to be God!

My response to this suggestion was probably the same as anyone's may have been. I laughed (quietly because Mark was snoring next to me), I couldn't write poems, I couldn't even remember the last time I read a poem. I surmised it was when I was at Primary School (later on

I actually found one of my English exercise books with various creative writing tasks in it; amongst them was a poem on Halloween. I was 11. It was ok, I suppose but nothing special, certainly not an early example of a poet laureate in the making). The very idea that I would create a poem good enough to share publicly at an event attended by about 400 people, some of which were very successful local businessmen and women was nothing short of terrifying.

Almost hypnotically I reached for my phone, opened a new email and quite literally words, phrases, rhymes and descriptions flowed out of my head to my finger and were typed into the email to myself. It took about 45 minutes, it needed no editing, apart from some typo errors. When I read it through I could not believe I had any part of it at all. Indeed, the truth of it is, I didn't have any part of it – it was not me. I recognised me in the style, but I was not a poet; I knew it was the Holy Spirit.

I have run out of excuses for mentioning God – Holy Spirit and Jesus; and I've ran out of concern if I offend some readers. I embrace all my friends and their sometimes opposing morality, beliefs and moral values – if I like you, I like you irrespective of your spiritual standing. We don't have to agree with one another to like, love and respect one another. I will always believe that the fundamentals of Christian beliefs are the only way, the truth and the only way to genuinely bring life alive. To be honest I can't tell this part of the story if I'm going to have to stop all the time and think of different ways to express my sensitivity to those of you who believe in alternative systems.

I sensed it was good, definitely good enough to read at the service. Mark had to be woken, I had to read it to him and tell him the experience I'd just had.

'Mark, wake up, wake up,' I said as I shook him excitedly.

'What, aye, what do you want, what's wrong now?' he mumbled from his sleepy saliva stuck lips.

I had to let him know immediately that something utterly bizarre had occurred. 'The Holy Spirit woke me up and he told me to get my phone and he told me just to listen and then I began typing and out came this poem – for the Carol Service!'

'Eh?' he said. 'What are you on about? Poem, Carol Service, fingers on the phone, Holy Spirit – it's only 5.45, it's Saturday morning?'

He had sat up by this point, I ignored his whining, and I started to read it to him.

The Shadow

I refuse to let cancer's shadow hang over me
Christ came to Earth at Christmas to give me the hope of eternity
He brought joy to my world that was tangled and bound
He broke into my darkness and spread love's light around
This gift of hope is a message to my heart
Hope that God loves me whether I'm near my end or not far from my start

So why rob my life of this gift of love
Which come with daily blessings from above?
And dwell on the pain that cancer has given me
Or the time it has robbed from my family
The scars on my body and words spoken of death
Could hang over my life until I take my last breath

I CHOOSE life and boughs of holly
This IS the season to be jolly
It's the chance to bless and serve others I meet
The sufferers of cancer, or the homeless on the street
And despite my sickness I live free from strife
If I allow this attitude of love to rule my life

Tinsel, Santa, carols and lights
Turkeys, gifts and elves in striped tights
My children chaotically adorn my tree
With candy canes and tinsel so tacky
I love it – I love it all, I love to see them so excited
We've been through so much but we stand united

Runny noses from the chilling sun

Steaming breath from winter fun
Rosy cheeks from frosty days

We warm our hands round the stove's hot blaze

I love to hear their smiles and giggles

Bottoms on my lap as they writhe and wriggle

Some days I dream of other lands way up high
Lands I heard of once in a lullaby
where sickness has no place and bluebirds fly
above the rainbow, so why can't I?
But I have a job still to be done
to push through this cancer until my battle is won

To make a trail for others to follow
In paths of hope not of sorrow
To treasure each moment as if it's my last
Christmas is coming I'm having a blast
Not to worry about what's next
No one really knows what to expect

So I refuse to let Cancer's shadow hang over me
I look to Christmas and what do I see? I see the 'hope' of eternity.

I swear I saw Mark trying to wipe a tear from his eye. 'Wow,' he said, 'that is very good, in fact it's brilliant.' I garbled on at him frantically trying to make it clear exactly what had happened; we were both as high as kites all day. It was the most exciting, hilarious, potentially life changing event that had happened since this whole wretched thing began.

Three days until the Carol Service when this beauty would be bestowed on four hundred strangers. I can be as praising as I like about this poem because it's not really mine. My hands wrote it, it reflects my heart, I can feel my situation running through its veins, but apart from that I had nothing to do with its creation. Those three days were exhilarating, I read it in church and received a standing ovation, I read it over and over again in the Maggie's Centre, volunteers were moved to tears and nobody was offended about the obviously Christian thread that is the foundation – this amazed me.

The night I read it was a night I will never ever forget. The beautiful Cathedral, soft candle light, a professional choir singing the carols we know and love filling the arches and lofty ceilings with their angel voices. People mesmerised, entranced, tangible peace as spirits rose, joy and hope infusing the atmosphere we occupied. My time had come and I walked to the pulpit, climbed the stairs and looked out into the semi darkness. I could almost see everyone – so many people silently waiting, watching, wondering what I was going to say.

Sir Peter Vardy had finished and Dame Margaret Barbour was to follow. I was speaking inbetween these two well-known figures. This was a moment in time, a moment that I could sound out to hundreds the poem that God had made. I know I did it justice, loud and proud, my voice rising and falling with the words and phrases I'd become so familiar with. The atmosphere was alive and electric as my words rang out in this ancient place, echoing into the vaulted ceilings, surrounding the carvings of the long ago saints and embracing the shadowy fluted columns finally resting in each and every person's heart.

The service ended. I was unable to leave my pew for the queue of people running right up the central aisle as far as my eye could see; people who wanted to shake my hand, cuddle me, weep on my shoulder, tell me their journey with cancer, ask me if I was a poet, how had I written it, where had it come from? It was like being a celebrity, but that honest streak in me was unable to take all this praise, I had to tell them the truth. One by one, sometimes a small crowd would gather I had to tell them my crackpot tale about 5 am and the Holy Spirit and the phone and I'd never written a poem in my life and so on and so forth.

I have no idea what anyone thought of all that waffle, but I could not have stood there and been fraudulent. I truly did not write that poem, so how else could I answer their questions without simply telling a bare faced lie.

Following this event I continued to write poems – this book was put on hold as I rolled along with about six months of poetry writing. The Shadow birthed a new and completely unexpected and unimagined skill – I can't say 'talent' because I know I'm no Wordsworth, I don't even know how my poems compare to other amateur poets – probably not very highly! But, I do know this, what they may lack in experience, finesse and any level of professionalism, they more than make up for in readability.

Poetry for the non-loving poetry readers, that's how I'd describe them, think 'Pam Ayres' style and you'll be getting close.

With a lot of help from some amazing people – Karen Verrill who provided the finances, Peter Wigglesworth the master designer printer and all round poetry writing counseller, and my marvellous agent Marky – in October 2017 we self-published 'Ode to a Titty', a collection of my poems. We launched it with an event in the Maggie Centre, rammed to the ceiling with family, friends, and strangers. I 'performed' a selection of the poems and explained how they had come about and out of which situations I had drawn my ideas and, even if I do say so myself, it was a roaring success.

I have done a few more events – we've sold hundreds of books – it reached the press and I was on local TV. I regularly receive emails from strangers all over the country telling me they have my poetry book and they just wanted to tell me how much it has encouraged them and inspired them to push forward in their own difficulties, and never ever give up hope.

I am daily excited and invigorated by what else may come my way. Never in my entire life could I have imagined or considered that one day I would write and be the proud owner of a collection of poems and a book that have inspired other people across the country to fight on and retain hope. I receive a manageable flow of invites to speak in different places about my journey and how I've been able, against all the odds, to discover new pastures and rebuild my broken walls. Whether the writing will continue or the poems, I know not. I have no ambition to be or do 'anything in particular' – the whole episode grew from the 'encounter' and obediently 'wiggling' my way into genuine 'freedom' in my soul. The only thing I'm sure of is that God is God and he is good; now that he is in the driving seat of my life I have evidence that empowers me to believe that ANYTHING is possible for my future, absolutely ANYTHING. That is FREEDOM.

The nearly ending

No one is more relieved to write those words than me – I've had to have a nearly ended daytime gin to celebrate. In fact, it's the next day, I was so elated that this epic journey has ended that one gin turned into another one and I never managed to come back to my computer.

I have quite literally nothing left to say. I'm reminded of that scene from Forrest Gump, he's explaining how he'd come about his epic run through America.

"That day, for no particular reason, I decided to go for a little run. So I ran to the end of the road. And when I got there, I thought maybe I'd run to the end of town. And when I got there, I thought maybe I'd just run across Greenbow County. And I figured, since I run this far, maybe I'd just run across the great state of Alabama. And that's what I did. I ran clear across Alabama. For no particular reason I just kept on going. I ran clear to the ocean. And when I got there, I figured, since I'd gone this far, I might as well turn around, just keep on going. When I got to another ocean, I figured, since I'd gone this far, I might as well just turn back, keep right on going."

Forrest: [running] I had run for 3 years, 2 months, 14 days, and 16 hours.
[He stops and turns around and sees a crowd of other runners who have followed him]
Young Man Running in front of the crowd: Quiet, quiet! He's gonna say something!
Forrest: I'm pretty tired... I think I'll go home now.

He stops dead in the middle of the road and that's the end.

That's how I feel. I started this marathon; I got to the end of the first chapter so I thought I might as well keep going. When I'd done that I decided I could do more so that's what I did. I reached many points when I wanted to stop but I'd got so far that I decided I had to keep on going. I've reached the end and like Forrest 'I'm pretty tired now, I think it's time to stop'. It's simply time for this to end.

Of course it's not really the end, it's just the beginning, the beginning of learning to walk in authentic freedom, beginning to live my life not feeling like I have to control it, the beginning of learning the true order of life, God, family then me out of which flows love, lots and lots of love. Love for God, love for others and love for self. 'All we need is love' – it's corny but it's true.

I could attempt to summarise what I've learnt and leave this on an inspirational high like a nice gift wrapped carefully with ribbons and bows, but I can't seem to think of anything. I'm still sick, very sick and due another round of whole brain radiotherapy. I went on a very tolerable chemo which managed everything very nicely for about two years. My brain, however, started to be naughty and I'm now – in November 2018 – awaiting to begin more radiotherapy on the six tumours that have grown. I'm still likely to depart this world much sooner than I'd like, I'm still a bit ditsy and often get things wrong and make mistakes; I'm still just me. But somehow Cancer has been good for me – did you take that in? Cancer has been good for me. The version of me that I am now after nearly ten years since the start is so much nicer than the one I knew before this all started. I am so grateful that it happened, so enormously grateful. Out of the ashes has grown beauty, the life I knew, destroyed, burnt to the ground, but out of the destruction has come such beauty in my life.

Life can hand you lemons it's true
But what you do with those lemons is all down to you
Look for the stars in the darkest night
Clouds may be hiding them, but they're still shining bright
Look around the problem, the solution is there
Choose life, love and laughter, never lonely despair.

(Extract from *'Ode to a Titty'* by ***Rebekah Simpson***)

The End... for now at least!

Also by

Rebekah Simpson:

'Ode to a Titty'

Poems of life, love and laughter

Rebekah's book of poems are available at £9 each inc P&P – if you would like to purchase a copy please email your request to Rebekah on: *dying.to.live2018@gmail.com*

If you would like to listen to some of Rebekah's talks please stream on-line at: *https://soundcloud.com/thebaychurch/sets/rebekah-simpson* and *https://soundcloud.com/thebaychurch/how-to-go-through-the-trials-and-not-even-smell-of-smoke*